Kidnapped in Iraq

Alexandre Goodarzy

Kidnapped in Iraq
A Christian Humanitarian
Tells His Story

Translated by James H. McMurtrie

SOPHIA INSTITUTE PRESS
Manchester, New Hampshire

*I know your works; you have the name of being alive,
and you are dead. Awake, and strengthen what remains.*

—Revelation 3:1

*You are neither cold nor hot.... So because you are lukewarm,
and neither cold nor hot, I will spew you out of my mouth."*

—Revelation 3:15–16

To my wife, Fimy, and my son, Joseph

Contents

Acknowledgments

Thanks to the Lord for this miraculous return to life. Thanks to my wife, son, mother, sister, and Hakim for having tolerated these difficult trials.

Thanks to Antoine, Julien, and Tariq for having been there with me.

Thanks to Philippe, without whom the book would never have seen the light of day.

Thanks to my friends for their faithfulness and support. Thanks to those who revealed themselves to my family in these difficult moments and those who chose to step back out of modesty.

Thanks to Agnès Geminet for her hand-drawn cartographic illustrations.

Thanks to Benjamin Blanchard, François-Xavier Gicquel, Luc Legarsmeur, Henri-Adam de Villiers, Étienne Mignot, Elisa Bureau, and Charlotte d'Ornellas for their support and corrections.

Thanks to Pierre-Alexandre Bouclay, for his help.

Thanks to Syria for having gotten its hands dirty for the world.

Thanks to the Syrians for who they are and for the fight they are waging.

Thanks to each person mentioned in this book for having confidently given me their testimony.

Thanks to all those who encouraged me to write this book, especially Jocelyne.

Especial thanks to SOS Chrétiens d'Orient, whose team went out of their way to get us back. I also thank their former colleagues, volunteers, and supporters, who prayed for us during our captivity. I thank the authorities and all those who, in the shadow or in the light, have acted to release us.

Thanks to all those I've forgotten to mention.

I don't thank my kidnappers, but I do hope for the salvation of their souls.

1

Kidnapped

On a bright, clear day, late in January 2020, I can see the houses, buildings, and mosques of the Iraqi capital—through a porthole.

Early that morning, I had kissed my wife and son, headed outside, and greeted my assistant, Wael, who had my car running and waiting. As we pulled out, Damascus was still waking up. He kept me laughing and kept me company as I progressed through the checkpoints on my way to the airport; the defeat in the last year of the Islamic State and then of Jabhat al-Nusra had made some things easier, but Wael still kissed me with an *Allah maak* (May God be with you) before heading back to the car.

My flight to Baghdad was running on schedule. It was mostly full of Iraqi refugees who had been living in Syria, in the Jaramana area, since the 2003 American invasion of their home country. I recognized some of them as pilgrims; the Shiite sanctuary in Sayyida Zeinab, the mosque in Roqiye, and Husayn's tomb, in the Umayyad Mosque in the Ancient City of Damascus, were all pilgrimage sites.

Our two-hour flight landed in Baghdad at 11:00. The customs booth was practically empty, but I pulled out my invitation from the Armenian Catholic diocese for inspection. I was also a pilgrim, traveling to participate in a pilgrimage project with the Christians and Shiites in the southern part of the country.

Kidnapped in Iraq

While the divisive factors had increased in the Middle East, given the diversity of the populations that make up the region, many political and church leaders had implemented joint projects to bring communities of the same population together. To help maintain a national unity that had been extensively weakened, especially during and after wartime, it was not unusual for representatives of different religions to come together during important celebrations: high-ranking Muslim officials came to greet the Christians at Christmas or Easter, and the Christians came to visit the Muslims during the feast of Eid al-Adha.

I had traveled to be one of the Christians there to help the Shiites, who were much more present in Iraq than in Syria, to commemorate Husayn's martyrdom on the day of Ashura. Although the challenge of Iraqis living together in peace had been ongoing for fourteen hundred years, we wanted to support them in their efforts, especially as the survival of local Christians depended on the region keeping the peace. On this particular trip, supporting them meant joining in a pilgrimage for Arba'een, the fortieth day of mourning. The three-day, hundred-kilometer trek started in Najaf, at the tomb of Imam Ali, and ended in Karbala, by the tombs of Husayn and Abu al-Fazl. For the Catholics among us, it was similar to the walking pilgrimage from Paris to Chartres.

But before I could join the pilgrimage, I had to get out of the airport. Calm as my flight had been, the airport is dangerous, and the waiting taxi drivers are often treacherous. When I saw a driver holding up a paper with my name on it—a stocky man with graying hair, about average height, and roughly fifty years old, exactly fitting the description that my colleagues had sent me—I knew I had a safe ride and stepped forward.

I eventually met up with Julien, the leader of the Iraqi mission. He had come from Erbil during the night with a young interpreter and adviser named Tariq, also known as Abou Dany. I also connected with Antoine, our assistant director of operations and safety and security manager. He had arrived from Paris just a few hours earlier. Julien and Antoine were visiting the Syrian Catholic diocese where our association had built a school a few years earlier. Although we had a full schedule, including visits to the city's different diocesan centers, starting with that of the Armenian Catholics, we had also made plans for that very afternoon to take a trip out to the large mountains near the city.

I was glad to get out of the city for a bit; an Iranian major general, Qasem Soleimani, one of the most powerful men in the country, had been assassinated in an American drone strike on January 3. Since his death, anti-American demonstrations had been occurring in the city every day. It was a dangerous place for any foreigners. Today was January 20, 2020. It was just seventeen days after Soleimani, the commander of the Islamic Revolutionary Guard Corps's elite unit in Iran, and his Iraqi first lieutenant, Abu Mahdi al-Muhandis, had been assassinated on their way to the airport. But the violence was nothing new. With one conflict following closely on the heels of another, the country had been at war for forty years, and assassinations and riots in the streets were commonplace.

We found a restaurant. I sat down with Julien, Abou Dany, and Antoine at a table on a sunny sidewalk to catch up and fine-tune our plans for the day. Antoine explained that, because of the violence, we were likely to run into roadblocks on our way back to Baghdad International Airport. He said we should shorten our stay significantly, and on his advice, we went right to the travel agency to adjust our tickets as soon as we finished eating. Although we were pressed for time on our new schedule, the travel agent moved slowly, and we watched impatiently as the minutes ticked by and the cars drove past outside. The agent finally wrapped up, and we hailed a taxi to head to our first appointment at the French embassy, mountain sightseeing forgotten.

As we left the embassy, I noticed some graffiti on a roundabout: "I love Karada" was written in large, colorful letters. I also noticed a big white GMC, which came up quickly behind us, then turned on a siren, accelerating to pass us. As we approached an intersection, another car swerved onto the road, cutting us off on the right, and the GMC suddenly stopped ahead of us, blocking our way forward. And that's when I realized that an identical GMC had materialized behind us, blocking any possible exit. We were trapped.

As my mind tried to catch up with what was happening, men sprang from the doors of the surrounding cars. They were strong, carried guns, and wore combat vests, T-shirts, and black ski masks. They had closed in on us in an instant and, shouting loudly, were pounding on our taxi with the barrels of their guns. In the front seat, Abou Dany, who was bearing the brunt of it, hesitated for a bit, then he finally opened the door and got out. They pushed him roughly to the car in front of us, and we could hear him shouting. Suddenly, the shouting stopped, and then I realized that one of the men was trying to open my door. I guess he didn't know that the left rear door on most taxis is sealed; it's safer to get out of a taxi right onto the sidewalk.

He gave up trying to force the door open and looked for another way in. The right rear door was already open, and Antoine had disappeared. My heart was racing. Julien, the driver, and I were still inside the vehicle. Julien got out by himself, with the barrel of an assault rifle pointed in his direction. I watched him being led to the car in front of us, into which Abou Dany had already disappeared. My mind froze, and for a moment, it was like someone had switched the volume off; I couldn't hear anything at all.

But I was beginning to make sense of these shadows that had so suddenly and violently torn away my friends. Two doors of the car were still open, and I knew that if I stayed there, they would get me too. I looked around for our driver and was bewildered to find him leaning nonchalantly on his steering wheel, apparently unconcerned with what was happening. I shouted at him, "Go! Drive!"

He didn't even turn his head.

"Get on out," he muttered. "Let's get it over with." And he gestured to the open door with a wave of his hand.

As his treachery sunk in, I stayed where I was and hoped for a vague moment that the kidnappers had forgotten about me—I knew it was a fool's hope.

A fat, sturdy little man came back and yelled at me sharply, telling me to get out. I was barely out the door when he grabbed me by the arm and pushed me toward the vehicle parked behind us. Once I reached the level of the rear door, I saw Antoine sitting inside, with his head leaning forward and his hands behind his back. His face was turned toward mine, and it spoke volumes. From that moment on, Antoine's expressions would be my barometer of misfortune during everything that followed.

I was quickly forced down beside him; we were stuck between two burly men twice as heavy and bulky as we were. With the four of us in the back of this GMC, Antoine and I were sharing one seat. He was sitting on the front edge, with his head almost stuck out between the two front seats. I'd been shoved down sideways behind him. The cars started with a bang and went at full speed.

The men pushed our heads down to make sure we couldn't see where we were going and then started rooting through our pockets, looking for phones and papers. I felt debased. As they shouted and threatened, wanting to make sure no one could use our phones to track us by GPS, they came from all sides, forcing their way through our clothes, making sure we had nothing left.

The volume switched off again; I watched, helpless, while our kidnappers took away everything that could ever help us be found again. I felt my face tense, and I wanted to shout, but nothing came out. God, help me, I thought.

As my two passports and one of my phones disappeared, the men continued shouting, asking me what I was doing here. Terrified as we were, we somehow began to get the sense that this was nothing new for them. The realization made me feel weak—like a victim between predators' claws—and I began to wonder how they would kill us. Would it be a long and tortuous affair, or would they end us quickly?

Though a part of me felt like weeping, there was no time for that. I had to think and concentrate. A survival instinct grew in me, in spite of myself. Every one of my senses was on alert, senses that together told me to be compliant. I didn't try to resist or show that I was stronger. I listened to what they said, glad that I could understand their Arabic and marginally relieved that, instead of planning our imminent deaths, they were wondering about us.

So much rushed through my mind as I wondered thousands of questions about them. Who were they? Did they work for the government? Were they Sunnis or Shiites? If they were Shiites, did they belong to the government, or were they uncontrollable militiamen acting only on their own behalf? Were they connected to neighboring Iran? Who sent them? I prayed that they weren't Sunnis. I hadn't heard them frenetically shouting "Allahu Akbar" or noticed any other hint of religious extremism. Besides, it was unlikely at this point that Islamists who were close to the Islamic State were working in the heart of Baghdad.

I judged that their motives must surely be political and villainous, doubting that they were ideological or religious. I pretended not to understand anything when they asked me their questions in Arabic, so they switched to broken English, asking me why I was here. Although my head had been partially covered by a hood, my mouth was still clear, and I answered that we were on our way to the Armenian Catholic diocese to meet Joseph Zabara, the administrator. I made my English deliberately simple in order to make it understandable to them.

They replied, "*Arman! Ente Arman?* You Armenian?"

"No, I am French."

"Ah, French! It's good!"

As they questioned me, I could hear them continuing to flip through my passport pages, examining all of my visas, and their questions were frequently punctuated by demands for cell phones and GPS trackers.

For fear that they would find my other phone on their own, I decided it was better to give it up and avoid the risk of angering them. I pointed to my leather jacket's interior left pocket without opening my mouth. As they rushed to get it, I heard them yelling in Arabic, "And you're only just telling us you have a second phone!"

I didn't answer. I wasn't even supposed to understand what they were saying. As they continued talking to each other, I felt Antoine leaning forward, right beside me. I could just barely hear him responding to his interrogation as our kidnappers talked loudly back and forth to each other across the car.

We drove on at full speed. I could tell from occasional stolen glimpses that we were following the other GMC, where Julien and Abou Dany were restrained. Our driver didn't seem to want to lose it by a meter. He tailgated them closely, preventing any other cars from slipping between us and them. Determined to stay on top of the Baghdad traffic, our kidnappers coupled their nervous and aggressive driving with blasts of sirens and horns. In case there was any risk of arguments with other drivers, the sight of their dark hooded faces, sticking out of the half-open windows, simplified things expediently. At one point, I caught sight of the GMC in front of us driving straight through a line of traffic, cutting off and scraping up the front of one car that had been passing through the intersection. No doubt the driver of that car got a sense of who he was dealing with and was not about to file an accident report. The two GMCs careened on, and as the noises around us died down, I knew we were leaving Baghdad behind us.

My hands were resting on my legs as we drove out, and suddenly, as though I might try to escape without warning, the kidnapper on my right put his hand on top of mine. But then I realized what he was after. He opened up my right hand, gripped it firmly, and removed my wedding ring, delicately putting it on his own ring finger. As someone else tied up my hands behind my back, I watched the thief folding and stretching his fingers, admiring and getting a feel for his spoils of war, checking the fit. I also noticed for the first time that he was wearing a big ring on his middle finger that had a silver crown on it, with a black and prominent stone.

This confirmed what I was thinking: these were Shiites. We might have a chance of surviving. But I wanted to be sure about it. If they were autonomous Shiites, who did not answer to the Iraqi state or the neighboring Iranian state, then nothing would prevent them from selling us to the Islamic State. Their methods were definitely crooked; I didn't have much faith that they were operating with one of the local governments. My mind stopped on that dismal assumption, and I couldn't think of anything else, except that I really did not want to die today.

As we traveled farther and farther away from Baghdad, the trip seemed endless, and I couldn't stop my mind from going to dark places. It definitely didn't help that they had stolen my wedding ring; it felt like they were ripping me in half, tearing me away from my wife, and like I was disappearing. Already in so much mental anguish, and anticipating the physical torture that I imagined ahead of us, I asked God to strengthen me. I could see us being suspended on butcher hooks, getting our faces smashed with iron bars, and being tortured with electric cables. In a place where decades of war and horror have hardened people to brutality and normalized every kind of violence, lives can be thrown away without a second thought. The notion of humanity is completely relative.

When it was dark outside, we stopped to change cars. One of the kidnappers held my head down to the ground, removed the hood they'd put on my head, and replaced it with a cloth blindfold. As he worked, I could make out the hands of several of the men who were surrounding us. I saw many rings—mostly two on each hand—with some pretty turquoise stones that I was used to seeing on Iranians' fingers. There is something refined about wearing these types of rings, which can also have black, red, or yellow stones. They are often worn by religious men, who hold the belief that they repel the evil eye. I could also see that our kidnappers' hands were thick and powerful, and my mind went back to visions of torment in which the rings would only add to our suffering.

The new car was smaller. We were cramped in the back, without much room for our legs, and the cords that tied our arms behind our backs forced us to lean forward. The front seats were quite far back, and our noses were pushed against them.

Cramped as I was, I realized that one of the cables was slightly loose on my hands, and I began to work one hand free as we sat in the waiting car. One of the kidnappers, getting ready to drive, was right in front of me, and he kept turning around to check that we were still secured. By now, my right hand was free, but I left it behind my back, letting him believe I was still tied up as he grabbed my shoulders and tested the knots by pulling on my arms. He turned back and settled into his seat, waiting for the other guys to join him. The engine was running quietly, and no one else came out. After he looked around and saw no one, he quickly turned toward us again and searched my pockets once more in case anything had been missed, hoping to find something he could keep for himself.

The questions started in my head again. Where were we going? Who were they? At least Antoine was still next to me, and there were no kidnappers crushing us on either side. But there were also no doors, and there was no exit, and we were still surrounded. My left leg ached from lying down on this side of my body for so long.

It was totally dark outside. I could tell, through the threads in my blindfold, that the man in front of us was watching me from his rearview mirror. I did everything I could to try to make him think I couldn't see anything at all, but he was more suspicious than our previous guards. He kept looking back at us and eventually found some cotton to tape over my eyes, under the blindfold. Now I really couldn't see anything at all.

I did, however, hear some voices coming closer to us, and then I heard someone else get in the car. We started driving again, for maybe another forty-five minutes. Periodically, we stopped for roadblocks; on the last one, they pushed us down, hiding us from the inspectors. This was not a good sign. If they were working for one of the governments, why would they be hiding us? I felt my spirits sinking even further as the car sped up, swerving around other drivers, and then veered off the highway for the back roads.

With my vision totally gone, I could feel my brain transforming, analyzing everything I could smell, hear, or feel. I tried to remember the turns the driver was making, if the road was smooth and we went quickly, or if it was bumpy and stony, forcing us to slow down. I tried to turn myself into a computer, wanting to store all the data I possibly could. Now we were slowing down, and the noises changed. They were more muffled. The car went for a few hundred more meters on this path, then it rolled to a stop.

The cotton on my eyes had slipped just a bit, and through a crack, I could see a fire and a large crowd of people waiting for us.

Someone unlocked the car doors, and we felt hands pulling us out, pushing us along as we stumbled on our stiff legs. We heard a heavy metal door open and could tell it was brighter inside, but we couldn't make out any details. We were forced down, and though we were surrounded by our attackers, we could also tell that all four of us were finally together again. We felt each other's presence. We were far from serene, but we took real comfort in knowing we were next to each other.

Now the question was what was next. So far, we were all okay. We were handling it. We were breathing. But we had to marshal our strength; we had to prepare ourselves for whatever was about to happen.

2

First Night, First Morning

We were exhausted. We collapsed together on the floor, where we had been dropped. Our hands were still tied, and our eyes were still blindfolded. We couldn't speak to each other yet. One of the guards placed two blankets on the floor and, closing the heavy iron door, shouted back at us, "Abou Dany, we'll be talking to you! If we have a question, you'll translate for the Frenchmen."

The door slammed shut, and the heavy bolt, sliding into place, made an awful sound. Subdued, we awaited our fate.

The room seemed big. We were hungry, and it was cold and dark. I was wearing only a polo shirt under my jacket. We tried to get the blankets, but they smelled like dirty goats, and the stench made my stomach turn. I scanned our surroundings to try to figure out where we were. It looked like we were in a garage, or perhaps a stable. The iron entry gate took up the entire width of the building. I could see an opening at the top of it; the wind rushed through, whooshing over us to some old, small windows, lined with broken shards of glass and covered with bars, near the top of the opposite side of the room.

The place must have been used as a kitchen. I could see cupboards for dishes, a gas stove, and a sink. The cupboards ran along the back of the room and the whole length on the right as well.

There was a wooden partition at the end, on the left, that hid a small, rough bathroom; there was also a cold-water faucet, a tiny shower, and a kind of gutter for raw waste disposal. We weren't allowed to go without asking the guards permission first, and then they had to come with us.

We slept on the concrete floor, on an old, filthy red carpet. The walls were once painted white, over a sealant that covered cob bricks. The ceiling must also have been white at one time, but now it was covered with a thick layer of grease, pockmarked with black, orange, and brown spots. Sticky dust occasionally fell from the ceiling in thin streams. The gas stove was also oily. Everything was greasy. The filth and the ugliness disheartened me even more.

Abou Dany stirred.

Julien, who could also see a bit, had his mouth hanging open. He seemed depressed, like me, by our surroundings. "It's really gross, isn't it?"

I nodded my head.

I tried to pray some Hail Marys and Our Fathers, but I kept starting them and losing track, not finishing them, or I'd start falling asleep and jumbling them with nonsense words. At some point, I realized that I was becoming delusional, caught between reality and a nightmare. I would occasionally fall asleep for a few short moments, then be jerked back awake by the pain in my hands; the guards had seen that my right hand was loose and had tightened the cables again before leaving us for the night. Even during the bits of sleep I managed, I was still alert, and the questions and fears revolved in my head, tormenting me. And I couldn't hold back thoughts of my wife and my little one, back at home. I was cold, tired, and afraid, and I felt shattered as I went over and over the last moments I'd had with my family, just that morning. Finally, exhausted beyond all measure, I fell asleep for real, my last thoughts on them.

We woke up early the next morning. Guards had come in, and we could feel them untying our hands, then retying them in front of us.

"You can take off your blindfolds and free your hands once we've closed the door. Understood?"

We nodded our heads in agreement as they explained that before they came back, we had to retie ourselves and put our blindfolds back on. They would call out to Abou Dany to tell us each time, "*Jahezin?* Are you ready?"

When our captors returned and breakfast was approaching, Abou Dany decided it was time to ask the most important question, the one gnawing at all of us. He didn't hesitate. I couldn't hear his exact question, but, thank God, I heard the guards' response: "*La ento mo daesh mnsawi shi!* No, no, we are not ISIS!"

But Abou Dany kept moaning and asking questions. He didn't trust them, and he thought for sure that he'd be killed. Because we were French, we might have a chance of surviving, but Abou Dany was in a much more precarious predicament. One guard said he wouldn't be killed, but Abou Dany continued laying out his fears, until suddenly we heard another voice bark out an order: "Now, shut up!"

The impact was immediate. We all froze, and no one spoke. Through my blindfold, I could see this guy getting down to Abou Dany's level. He sat cross-legged on the floor, his own blindfolded face leaning forward.

"*Skot ow beétlak! Smaanak ktir!*" the man spat at him. "Now, you shut up, or I'm going to kill you. We have heard enough of you!"

I felt Abou Dany withdraw like a hermit crab.

I had already been afraid—and still was—that they would discover my Iranian roots and send me to Iran. But Abou Dany had a much greater reason to fear for his situation, here in his own country.

He told me later that when we had stopped to change cars, he thought they would execute him, throw him in a ditch, and then continue on driving with the three of us Frenchmen. Abou Dany knew that he was a threat to these men. He could understand everything they said, including the phone calls and radio conversations. He could pick up on the subtleties of their language and could understand the different codes that were used, even the accents that identified each man by region. He could decipher the cues to their social standing and their religion. And it wasn't just the people he could identify; he could tell where we were just from the air he was breathing, not to mention the food around us. His recognition and knowledge of all these crucial details could be fatal to the kidnappers if we ever escaped. Sooner or later, he knew they would have to kill him.

On our end, relieved that at least we were not in the hands of ISIS terrorists, Antoine, Julien, and I were still trying to understand what could have happened. Images of being dressed in orange suits, waiting for execution by extremists holding knives at our throats, were receding.

At the same time, if these were some of the many independent Shiite militiamen who were scattered around Iraq, things were still complicated. They had, after all, just lost the Iranian General Soleimani, their spokesman and unifier. Without him, groups formed together, based on whoever was closest geographically. Their most pressing concern was to locate the spies who had facilitated the assassination of Soleimani and of the leaders who had been killed with him.

All of the militia upheaval meant that anyone looking for hostages would have a hard time tracking us down—and it meant that these militiamen didn't have any one authority that they answered to. Did that mean money would be their single largest motivating factor? If so ... my mind went back to the worst scenarios. If they acted only on their own behalf, nothing would prevent them from selling us to ISIS, which had never completely disappeared from Iraq. Their active cells were reforming in the south and the east, and even around Baghdad.

3

"You Are Spies!"

I guessed we'd been prisoners for about forty-eight hours. It must have been January 22. At the end of that day, we heard the guards coming back, and they asked us to put on our blindfolds with our backs to the door. There was, evidently, an important person arriving. We heard them set up a chair for him, and then he came in and approached us with an audible "*Salam Alaikum,*" to which we responded.

He sat down and started asking us some questions. He had a strange voice, one I would not forget. "Who are you, and what did you come to do here in Iraq?"

We explained that we were humanitarian aid workers and that we were mostly working in Iraqi Kurdistan. We told him that we had been in Baghdad to register with the local authorities so that we could work in the rest of the country.

"You are spies, and you have come to give money to the demonstrators to help them destabilize the country."

"No, sir," Abou Dany said respectfully. "You're mistaken. That has nothing to do with us. We would never do something like that. We're a humanitarian organization, and we work to help communities that are victims of war. Call Monsignor Zabara, who supports our presence in Iraq. Contact the French ambassador, and you will see."

"No! You are spies. You incriminated yourself when we saw you giving money to a man named Youssef," he continued. "And, as far as your ambassador is concerned, he isn't here. He's traveling in the United States."

"No, sir! That wasn't us. We're Christians, and we're rebuilding homes in villages that have been destroyed."

"Why are you not helping your own country?" the man said, cutting off Abou Dany and turning to us. "The French people don't seem very happy with their own economic situation. You should stay home and use your money to help them instead of coming here to help the Iraqis."

Behind my blindfold, I was a little puzzled by how the discussion was going. At this rate, I wouldn't be surprised if he started lecturing us on the yellow vest protests back home.[1]

But instead, he quickly changed the subject again. "Why do some of you have two passports?"

Antoine and I were still seated, with our backs to our interrogator and our heads down. But, worried for Abou Dany, we asked if we could explain. Antoine told him about our association, SOS Chrétiens d'Orient, and described our purpose. And then I told him about humanitarian aid workers being entitled to two passports.

He asked for our full names, and he demanded to know if we were all actually French.

When we told him that three of us were Frenchmen and one of us was Iraqi, he responded, "But not that one. He doesn't look like a Frenchman."

---

[1] Starting in 2018, a grassroots movement grew across France to protest newly instated high fuel taxes. Protests sometimes became violent; participants wore reflective yellow vests as they marched.

We couldn't tell who he was talking about. Abou Dany asked him which one of us he meant, and he indicated me.

Abou Dany translated all of this, and I responded that I was quite French, no matter what I looked like. But the man would not believe me, so I let it drop, afraid to press the issue.

Finally, he asked us all to repeat our names again, one at a time, and questioned if we had ever been to Israel.

"Alexandre Goodarzy. No, I have never been to Israel."

He said that they would do some background checks to verify everything we had said, and then we heard him get up to leave. As he went, he said that if our story checked out, he'd be back in seven to ten days to oversee our transfer to a warmer, cleaner place that had a television. And, for a moment, we began to hope.

That night was long. I could hear the hyenas outside, giggling by the dozen, all around us. The guards kept shooting at them. The sound of their automatic weapons jerked us awake again and again, reverberating against the iron door that kept us closed in.

As the days passed, we could hear construction machines working all around us. The smoke and dust were suffocating, and mixing with the cold air, it came through the high windows, choking and freezing us.

I prayed more when I heard the backhoe behind the wall, digging into the ground. I imagined that it was digging our graves, and visions of us being thrown into the ground and buried alive rose in my mind. When I heard loud cargo trucks, I couldn't stop myself from imagining us hidden in a big trailer, transported secretly to Iran. My thoughts overwhelmed me as I remembered dozens of stories of hostages, some who had remained captive for a long time. I tried to recall the tricks they had used to survive, to not break down, to remain intact, but my mind refused to cooperate.

Sometimes we caught each other praying, almost as if we were embarrassed. It wasn't so much embarrassment at the prayer as it was embarrassment at the acknowledgment of weakness and fear. We didn't want to let each other know how close we were to breaking down.

It was inevitable, though, that after a few days, we all prayed together, out loud. We knew we needed it and had gotten past the point of being ashamed to show fear. And every time we prayed the Rosary, said grace before meals (such as they were), or offered any other little prayer throughout the days, we prayed not just for our own safety but also for the good of our jailers. We put their lives and souls into Christ's hands and prayed that they would come to see the Truth, that Truth would reveal itself—Himself—to them. And we prayed that they would see that we were innocent.

As it turned out, the guards had moments of decency, and they were even reassuring at times. But I couldn't tell if they were sincere or if they were just playing with us. There is an old saying that petting the cattle before cutting their throats makes the meat more tender. My ability to judge their intentions was limited because of our blindfolds. I couldn't see their eyes, and so I couldn't really get a sense of their characters. Only the intonations of their voices gave us any indication of what sort of men they really were.

We spent the days and nights lying on a rug that barely covered the floor, with one of those stinking old blankets to warm us up. Every night, I was bitterly cold and felt increasingly filthy. As I listened to the hyenas howling and the soldiers shooting at them, I put my head under the dirty blanket, trying to block out the sounds. But I couldn't breathe; I was suffocating. Gasping, I pulled my head back out into the air that froze my lungs. And I dozed fitfully, never fully awake, never fully asleep, surrounded by stench and noise and cold and fear.

4

Shadows and Voices

January 26, 2020, somewhere in Iraq, not far from Baghdad.

I was keeping my mental calendar. Today was Sunday, January 26. I forced myself to repeat the date every day to keep myself grounded, to hold on to some part of reality.

A blackout plunged our room into darkness, followed by a moment of silence that was broken by the mechanical noise of a weapon being reloaded. The door opened, and a voice from outside shouted at us to get up, one by one, and follow them.

There were many of them that night. As Abou Dany translated, we stood up, hearts beating. I was sure they were going to kill us that night, that it was all over.

Antoine had already been snatched up. I could feel him leaving the room. I wanted a chance to say goodbye to the others, but a hand grabbed my arm, pulling me outside into the cool, black night. I got the sense that the man who had grabbed me was young. He guided me surprisingly carefully, making sure I didn't run into anything, and, after walking about ten meters, told me to lift up my foot to step into a truck.

I was trembling with a mixture of cold and fear. I pulled myself together. I couldn't let it get to me like that; I couldn't be so weak.

I prayed for strength and peace and suddenly felt my spirits calm and resolve. As I listened to the sound of the truck, I knew I was in a tractor trailer. It sounded large and empty, but when I sat down at the far end, I could feel someone next to me. It was Antoine. He gripped my arm, letting me know he was alive.

The others soon arrived, one by one, climbing into the truck to join us. The young man who had led us each here sat down and asked us, "Why is he sad?"

"Who?" Abou Dany asked.

"That one, all the way to the right."

He was talking about Julien. Abou Dany turned to him, translating the question.

There was a pause, and then Julien blurted out, "I miss my family." He wouldn't say anything else.

When Abou Dany translated his response, our captor told us, in a friendly and understanding voice, "Don't be sad. You'll be a hero when you return to France. I shouldn't tell you this, but you'll be released in two days. Be patient. The end is near."

Then he changed the discussion by talking to us about soccer, asking us about our favorite teams and sharing the French players that he liked. The conversation was jarringly mundane, but it was predictably interrupted by someone shouting outside, ordering us to come back inside our old garage.

When we pulled off our blindfolds, we saw that all of our blankets had been rolled up, as though they had gone through them and set them aside. Why were they looking through our things, and why did they have to take us out to the truck first? But we knew it didn't do any good to ask questions. We put the blankets back in their places, one on the rug to protect us from the cold ground, and two on top to protect us from the wind and drafts.

I readjusted my pillow, such as it was—a thick piece of fabric, unstitched and stuffed with cotton. It smelled like rodent urine, and we could see mouse droppings in it.

We spent another whole week wondering what would happen, thinking about every possible outcome, mentally torturing ourselves. The days ran together and time dragged, but we always knew how cold it was. The guards would occasionally bring us a cigarette or two, and then they started bringing us whole packs. I hadn't smoked in fifteen years, but I did now. And each night, as darkness fell and the cold sank in again, I tried to stay warm under my blanket and wished to be anywhere but there. All week long, we fought back tears, tried to hold on to a sense of peace and composure, and did our best not to let our hearts break in despair.

Late one day, I turned my head to look at the narrow opening above the door, and I saw the eyes and the top of the head of one guard. Our gazes met, and I quickly turned away again, worried that I'd get in trouble for seeing his face, for not having my blindfold on. I called out an apology, but he answered in a friendly manner. "No problem."

I recognized his voice. He often came to tell us not to worry, trying to reassure us that we'd soon have a resolution. Now he was coming to tell us that he would be leaving. He was being reassigned, and his place would be taken by someone new. He wanted to say goodbye, and he surprised us all. "Pray for me when you go, and please, don't blame me for whatever happens."

Shortly after he left, the guards took away our blindfolds and gave us ski goggles to wear instead. They had been spray-painted black, inside and out. I wondered if this meant they were moving us somewhere new.

After seven days of waiting, the man they called "the officer" came back to see us. He was the one with the strange voice, a voice that sounded old and cruel. The paint on the goggles was slightly chipped in some spots, and I could see him just a bit. I knew that he was in charge of all of the guards and us, but to my great surprise, he was much younger than I had imagined. He was dressed in a mostly navy-blue cotton outfit. His pants were tailored, and he had trendy city shoes. He was elegantly dressed, with a sartorial taste that would distinguish him in any fashionable city.

I rotated my head slightly to try to get a good glimpse of him but realized suddenly that he had turned to look at me; he must have felt me watching him. I turned my head away, hoping he hadn't realized I could see him. I think he must have decided that I couldn't. The only thing he said was that we were being moved to a new location, one that would be "in line with European standards."

After the officer left, his men tied us up again and took us to the vehicles. Night had fallen, and I was shivering in the cold as they led us to a small car. The interior of the vehicle felt cramped as we were all put inside. But it was a short trip, no more than ten minutes, all on a dirt road. I saw some big spots of light to my left on top of a building and thought that surely we must be on a military base. They took us out of the car and brought us into what they called a trailer.

As they left us, and we took off our ski goggles to look around, my heart sank, and my stomach worked itself into knots. I was certain that this would be our last "home" on earth. It was one of the Algeco trailers, temporary structures often used by humanitarian aid workers as medical booths. It didn't take us long to look around, and we put our goggles back on as the men returned, this time with the officer.

"So, is this okay with you?" he said. "You won't be cold here. Notice too that it's clean, and you'll have a television."

It was a bad joke—there was no television, but there was a camera filming us. *We* were the television.

We decided to ask again about the French embassy and told the officer that we insisted on contacting them. We wanted to talk to them and to ask them to get word to our families, to let them know we were alive.

But he rebuffed us, responding calmly and evenly, "The ambassador has not yet returned to the embassy. It would appear that he is not at all worried about your absence. As for your families, you can forget about them. You've had a whole lifetime to enjoy them, but all of that's over now. You won't be seeing them again. Your lives will end here."

These words exploded in my head, and I thought my heart would burst. He had just confirmed all of our worst fears and destroyed our hopes of survival.

As he prepared to leave, he turned to say one last thing. "Life is full of such trials. This is what makes us men."

Left alone again, we took off our goggles and looked at each other. Incomprehension mixed with despair was visible on each face.

We were in shock, and I think we all wanted to cry, but we tried to gather our wits and focus on the possibility of rescue that might save us. We thought about SOS Chrétiens d'Orient again and tried to gauge their response time—how long would it take them to decide to gather a team and start searching for us? Julien thought of Erbil and the volunteers there, and the anxiety that they would experience when they learned what had happened to us. But Antoine spoke about everything that would work in our favor. He sounded reassuring and confident about our association and the services that were in place both in France and in Iraq to assist us. He never doubted, and he strengthened us each day. I owe him a lot—perhaps even my survival.

Kidnapped in Iraq

But if Antoine was the assertion of hope and persistence in trials, Abou Dany was the opposite. This is putting it mildly. When we had first been captured, he stayed under his blanket for several days, refusing to talk or eat. He thought we were living on borrowed time. Given what the officer just told us, maybe he was right.

As for me, I didn't know what to think. I knew I was confused. It was hard for me to look at Abou Dany. He was always scared. I was well aware that he knew his country better than anyone else. He understood the danger we were in more than the rest of us. He had grown up always surrounded by war and by ugly stories of Iraqi civilians who were kidnapped and didn't reappear for months—even years—or, worse yet, never returned. While we were clinging to the hope that France would never abandon us, and would never abandon an Iraqi who works for a French NGO (nongovernmental organization), he was focused on the certainty of long imprisonment or death and either mocked us or didn't say anything at all. He clearly had no faith in anything positive that we said to him.

I listened to Antoine and Julien. They were talking about everything that had been in place before we went missing, all of the people and organizations that might understand why we had been taken, and where. The Quai d'Orsay knew that we were going to Baghdad. They had even confirmed that French people were being targeted. Some members of the French embassy had been informed about our visit and had told us that we could come. In any case, nothing drastic had changed to make us think we should have canceled our trip. The general state of things certainly was not worse than it had been. We had been advised not to leave on the day of the pro-Iranian demonstration that was being held on Friday. Our director of operations had estimated that we should rely on the advice of the on-site embassy.

We inspected the room again. It was six square meters. It had four mattresses lying next to each other on the floor. There were heavy chains on the wall, which were joined together right above each bed. We could see padlocks and a camera by the door. Where there should have been a window there was a rectangle of soldered iron, blocking out all light. The only time we got fresh air was when the guards opened the doors to check on us.

My stomach churned with misery. Again, I wondered how long we were going to stay in this cage. There was no room to move, but we had no reason to get up anyway, except for asking the guards for permission to use the toilet and shower. Back at the garage, when we were able to shower, it was always in the cold, with no way to dry ourselves, and always with the same dirty clothes waiting for us. But here, on our second day, they gave us shampoo, razors, toothbrushes and toothpaste, underwear, and tank tops. We hadn't had clean clothes in ten days.

They also loaned us a backgammon game and two decks of cards. While this might have been taken as a sign of good treatment, we also knew it was a bad sign. If they were trying to make us comfortable, we could guess that they were planning on keeping us here a long time.

The long days went on in endless hours of sitting and lying around. They kept bringing us cigarettes, now by the carton instead of the pack. Each time a new carton arrived, we knew that they planned on keeping us there that much longer. Our smoke filled the cramped room, and it irritated Abou Dany.

Whether it was for Abou Dany or for all of us, we didn't know, but one day the soldiers used a knife to cut a small rectangular opening high up on the wall of our cage. It was above my mattress, and I watched the big, sharp blade of the knife moving through the wall, in and out. It gave us one small window into the outside world, one continuous breath of fresh air—and a way to keep track of morning and night, to hold on to the notion of time.

Antoine, who always found the best in everything, showed us that at a specific time each day, if we stood in a certain spot, a beam of sunlight would come directly through the window, warming our faces one at a time. It lasted only a few minutes, and standing there was like catching the rare moment of an eclipse, not to be missed.

I tried to pray and didn't stop thinking or regretting. This was my last trip—the last one.

Some of the hardest moments were when I would think about my wife. I would try to pray as my mind ran in circles, full of regret and sure that I'd never take another trip. I pictured Fimy again and again, standing on the doorstep and saying goodbye to me with her big, sad black eyes. It was the same look she had given me the night before, gently asking me why I would travel to Baghdad, asking me to think again, and begging me not to go. She had been so right, and I ached all the more for the grief I knew I was causing her. I hated not being able to see her, not being able to say goodbye, leaving her all alone. I couldn't erase that final image of her from my mind: her worried face, broken with misgivings, as she stood in front of our home and watched me leave. Half of her lovely face was illuminated, and the rest was in shadow.

And I thought of our baby—my son. He had been asleep when I left, with his closed fists on either side of his sweet head. He had a little heart-shaped mouth. I remembered cuddling him and breathing in his warm baby smell, so rich on his cheeks and neck, one last time.

I sat against the wall in our cell, and I remembered the last few years. Each day, I buried myself a little more in the past. I had so little control over the present, and none at all over my future. But if I thought about my family, I was holding on to something tangible and very real. I told myself for hours that my life couldn't end in this can, that God had other plans for me, and that this was simply another trial. I also thought back to Cholet, where I had been a history and geography teacher. I thought about my students and about my mother and sister. I thought about the violent suburb where I had grown up and about my Iranian father, who had arrived in France in 1980. I also thought about my encounter with God; I had been rescued by His care, after I had cursed His name for so many years.

The days went by. Nothing happened, and we waited. I thought back on my first meeting with SOS Chrétiens d'Orient and my commitment to them, which had led me here. It had all started with the monastery. I found that monastery, and I withdrew from the world for nine months. Nine months ...

5

A Brief History of Modern Syria

I was thirty years old when I left the monastery. I'd been there for nine months, working through anger, exorcising my demons, and learning to live again after a youth that had been shaped by violence. The monastery gave me a new birth.

Toward the end of my time there, knowing that my departure was imminent, I started sending out résumés, looking for a teaching job. With my bachelor's degree in history and languages, and my master's degree in geopolitics, I went to the board of education to find out if they needed history and geography teachers. I was quickly asked to serve as a substitute teacher, teaching Middle-Eastern history and geopolitics—first in Ensemble Dom Sortais, then in the Pinier Neuf school, in the city of Beaupréau, near Cholet. I found it strangely satisfying to teach on the Middle East. I appreciated being able to provide some nuances and clarifications on the explanations that were given by the mainstream media about the ongoing tensions in that part of the world.

I also applied for a job at the Catholic university in Angers, where I had taken some courses in theology. In fact, the weekly schedule for "postulants" in Cholet's Franciscan monastery had included two visits to Angers for some of the coursework at the Catholic university.

At the same time, I was still trudging along with the Church, preparing for the sacrament of Confirmation. Baptism had been a cleansing with water; Confirmation would be a purification and strengthening through the fire of the Holy Spirit.

One day in February, right after exams, some students asked me to join them for a drink. They were hardly younger than I was, and I gladly accepted. While we were sitting and chatting together, one of them started talking about a Christian organization that had gone to celebrate Christmas with Syrian Christians. I was impressed with the idea and wanted to hear more.

The Syrian war had caught the attention of the international community with its initial conflagration in 2011. I'd been following it and had watched hours of videos and documentaries on the political and geopolitical events triggered by the bloody chaos.

I had already traveled to Syria four times before. Each time, I had been running away from my own city and neighborhood, and life in general, ready to see something else. I had loved the country, its people, its natural goodness, and its certain way of life. In Syria, tradition survived modernism; in France, it felt like a daily collective suicide, with our traditions by and large willingly surrendered in favor of anything new.

That said, democracy was a distant concept for Syria and all of the countries around it. Syria had become an authoritarian regime in 1970, when an air force general named Hafez al-Assad had taken over. For thirty years, he had ruled the country with an iron fist, and he did in fact bring it stability and prosperity. Hafez had four sons and one daughter—he had prepared his oldest son, Bassel al-Assad, to succeed him. But when Bassel died in a car accident in 1994, another son, Bashar al-Assad, became his heir.

Unlike Hafez, Bashar was an ophthalmological medical student in London and had never worked in the political sphere. He had no experience and was the last person that anyone would have guessed to be named as his father's successor. Nevertheless, when Hafez died in 2000, Bashar stepped into his role at the age of thirty-five.

With the political unrest that followed the death of Hafez and ushered in the Damascus Spring, Syria became more liberal. As Bashar al-Assad sought to maintain order, his father's old guard — also heirs of an authoritarian regime — reminded him of local political realities. They were looking at a number of hot-button issues in the region, including Ariel Sharon's contentious visit to the Temple Mount in Israel, the pressure that the United States was putting on both Iraq and Syria, and the long-standing and increasing tensions with Lebanon over the exact location of the border between them.

Fast-forward to 2011, and over the course of just a few months, in the eyes of the world press, the ophthalmology student became worse than Hitler, Stalin, Mao, and Milosevic combined. His nuance had suddenly disappeared, and he was no longer a young man courting democracy with his beautiful modern wife but was instead an authoritarian monster thirsty for the blood of his youth. Everyone forgot about his visits to France to honor Bastille Day, and the fact that President Chirac had awarded him a Legion of Honor medal.[2] He was up against a group of officers and sub-officers who had risen up as one man to provide the democracy that the Arab people were clamoring for loud and clear. It was as beautiful as a Corneille tragedy. I had never seen the media so united in the assassination of a man's character; it was, quite frankly, disturbing. But the truth was there, if people could only

---

[2] Then French President Jacques Chirac awarded Bashar al-Assad the Legion of Honor medal in 2001.

look past the media storm. Syria had a Sunnite majority, and it also contained a number of minority groups—Christian, Alawite, Druze, Ismailian, and Shiite. Hafez al-Assad was a member of the Alawites, one of these despised minorities.

Syria was a secular republic that functioned through a flawless crushing of the opposition. This opposition, which was mainly Sunnite, gathered itself together into a group called the Muslim Brotherhood, created by Hassan al-Banna in 1928. Though this group had first taken off in Egypt, it soon expanded into several Arab countries and then spread throughout the world. This "brotherhood" gained a reputation for being reactionary, feudal, and medieval. They are the most violent and brutal militants in the Arab world and are largely recognized as a terrorist organization. But they are also the organized ones, as they would demonstrate by their growing footholds in Egypt and Tunisia in 2011. Notably, this organization was also opposed to the power of the Assad regime.

Learning that Catholics had willingly gone to such a place left me speechless. I didn't know what to think.

6

God's Mission

Confirmation is an important moment in a Christian's life. It is the day the Lord sends us His Holy Spirit in order to go on a mission, to be soldiers of Christ—the day we commit to Christianity. There were about ten of us who received the sacrament that day in the Angers Cathedral. Bishop Delmas had called us, in turn, by our first and last names. Our names resonated in the vastness of the stone cathedral, and we answered, one by one, "Here I am."

When it was my turn, I responded confidently and decisively. I understood that Confirmation meant being entrusted with a mission, and I took this expedition very seriously. I was moved by a zeal for the Lord, and I wanted to bring this impulse to a fruition. I asked Him with all my heart to tell me how I could be useful to Him.

The year went by. I was back on duty in my two high schools in Cholet and also worked as a substitute teacher at the Catholic University of the West in Angers. The course load was heavy, and as I grew exhausted by the busywork, my morale dropped, and I found myself despairing a little more every day. It wasn't that the students were disagreeable. On the contrary, they were rather attentive. As I worked my way through a geopolitical history of the Middle East, I knew that I had their interest and respect.

But the general atmosphere in France was eating away at me. Nothing great, beautiful, or powerful was happening in our country. Each day took us further away from the grandeur of our past and rooted us more firmly in mundanity and mediocrity. The Europe we had been promised was starting to disintegrate, and our culture with it. Increasingly, our society was looking like one enormous retirement community, with all of our own people growing older while we depended on the Sudanese, Syrian, Afghan, and African immigrants to empty our garbage cans, wipe our elderly, and clean the filth that we could no longer be bothered to pick up.

We were one big hospice. We were born here, ate here, occasionally had children here, and all the while, through our actions and inactions, committed ourselves to maintaining a declining economy. And then we died, without having risked, experienced, or overcome anything, except for weekend traffic jams and supermarket lines.

When we marched in the streets, it was to protest for a more secure retirement. I saw twenty-year-old kids participating in such a procession at the Place de la Bastille, shouting to anyone who could hear them that "Our futures must be secured!" Twenty years old. They'd never accomplished or experienced anything big, and they were already thinking about their retirements. They were old before their time, before they had earned any right to be. That was our French youth. It was distressing, and a little shameful. I found myself feeling something undefinable, somewhere between scorn and embarrassment.

They were all afraid—afraid of losing little things that made their daily lives incrementally easier. A little personal housing allowance here, a bit of help there, a little welfare, some assistance with transportation, a pittance from the government that made us think we were living when we were only surviving. This was a population that was used to being helped instead of doing things on their own. These lives were sustained on an IV drip of government subsidies. But they were subtle, seemingly inconsequential little benefits that kept everyone comfortable, calm, and lazy enough that no one ever thought of questioning or bucking the system. Things had been this way for forty years, decades before most of our younger generations had been born.

The government had bought the zeal and fire of youth, which naturally longs for grandeur, challenge, and greatness, with welfare and Christmas bonuses, transforming the will of would-be indomitable generations to a morass of indifferent torpor.

The *furia francese* had been floored not by weapons or an occupying army but by an even worse enemy. The French fury, which we had feared for centuries, had given in to *comfort*. We were no longer dying in battle; we were instead overcome by rampant obesity and strokes.

We no longer believed in anything, especially not in ourselves. There was not a day without repentance: public and widespread apologies for being who and what we were, and for the so-called crimes of the generations of our people who had come before us. This included repentance for being French, for being white, for having colonized countries and brought them water, electricity, and literacy, and for having built roads and capitals that could not have been built without our aid. The Church did not escape such treatment, as even the pope made a show of publicly repenting of ecclesiastical crimes. In short, we all had to lower our heads and castigate ourselves. This was, after all, the fashion of the time.

One day, as I was finishing one of my classes about Syria, a student named Pierre-Augustin approached me to ask if I was aware of a Christmas trip to Damascus happening at the end of December.

I was confused for a moment, as I hadn't heard anything about it, and I wondered why he would ask. But suddenly I remembered.

"Oh," I said. "Wait, is this the same Christian association as the one that went last year?"

"Yes, that's it. They're doing it again this year. SOS Chrétiens d'Orient."

I was glad to hear their name. I turned it over in my mind and wondered about this group. How had they started? Who were they? Where did they come from? I realized I was in awe of them and, at the same time, a little envious.

I thought about my recent Confirmation and what it meant to be sent out into the world on a mission for Christ, a reality I had taken very much to heart without yet knowing how I could actually live it out. This, I thought, was a chance to live out that mission. I couldn't stay in France while such things were happening elsewhere. I had to return to Syria, to be a part of this. My last trip to Syria had been in 2007. Except for traveling in Iran, Tajikistan, and Afghanistan as a student in 2009 and 2010, I had not been back in the region. I really wanted to see Syria again, and here was a wonderful reason to go.

When I got home, I picked up the phone and dialed the association's number. I couldn't wait to find out if I could actually do this. A man named Benjamin Blanchard answered my call; he wasn't just working in the office—he was actually one of the two founders of the whole association. We talked for a long time, and I explained to him who I was and told him that I wanted to go with them to Syria. At the end of our conversation, he agreed with me that it was a good idea, and I began my preparations right away.

7

Christians of the Orient

Christianity in the Middle East has been riddled with conflict for two thousand years. At the beginning of the fourth century, after three hundred years of persecuting Christians, the Roman Empire became Christian. This turnaround happened at the hands of Emperor Constantine, who had just won the Battle of the Milvian Bridge after a miraculous apparition of the Cross. The Roman persecution of the Christians ended in 313, and Rome no longer acknowledged a pantheon of gods. It had one God, for one empire, and Christianity became the religion of that one enormous empire. However, as it happened, the empire was so large that it was divided in two: Rome was the capital of the Western Empire, and Constantinople was the capital of the Eastern Empire.

In 476, Rome fell to barbarians. Since it had opened its borders, the empire could not sustain itself; it was still too vast and not homogeneous enough. While the scattered tribes of early Europe sought protection under the Roman Eagle, they were a disunified mass that signaled the collapse of Rome, not its continuance. But in the East, Constantinople marched into the future, bringing with it the message of Christianity and rooting it in the Middle East.

Kidnapped in Iraq

When Rome had stopped her persecutions, some Christians who still looked for dedication to their faith through bodily mortification embraced what was known as white martyrdom. This was the asceticism of the thousands of monks who lived as hermits. In the east, they were found in cave dwellings in northern Iraq, especially in Alqosh, and in Maaloula, which is in Syria. They were also in the Petra area of Jordan and in the Kadisha Valley in Lebanon. At any given time, there might be hundreds of these monks living in neighborhoods in the same valley. However, this period would end with the arrival of Muslim fighters in the middle of the seventh century.

Hejaz's Arab tribes were unified under the leadership of Khalid ibn al-Walid. They had attacked the Persians in 633 and the Byzantines in 634, two empires already weakened by centuries of conflicts. In 636, the Byzantines were defeated in the south, and the Arabs pushed on to the Holy Land in 638. Syria was completely conquered in 639. Meanwhile, they were also gradually overcoming the Persians; within ten years, they had completely dominated them.

Within a decade, the Arab-Muslim military encroachment took hold of territories that had taken Christians more than three hundred years to convert, oftentimes by the sacrifice of their lives. One hundred years after Muhammad's death, the Arabs were in Poitiers.

The Christians in the Fertile Crescent, especially in Syrian territory, didn't overwhelmingly convert to Islam. Many of the smaller communities remained committed to their faith and traditions (we're talking about two hundred thousand Arab Muslims in the midst of two million natives), but a special tax called a *jizya* was levied against them. While perhaps the Christian churches weren't directly destroyed by the Muslims, with the *jizya* and

42

other strictures, it was not easy for them to flourish or even to be maintained.

In the meantime, the Muslims were torn between those who became Sunnites and those who became Shiites. And while the Muslim population grew for several centuries, the Christian community was slowly eroded by a variety of factors: taxes, mixed marriages, polygamy, society's Arabization via its Islamification, and the internal quarrels took over a good part of the Christian population.

In 1055, the Turks, who came from the steppes of Asia, arrived at the gates of Baghdad. They had been newly converted by the Samanid Persians, who provided a boundary between the Islamic Abbasid Caliphate and the nomadic shamanistic and Zoroastrian world. They had come to Baghdad on pilgrimage, and they asked to be allowed into the city.

If the Arab conquerors had some kinship with the subjugated people and, consequently, were somewhat tolerant toward the communities that had not become Muslim, the Turks, who came from faraway places, had no such scruples. There were no common genes or shared histories with the caliphate's minority citizens. Whereas the Arabs had managed to develop a common culture by being reconciled with the cultures of the defeated empires, the Turks arrived with the zeal of new converts, and they were not interested in reconciliations and mutual understandings. Once they came into Baghdad, they forced al-Qa'im, the caliph, to recognize the Seljuk leadership. They also dictated that, in order to secure true Turkish succession, Turkish caliphs could only marry Turkish women. Their rules regarding succession did not end there; if one of their own Turkish caliphs was deemed unable to procreate, he was beheaded and replaced.

From then on, the Seljuk Turks took control of the entire Middle Eastern Muslim community. The roads in Jerusalem were closed to individual pilgrims, and many of them were massacred. With this as a backdrop, Western Christians rallied Pope Urban II to wage a just war—to end the massacre of Christian pilgrims and to liberate the holy places of the East. These would be the first crusades.

With the fall of Constantinople in 1453, the Ottomans put an end to the Eastern Roman Empire and took up the caliphate's torch. Their expansion was marked by a constant threat to Europe from the Balkans and northern Africa. Two centuries later, their advancement was stopped at the walls in Vienna in 1683.

This stalemated, hostile environment would last for five centuries, until the First World War, when the Ottoman Caliphate finally collapsed. And this, in turn, precipitated the revenge of old European nations, which completely divided the Turkish Empire. After World War I, the Arab states that were built on the ruins of the Ottoman Empire were not only designed to lead the people toward modernism under the auspices of the League of Nations and the United Nations; their state leaders were also supposed to ensure the protection of Europe from illegal immigration and radical Islamism.

Yet if the West's paw in this new societal model had seduced men like Nasser and Assad, it had also pushed whole sectors of these societies, which toppled under the influence of the Muslim Brotherhood, to be radicalized. Part of the authoritarian regimes' mission had been to warn the West about the extremities of the radicalized factions. These regimes shared an interest with Western powers in preventing extremists from gaining any real foothold. In the eyes of the Muslim Brotherhood, the authoritarian regimes were guilty of pandering to Western powers, and in reality, the more these regimes tried to adopt a democratic system, in homage to modern Western development, the faster they spelled their own downfall. Adoption of a governmental system that allows the law of the majority, by a ruling power that is in fact in the minority, was a move toward political, societal, and governing suicide that would cause ripple effects in all of the surrounding states.

Bashar al-Assad's Syria would pay the consequences of such an experiment in societal development. He would be found guilty of being faithful, in his governing style, to what the Europeans of an earlier era expected of him—namely, to head a secular authoritarian regime, as Libya, Saddam's Iraq, Egypt, Algeria, and Tunisia had previously been. While in the years following World War I the plan had been that these countries would protect Europe from immigration and Islamism, in the eyes of the modern European leaders, democracy was encouraged to such a degree that it took precedence over security. In a movement of sheer masochism, the West encouraged political developments that would destroy systems designed as a safeguard against extremism; smooth power transitions are possible, but not in such circumstances as they encouraged. In 2020, ten years after the Arab Spring, the results were widespread and undeniable: Islamist terrorism and uncontrolled migratory waves, while the democracy that was supposed to be the gateway to modern freedoms had been quashed in almost every country in question.

Only one would resist. He was our best enemy—the one we loved to hate. Syria's al-Assad would remain faithful to the policy of containing Wahhabism and the Muslim Brotherhood's ideology. His followers have died there, working to preserve the Western way of life for the rest of us.

Today, after fifteen hundred years of history in the region, the Middle Eastern Christian world has not quite 3.5 million Christians, spread out over Iraq, Syria, Lebanon, Jordan, Palestine, and Israel—namely, around 750,000 square kilometers. By contrast, in Egypt, a country of just over 1 million square kilometers, there are 20 million Christians.

8

Christmas in Maaloula

After my phone call with Benjamin Blanchard, I waited impatiently while the weeks went by, and my anticipation grew as the Christmas holiday began. It was almost time for the big trip, and I was finally going to return to Syria. I was grateful even at the prospect of temporarily sharing my faith alongside those who had held fast to it in very dark times. The Christians of the Middle East lived in persecution, and thanks to their steadiness and courage, I would experience a spiritual witness unlike any I had ever seen. They lived their whole lives in the sort of Confirmation mission that was my goal.

There were eight of us at Roissy Airport: Benjamin, Damien, Jérémie, Anne-Lise, Anne-Marie, Gérald, Thibault, and Caroline. While we didn't have a direct flight—we had a layover in Algeria—we would actually be landing at Damascus International Airport. I'd never been able to come that way before; on my earlier trips, I'd come into Syria through Lebanon or through Turkey and Jordan.

Just as we left the plane, however, we hit a snag in customs. Our visas, which were supposed to be ready and waiting for us, hadn't been prepared. Thanks to Father Toufic, a Lebanese priest who was the pastor in Maaloula, we finally got through. He had lived in Syria for a very long time and knew how to talk to people. After seven hours of tense investigation and discussion with the authorities, he was able to clear things up, and they let us through.

We had a tumultuous drive into Damascus. While it's a normal thing through most of the Middle East for everyone to ignore the rules of the road, it used to be that Syria was more orderly. Not that day. With the sheer number of cars, the frequent roadblocks, people driving in the wrong direction, men in fatigues, and civilians with Kalashnikov rifles, it felt like we were in a rodeo. But everyone seemed used to the mess and not particularly bothered by it.

Father Toufic explained that the population in the city had gone from five to seven million residents in only a few months. "The communities in the different regions of Syria have come to take refuge here, but even here, it hasn't all been peaceable. Just a few months ago, we were having frequent problems with car bombs."

The crowd brought back old memories. During one of my visits to Damascus, in 2006, the city was already bursting at the seams with refugees from all of the neighboring countries: Iraqis continuing to flee their country, Lebanese running away from the thirty-three days of bombings that pitted Hezbollah against Israel, and Iranians who were there on a pilgrimage. On that trip, there had been no room in the hotels and dormitories surrounding Old Damascus.

We made our way toward Jaramana, an area in the southeast of Damascus. It had grown with the arrival of many Iraqi refugees, who had left their homeland after the American invasion in 2003 and Saddam Hussein's subsequent death in 2006. Kashkol was the small section of Jaramana where we'd be staying; in English, *Kashkol* translates roughly to mean "melting pot." There were Christians there from every rite, as well as Muslims, Sunnites or Shiites, Druzes, and Alawites. They had all left regions threatened by Islamists, and they had found refuge in the capital, which was still a place of law and order thanks to the government and the Syrian National Army.

We weren't just thinking about the Iraqi refugees. Father Toufic also told us about the plight of the Syrian refugees, so many of whom had been displaced because of the civil war. Somewhere close to 13.5 million Syrians had been forced to leave their homes. Before the war, Syria's population had been about 22 million.

The car stopped in front of the Mar Mikhail Monastery, where we would sleep, in Kashkol. We were right up against the edge of the city line into Eastern Ghouta, which lay along all of eastern and northeastern Damascus and continued into the Syrian Desert toward the east. There was a lot of destruction here that the Islamists had caused. Large earthen trenches marked out the area. There were a few businesses here and there, poorly lit by generators. The generators were noisy, but at least they provided some light in a dark place. At the end of the roads, marking dead ends, there were stretches of no-man's-land marked by some sentry boxes that bore the colors of the Syrian Arab Republic. And in the dark of no-man's-land, there were bearded men.

Night had just fallen when we arrived, and the neighborhood was immersed in complete darkness, broken only by the lights from a few street vendors. Caroline and I ordered some *shawarma* for the rest of the group, as we were the only two who spoke Arabic. The shopkeepers smiled when I talked. I was sure my language sounded odd and formal, exactly like a textbook, and I could see they were amused. But at the same time, I sensed that they were touched to hear foreigners speaking their language, even if it sounded unusual.

The next day, we left to visit Old Damascus's different patriarchates in Bab Sharqi and Bab Touma. The districts in Bab Sharqi, al-Qassaa, the Abbasid roundabout, Tahrir Square, the street in

Aleppo, and the French hospital were residential areas that were mainly Christian.

Father Toufic explained that Bab Touma, a zone where Christians and Shiites live together, was targeted every day. And then he laughed as we all jumped at the sound of mortar attacks. "Don't worry," he said. "That's the sound of a skirmish wrapping up, far away. You're in no danger from that. You'll soon learn to hear the differences." Not entirely at ease, despite his reassurance, I nodded silently.

On our second morning, we were all ready to go in front of the monastery gate. While we chatted about our night's sleep, and the fear of sleeping under shell and machine-gun fire, I noticed a man who had a gun on his belt that was sticking out of his shirt. He had just made the sign of the cross while looking at the monastery, and he was kissing his fingers.

Our minivan driver, Samer, was from Maaloula. He was about thirty years old, and he was big and strong. The gentleness and kindness of his face—you could sense that he was a good man—was impossible to miss; you didn't expect a face like that on someone with such an imposing stature. Father Toufic told us that Samer had been part of the volunteers of the National Defense of Maaloula, an armed group that had participated in the village's defense against the Islamists.

Maaloula is in the Qalamoun Mountains, also known as Anti-Lebanon by the Lebanese, who are on the other side of this natural border. It's a small, ancient city that's attached to the mountain. One of its defining features is that its residents still speak Aramaic, which was the language spoken when Christ was alive. It is northeast of Damascus, and it takes about forty minutes from the city to get there by car. You have to go through a main highway that runs along the areas of Jobar and Harasta, which are in Eastern

Ghouta, on the eastern periphery of Damascus. As the dividing line between the militants and us, it was an extremely dangerous road that saw frequent attacks. We had to move quickly, knowing that if we lingered, we would be targets for snipers. One of the Islamists' favorite strategies was to hide in the rubble along the road, shoot to wound one traveler, wait for help to arrive, and then attack again when there were more potential victims, making sure to inflict the greatest possible number of casualties.

As we left the city and made our way onto this road, Samer made the sign of the cross in front of me. I did the same thing, and he accelerated as much as he could, driving strategically to get through this dangerous stretch as fast as possible. Father Toufic was blessing the road, and some of us started to say a Rosary. Others tried to diffuse the tension by talking quietly, and I could hear them laughing uneasily.

The road took us past Douma (in northern Ghouta) and Adra, which had been occupied and bloodied by al-Nusra—the same men currently occupying Ghouta. They had taken some serious hits in their clashes with the Syrian Army, and from the distance of the road, the city didn't seem inhabited. In 2012, al-Qaeda had taken possession of it, and anyone who had been working in the public sector had been executed for colluding with the regime. The women had been dragged by their hair through the snow—naked—before being beheaded. Their heads had been hung in the trees. And, depending on how you looked at it, that wasn't the worst of it; knowing what awaited them at the hands of al-Qaeda, the city's Alawite men had brought together all of their women and children and, standing in a tight group, committed group suicides by releasing grenade pins. Samer explained that it was either that or watch each other be raped and dismembered, knowing that it was your turn next.

We made it through some roadblocks that controlled the traffic, and the car slowed as we moved forward on a narrow road. But I could feel fresh air, and we were starting to catch glimpses of Maaloula. *Maaloula* means "the door" in Aramaic, and it felt like we were gradually moving through the door into the city as we moved along the curving roads that clung to the mountains, coming closer to the village that was set in stone, giving an impression of a cocoon where peace and serenity prevailed.

"Don't let this silence deceive you," Father Toufic said. He said that all of the villages in the Qalamoun Mountains, from Damascus to Homs — including Maaloula— had been invaded and occupied by the Free Syrian Army (FSA), and then in turn by the men of al-Qaeda. Although al-Qaeda was called Jabhat al-Nusra in Syria, Father concluded that it was the same horror under another name.

The occupation had lasted from December 2013 to April 2014. This was before the Syrian Army and the Lebanese Hezbollah freed each of these cities and villages from Islamist terrorism. As we drove along, we saw flags of the Syrian Arab Republic and the Lebanese Hezbollah everywhere. They were planted at regular intervals to remind people that the area was being guarded and monitored.

We entered the village through an arcade that still bore the scars of a suicide bombing that had occurred a few months earlier. A Jordanian suicide truck bombing had killed fourteen soldiers. After only a few turns into the village, we could see its ghostliness and destruction. When we looked down the mountain to the fields below, we could see that they had been burned. And when we looked up the mountain, above the city, we could see the pockmarked face of what had been the five-star hotel Al Safir. It used to be a warm and welcoming spot for the thousands of summer tourists that Maaloula drew in. The ancient village and its people had intrigued, attracted, and amazed travelers, both through their history and their beauty. But after being used by the Islamists as a command base, and thus subsequently destroyed by the Syrian Army as its soldiers moved in to drive out the terrorists, the hotel was cold, dark, deserted, broken, and even frozen over in some spots.

Father Toufic took us to stay at his home in the St. George Parish rectory, which SOS Chrétiens d'Orient had rebuilt. Benjamin had carried a donation for St. George's all the way from Paris, and now he could finally put it where it belonged: it was a new statue of St. George slaying the dragon. The original one had stood by the entrance of the church, but it had been destroyed by the Islamists.

It was December 24, and we gathered inside the church, ready to celebrate Christmas. It was cold—even inside—but we were all wearing the same white sweater, a mark of SOS Chrétiens d'Orient. We had already seen the distortion of the church's façade, where the mosaic image of Christ had been damaged by bullet holes. And now we discovered the carnage inside: icons slashed with knives, their eyes gouged out, claw marks that made it feel like the devil himself had been there in a bout of fury, and paintings that were charred or blackened from fire. Even the church doors had been damaged; where once there had been images of the chalice, the cross, and other Christian symbols, now there were great holes, dug out with knives. Not a single icon or painting in the entire church had been spared.

As Midnight Mass started, the eight of us looked at each other, knowing we were the first foreigners to visit this parish since the start of the conflict. While a few young people had taken their places for Mass, there were not many of them. I didn't know if it was because the village was still almost empty or if the Nativity simply didn't interest them.

Kidnapped in Iraq

The day after Christmas, we got a good chance to see Maaloula on foot, walking easily through the main town on a broad street. We made it up the steep hills to the St. Sergius Monastery. From there, we could admire all of Maaloula, spread out at our feet. Beautiful as it was, it was still impossible to ignore what the village had been through; as we climbed up, we saw a Syrian tank lying on its side in a ravine along the mountain.

St. Sergius, clinging to the mountain face above Maaloula, offered a stunning view of the whole village. Samer was there, too, checking in with his brothers-in-arms. They were all in a military uniform, and from this vantage point, they stayed in close contact with the Syrian Army, safeguarding Maaloula's security from the monastery. Father Toufic took us up to the roof, showing us the mountains that led to Lebanon. Then he turned slightly, pointing in another direction, showing us the little city of Yabroud. It was from there that the Islamists had taken Maaloula, trapping the Syrian Army below.

Before coming back down toward St. George's Church, we went through a small canyon to visit the Convent of St. Thecla. Some people say that the narrow gorge in the mountain was formed when the earth opened up to hide Thecla, a young girl who had been converted through the efforts of St. Paul the Apostle, when she was hunted down by her own people after her conversion to Christianity. The convent itself had been seriously damaged in the conflict, and the thirteen sisters and their three attendants who lived there had been kidnapped by the Islamist forces. They were later used as a bargaining chip, as the Syrian government would eventually release 150 imprisoned women and children in exchange for their release.

In the evening, we spent time in one of Maaloula's homes, which was in the heart of the village, known as Old Maaloula.

The streets are narrow, and the cave dwellings seem to have come out of the rock itself.

The next day, we left Maaloula and traveled north to end our trip in Homs, Syria's third-largest city. We wanted to visit the Christian district of al-Hamidiye. The Christians there had been mobbed by the Islamists of the surrounding neighborhoods, and eventually they had escaped rather than leave themselves to the mercy of al-Nusra militants. When the Syrian Army was able to respond after the fact, it had retaliated seriously by sending in the air force, and the resultant wreckage was bleak. As we made our way from one church to another, the widescale destruction of streets and structures unfolded before our eyes.

The first parish we visited was the Melkite Greek Catholic church. The jihadists had requisitioned its cathedral as a base. The tiles in the outer courtyard of the cathedral had been torn up to plant hemp, and the church basement had been transformed into a private hospital. And as they were running away from the approaching Syrian Army, the jihadists had left a bomb hidden under the bishop's pulpit. Its explosion killed two parishioners.

Before returning to France, we connected with a priest named Father Zahlaoui, who was from Notre Dame Parish in Damascus. He wanted to send a message to the members of our association, and another one to France. When Thibault and I held our cameras, recording his words as he looked directly at us, it felt as though he was speaking to us personally. He stood at the top of the altar steps, surrounded by his choristers and church musicians, and spoke eloquently and at length about what Syria was—and what it would be if it did not have its Christians. What would Syria look like without a government that protects its minorities? What would a nation look like without its music, literature, and culture? This is what it was all about.

Kidnapped in Iraq

I thought about that priest on our flight back to France. I felt connected to him by what seemed like a promise. He had spoken so passionately and with such great assurance that his country would be victorious over these enemies of real beauty and civilization. And deep in my heart, I knew that even in our own country we had similar threats to our defining culture, but they were comparatively subtle and easy for the mainstream to dismiss. Father Zahlaoui focused on one question: "Why?" All of this struck me deeply and stayed with me.

Several years later, on May 3, 2017, I would write in my journal the news that Father Toufic shared with us: of six Maaloula hostages captured in 2013, the bodies of five had been found beheaded. Father saw to their burial.

9

Return to Gray Cholet—Resignation

Back in Cholet, as I prepared my classes for the January term, my head was full of images from our trip. I liked my job, but I was no longer peaceful there. What I saw in Syria deeply upset me—so many Christian communities in truly dire straits. My heart and thoughts were focused over there. I knew that we had been given a kind of duty: we needed to be a voice to the rest of the world, drawing attention to the constant tragedy being experienced by all these people who were silently suffering and dying.

What had been the point of our trip if all we did was come home and go back to our regular lives? How could we bear witness to their plight if we hid in indifference instead of speaking up for those who couldn't speak for themselves? We had a mission, and we could not ignore it.

Despite my inner turmoil, my classes went on peacefully. When we came to the topic of the Middle East, I would sometimes go on tangents, speaking about the countries there, about the various people and the issues facing them, not all of which was relevant to what we were actually studying on any given day. I called on the students to look beyond what they saw on television. The answer of one student was biting: "Why don't you go live there if you like it so much?"

Her remark made me aware of something, and I realized that, in a strange way, she was actually making a good point. The message I wanted to offer was not something that could be heard here. Our own society had become so incoherent that my students could not collectively comprehend what I was saying. This student was right. I had to be coherent in this incoherent society.

During this time, I was taking a training course with the Nantes Board of Education that was supposed to improve my teaching methodology. For all of us going through this course, it was clear that this wasn't about the subject matters we specialized in but, rather, the way in which we taught. I thought the method was disagreeable, closer to an institutional dumbing down than anything else. It sacrificed a focus on actual history—so many beautiful passages in French history, truly educational moments of cultural development that defined us, that mattered—for social methodology. I no longer felt at all at home in my academic discipline. It was getting harder and harder to ignore the fact that I needed to be a part of something France was trying to erase even from our history, not to mention our present—something noble, something to be proud of.

I hadn't stopped thinking about Syria, and finding a way to go back there had become an obsession. While the Christmas mission that I'd participated in had been temporary, I found out about another long-term mission that had been set up in Iraq.

I called Benjamin Blanchard to suggest that, if they had a need for it, I could go there for a whole year. I was thinking I could do volunteer work, studying for a thesis, and also write some articles as an independent journalist.

Benjamin got me in touch with Tanneguy, who was the leader of the auxiliary mission in Iraq. As the three of us spoke over the phone, Tanneguy told me about the situation there and mentioned that most volunteers stayed for one to three months. He was quite surprised to hear that I wanted to make a commitment for a whole year and noted that no one had ever suggested such a long time before.

At this point, Benjamin made a brilliant suggestion. "There's already a long-term mission in Iraq that's going rather well, with François-Xavier and Tanneguy managing it just fine. Why don't you set up a long-term mission with the Syria group? Would you have any interest in that?"

My heart leaped, and I said yes without a moment's hesitation.

The next day, after a restless night, I left, as I did every morning, to teach my classes in the two high schools. But unlike every other morning, I knew this would be my last time teaching them. It had been instantly clear to me that this was the right thing to do; this opportunity felt like an answer to my prayers. As I explained my decision to the assistant principals at each school, sharing my perspectives about Middle Eastern Christians, it seemed clear that they understood my decision and, honestly, that it made a lot of sense to them.

Just two months ago, one of them had called me to his office to give me a word of caution and warning. Apparently, my enthusiasm and love for our French history had earned me a reputation among the students not of being a patriot but of being an "exhilarated extremist." I suppose it was no longer socially acceptable for our students to remember that French history was "extreme" in every sense of the word. Although the assistant principal had been kind throughout the incident, he did advise me, "The students are worried about the way you wax so eloquently on the history of France. They're not used to hearing that."

I suppose it would have been more acceptable if I had publicly defiled and apologized for our past, like some willingly "repentant" teachers who in fact hated the country and themselves. But this was not in my nature, and both of the school principals knew it. My colleagues wished me well, and I moved on to the next stage, confident in my decision and without any regrets.

10

Iraq—Christians Driven Out Everywhere

I met Samuel, another volunteer, at Roissy Airport. We were going to make the trip together. While I was in the plane, I thought about the last twenty-four hours. Just three days ago, I was still teaching history and geography in Cholet, and already here I was, on my way to learn how to carry out my new mission in life. Benjamin had explained our plans at the headquarters of the association; I would be in charge of communication for SOS Chrétiens d'Orient, on location, and I'd supply the website with pictures and videos documenting the work we were getting done. Before going to run the mission in Syria, I'd start with four months at the permanent base in Iraq, learning the ropes.

I'd never been to Iraq, let alone to Erbil, in Kurdish territory. The country had been at war since 1990, making such a trip impossible. So while I had managed to visit all of the other countries in the region, this was my first time here.

I recalled with some discomfort that, during one of my trips to Syria in the early 2000s, I had gone to Aleppo from Deir ez-Zor in a bus that was carrying a lot of Iraqi passengers. I ended up talking with some of them about their country, and I told them how much I wanted to travel there. Their faces became somber and serious, and one of them took my hand and cut me off in the middle of what I was saying. "Don't go there," he said. "Don't make such a mistake. They will hurt you." And he ran a finger across his throat, shook his head, and whispered, "Al-Qaeda."

When I thought of Iraq, it's true that this was in my mind, but so were a thousand other things that defined it. I thought that Iraq was Mesopotamia, with the Neo-Babylonians in the north and the Akkado-Sumerians in the south. It was the Code of Hammurabi. It was Abraham's birthplace. It was Nebuchadnezzar, the prophet Daniel, the captivity of the Jews, and their release by the Persians. Iraq was also the Assyrian people before becoming "Little Iran" and the Persian Empire's key and gate. It was also Ctesiphon, the Parthians' winter capital. In medieval times, it was still the Abbasid Caliphate, Harun al-Rashid, and Bayt al-Hikma. It was the center of Shiite Islam with its military garrisons in Kufa and Basra, but especially with its holy cities Najaf and Karbala.

When we arrived at Erbil International Airport in the middle of the night, Tanneguy was waiting for us. I got the sense he was a serious person, but he was friendly and pleasant. He offered us a drink, then told us everything we needed to know about how things were set up there and gave us a few basic safety tips. He mentioned that the other volunteers were all asleep, and as he showed us to our rooms, he said that we'd meet them tomorrow.

The five other volunteers all came from different backgrounds: Matthew, the Armenian; Nicholas, the artist; Bertrand, the rugby player; Melanie; and Lucy, my future general secretary in Damascus. As I got to know them and spent time working alongside them, I was increasingly impressed by how well they got along. We lived in tight quarters, in what was in many ways a small world—and they were very different, both in background and in character.

Our base of operations—in the Christian section of Ankawa in Erbil—was centrally located among the four camps of displaced

Christians with whom we worked. Our activities were essentially directed by the information we received from Christian families, who let us know what people needed. That might be basic things, such as food and hygienic products, or more complicated help with sorting, processing, and understanding paperwork. On easier days, it meant simply spending time with people of all ages who were living in the camp: coloring and songs with the little ones, ball games with the teenagers, and dominos with the elderly.

Erbil was the capital of the autonomous Kurdistan Region of Iraq. Since the dawn of time, it had sheltered the Kurdish people. The Kurds were an Indo-European people who came from an Iranian family line. Since the antiquity of the Kurds, they had lived in the mountains, whereas the Persians had settled in the Piedmont Plain. The Kurds were mercenaries who worked for the much greater dominant powers. They had always lived on the fringes and were used to being used for other people's dirty work, never being allowed to form themselves into their own sovereign state. This history went back all the way to the sixteenth century, when the Kurds from the Barzani tribe had fought as mercenaries for the Ottoman Turks—against the Kurds from the Talabani tribe, who were mercenaries for the Safavid Persians. The Barzani-Talabani rivalry had persisted in Iraqi Kurdistan to this day, with the Barzanis in Erbil heading up the pro-Turkish Kurdistan Democratic Party (KDP), and the Talibanis in Sulaymaniyah heading up the pro-Iranian Patriotic Union of Kurdistan (PUK). The Syrian Kurds were separate.

Overall, there were almost thirty million Kurds, and they were splintered between Turkey, Iran, Iraq, and Syria. The frustration of not being an established state did not dissipate with their diaspora to these four different countries, a frustration that was in fact all the more acute because their presence in the region had predated the arrival of both the Turks and the Arabs. The Kurds were a fated people. When the Treaty of Sèvres was replaced by the Treaty of Lausanne in 1923, they were the only significant group not given a sovereign state. The Europeans, who were overseeing the territorial divisions and assignments, never took the Kurds seriously because of all their internal tribal divisions, which had been so deeply rooted for centuries; their divisions were as numerous as the countries among which they were scattered, and they lived with those divisions every day.

When Kurdistan finally came to be created in 1970, it was only in the face of a great deal of opposition from the Turks. Indeed, the land to form Kurdistan was in fact a large portion of Turkey, and the Turks referred to it as "eastern Turkey." The Turks hated the Kurds, despite having hired them to clear any Christian presence out of the region through mass genocide. Assyro-Chaldeans, Syrians, and Armenians had been massacred there during the First World War in what would be known as the first genocide of the twentieth century.

One friend told me a story that his grandfather used to tell him during his childhood. This old man had survived the massacre of his people during his youth, and he shared a legendary tale of the time. As one Armenian man was about to die, he warned his Kurdish murderer of the treachery of his Turkish "employers": "We are their breakfast. You will be their lunch." The Christians who live in this area now are descendants of the survivors of the 1915 genocide, and they rub shoulders with the descendants of those who had cut their throats a century earlier. I understood the apprehension and mistrust of the Christians toward their hosts.

By the mid-1980s, bloody wars between the Turkish Army and Kurdish guerillas were continuing on. Some Kurds had fought for the Iranians in Iraq, and others for the Iraqis in Iran, from

1980 to 1988; there was a conflict between Arab nationalism, led by Saddam Hussein, and the first manifestation of political Islamism, led by Imam Khomeini. The consequences were dark. In one instance, five thousand Kurds were gassed in Halabja on the Iranian border in 1988, thanks to the orders of "Chemical Ali," Saddam Hussein's brother-in-law.

Meanwhile, in Syria, the Kurds' citizenship was revoked in 1962, a policy that wasn't reversed until 2011. Many scholars believe this reversal was not at all undertaken in a spirit of restitution and was instead nothing more than a political ploy to try to bolster support for the standing government in the face of the Syrian Civil War.

After the American invasion of Iraq in 2003, the Kurds were famous on the world stage. In 2005, Iraq exploded into three fragments—Sunnistan to the west, Shiastan to the east, and an autonomous Kurdistan to the north. The Kurds' region, which was full of petroleum, made them rich overnight, and they could finally take charge of their own destiny.

Erbil had been a dusty little town in the mountains, but in the early 2000s, it developed into a modern city, with glass and steel buildings competing for prominence against an increasingly impressive skyline. In 2014, however, the war against ISIS stopped this economic ascension and froze the construction development in its tracks. It transformed from a modern, growing city into the epicenter of international human aid. Displaced people set up camps in random spots all over the city: vacant lots, strip malls, an empty supermarket, and buildings that were only ever half-finished. Placed all over the city, the banners of the United Nations High Commissioner for Refugees (UNHCR) were visible from miles away. They marked out individual homes in living quarters that resembled squats or slums. The refugees looked like nomads. They wandered from one plastic canvas to another, without knowing where to settle. There were only a few kilometers between them and their native land, but thanks to the ISIS occupation, no one was going home. The camps had also become temporary homes to many Yezidis fleeing from the advance of ISIS fighters. There were horrible rumors about what they had experienced—slavery, rape, torture, and all manner of horrific inhumanities.

The elites had left the country a long time ago, and the years of persecution and loss of everything that defined Iraqi Christians meant that they were homeless in their own country. Many of them looked back with nostalgia to the time of Saddam, saying that he had been a true shield against Islamism. Since his death, the extremism of many Muslims had gone unchecked, and the chaos induced by their radical fantasies of a caliphate was a daily reality instead of a distant nightmare. One Syrian Orthodox bishop, Monsignor Daoud, was invited to a lecture series in France and made the trip from his home in Mosul. When one of the conference attendees asked him if any Muslims had helped him and his fellow Christians during the war, his direct answer made the whole audience laugh: "Yes! Those who hadn't read the Koran." The implication, of course, is that "well-informed" Muslims whose allegiances are not tempered or held in check are intrinsically inimical to Christianity and show that enmity, sometimes brutally, in their everyday actions.

I stayed in Erbil for a total of four months. I was sorry to leave our team at the end of my time there, but I was also eager and anxious to take all I had learned in Iraq and put it to good use back in Syria.

11

Damascus in Wartime

When I arrived in Syria after my time in Erbil, the Syrian Civil War had started four years previously, in 2011. While we were driving from the airport toward the center of the capital, I saw large posters of Bashar al-Assad hung up all over the city. The taxi driver was quiet, keeping his eyes on the congested road. I said to him in Arabic, "You all must really like your president. You have pictures of him everywhere!"

He glanced at me in the rearview mirror to see if I was kidding him or operating from some ulterior motive. I realized I had made him a little nervous, and to reassure him, I added quickly, "I'm coming from doing charity work in Iraq. Before that, I was in France. I'm French."

He instantly relaxed and all at once started talking nonstop.

"Doctor Bashar al-Assad is our hero. If he wasn't here to defend us, we would have all died a long time ago. Did you know that the Islamists have been in our country for a long time? His father, Hafez—may God bless him—crushed them in Hama in 1982 when they rose against the government. Sir, we are a secular country. Religion is a personal matter, but we have all watched the Muslim Brotherhood try to rise to power for forty long years, wanting to impose their way of life on all of us. Luckily, our president is here.

If not for him, my wife couldn't drive, go to cafes to smoke hookah, or go out by herself. That's the truth!"

I thanked him for the drive—and his conversation—as he dropped me off in front of a picturesque hotel in the Bab Sharqi neighborhood of Damascus. That night, I met up with Antoun, also known as Tony, one of our Maaloula contacts. It was good to sit and have a beer with him, to catch up on everything that had happened in the six months since our Christmas trip. He shared with me that, like many Syrians, he was still at a loss to understand how the country had toppled in the war, and what fatal chain of events had dragged them all down.

"You know," he said, "at the beginning, there was some un-derstanding, some ability to get along between the relatively peaceful anti-government demonstrators and the more extreme Free Syrian Army. There were those who had chosen to wave signs, and there were those who had chosen to bear arms, but we all knew each other, and we were neighbors. Even the most virulent ones were at least somewhat kind toward us Christians. They told us, 'You Christians, you stay out of this conflict. It's between us and Assad!'

"And so that's just what we did in Maaloula, at least in the beginning. We didn't want to get involved, and we kept out of it as long as possible, but we made the fatal mistake of letting the Islamists settle on the mountain heights above our village. It would take several months, and many deaths, for us to decide to defend ourselves against the fanatics. Plenty of people have criticized us for waiting too long to fight back, and they have a point. But after centuries of their conflicts, we are just plain tired of getting caught in the crossfires in these endless confron-tations between Muslims and other Muslims. We understood too late, like thousands of other Syrians, that the problem this time around was deeper, and that the political rifts were hiding a much greater dispute—one that would devolve into such a denominational conflict."

I knew he was right. Arab nationalism was supposed to transcend tribalism and denominational community differences. And yet, for better or worse, the Alawite Assads had risen to power through tribal ties and conflicts. This was why many Sunnites, who were close to the Muslim Brotherhood, wanted to remove them from power—even worse, to exterminate them, in the manner of *Majmoo' al-Fatawa* by Ibn Taymiyyah, who was thrown on the "Alawite heretics" in the thirteenth century.

Tony continued, telling me that ever since Hafez al-Assad had become president in 1970, he had worked to compromise with the Sunnite majority, knowing that it was a potential source of great conflict for his regime and a threat to the stability of his country. During the thirty years of his reign, these efforts at maintaining peace and bolstering the legitimacy of his government included building more mosques than there had ever been during the fourteen hundred previous years of successive Islamic caliphates. Perhaps more significantly, however, to the displeasure of the Sunni majority, he also established the Alawite denomination as the religion of Islam; before his accession to power, this branch of Shia Islam had never been considered as such.

He had then ensured that no non-Muslim person could be eligible for the presidency, closing the door on Syrian Christians despite the fact that their residence in Syria had predated all of these warring Muslim factions—this had been a Christian homeland. Although, just as the taxi driver had said, this was supposed to be a secular country, Sharia law remained one of the bases of the Syrian Constitution. As the decades of the Assads' power continued, many Christians became aware that while their presence was tolerated, their protections were limited and were ensured by only a few good people. If Bashar al-Assad were to fall, the Christians would not be the only religious group whose future hung in the balance: What would happen to the Druzes, the Alawites, the Ismailians, the Twelvers, and the Kurds?

Tony's questions were my questions too. I knew that we needed to discuss them during the SOS Chrétiens d'Orient meetings that I was working on setting up.

One Syrian priest had told me that everyone made a mistake thinking that the war against Sunnite fanaticism had only started in 2011. He assured me this was false; concrete conflict with Sunni extremists had occurred much earlier in the Assad regime. "The country was already at war in 1979," he said. "That was the year that an officer on duty at the Aleppo Artillery School issued a special order to some cadets to attend a morning meeting at the mess hall. The order was issued just to the Alawite cadets. When the eighty of them arrived at the hall, they discovered too late that the officer had let in militants with the Muslim Brotherhood. All of the cadets were shot down unarmed, massacred in accordance with Ibn Taymiyyah's fatwa. This is the truth. But even here in Syria, nobody wants to talk about this."

Even if, as he said, no one wanted to talk about it, the Muslim Brotherhood would eventually pay dearly for their crime. While there were smaller-scale incidents in the intervening years, things would come to a head in 1982, when their headquarters city of Hama was attacked by Hafez al-Assad—and their people slaughtered as they were pulled out of the wreckage of their razed city. The number of those who were killed has never been clear; some say as few as three thousand, but other reports say twenty thousand. The city of Hama and the Muslim Brotherhood have never fully recovered from it—not even today.

These old hatreds rapidly resurged during the civil war. The Sunnites, who represented the armed opposition, quickly joined forces with foreign fighters to boost their numbers. Some factions of the Free Syrian Army even welcomed and fought alongside the jihadists from Libya, Tunisia, Qatar, and Saudi Arabia. But they had made a deal with another devil: it only took a few weeks for the Free Syrian Army to be neither Syrian nor free, as its fighters started receiving orders from religious Shiites in foreign countries, dictating their actions. Soon their slogans no longer had any ring of freedom or democracy; they instead resonated with the sounds of "*Allahu Akbar.*"

The Christian residents of Maaloula, Dmeneh, Rableh, Qusayr, Yabroud, and Maamoura no longer recognized the Muslims they had grown up with and lived with in the villages of Qalamoun — the mountain region between Damascus and Homs. When the Muslims would leave their mosques on Fridays, some of them would shout out through megaphones, "Alawites in the tomb and Christians in Beirut!" In other words, they called out not just for violence to the Alawites but also for Christian exile. And then their messages began to worsen: "Widen the Alawites' graves — throw in the Christians too!"

But things got much worse when ISIS rose to power in 2012. The Syrian Abou Mohammad al-Julani, who was based in Iraq, had come to Syria to lead the al-Nusra Front in January 2012. When Baghdadi, Iraq's ISIS leader, pushed to have the al-Nusra Front be recognized as an ISIS extension in the east, al-Julani had refused. He preferred to support the Egyptian terrorist Ayman al-Zawahiri, who had taken over leadership of al-Qaeda after the deaths of Abu Musab al-Zarqawi and Osama bin Laden. By 2012, al-Nusra had put down roots in the local Syrian communities that had a Sunnite majority — that is, the very ones who made up the Free

Syrian Army. Al-Julani simply needed to use Al-Nusra to absorb the Free Syrian Army. Al-Nusra's connection with al-Qaeda, its abundance of weapons, and its international size would combine to make it the perfect ringleader for all the foreign fighters who were in a hurry to join jihad.

It was in this context—al-Julani wanting to lead through al-Nusra and pushing back against Baghdadi's efforts at ISIS takeover—that the bloody rivalries between al-Nusra and ISIS arose. The violent demonstrations between these two jihadist entities exploded when ISIS, which came from Iraq in the summer of 2014, encroached on the positions of al-Nusra in eastern Syria, especially in Deir ez-Zor and at the gates of al-Hasakah.

And it was in this context that I came to Syria. ISIS was advancing, conquering wide regions, while al-Nusra would not surrender.

The country had changed enormously since my first visits, before the 2007 war. Thousands of jihadists were pouring in from the open borders of Turkey, Iraq, Lebanon, Jordan, and Israel. They had set up fronts in every corner of Syria, dotting the map of the conflict with dozens of terrorist training camps and breeding grounds.

If, by any chance, ISIS were defeated, it seemed likely that all of these foreign factions would splinter to form their own microstates for the Druze, Alawite, Kurdish, and Arabic Sunni communities. However, notably, there would not be any land for the Christians. There were certainly areas where the Christian population was concentrated in Syria—Qalamoun, the Valley of Christians, and Jazira. But unlike the well-defined territories that the other minorities held, there were no large or significant territories where Christians had a continuity of roots and majority.

In every region, the Christians were the minority among the rest of the groups—the Sunnites, Alawites, Druzes, and Kurds. If

ISIS fell, the Christians would of course no longer be subject to ISIS persecution, but they would also be at the mercies of every other faction, and they would be stateless. But they also believed that the only way to hold on to their homeland, which they had worked on shaping for centuries, was to find a way to stay in Syria. No Christian, not even one most opposed to Bashar, wanted to become a *dhimmi*.[3] It was as simple as that.

On the other hand, we also understood what our own French President Nicolas Sarkozy meant when, on September 5, 2011, he explained to Monsignor Bechara Boutros Rai, the Lebanese Maronite patriarch, that the Christians in Syria and Lebanon should take refuge in Europe; they no longer had a place in the Middle East, and they should follow in the steps of the two million Iraqi Christians who had already gone into exile. Now, while we might have understood this position, we did not agree with it: SOS Chrétiens d'Orient was fiercely against this "refugee policy," which had no natural resolution. And, even more than the long-term impracticalities that it perpetuated, we also objected to the inhumanities and the breakdown of civilization that necessarily came with encouragement of such diasporas. We knew what the overall message actually was, what it would lead to, and what motivated it: "Don't stay at home! Flee your country. Become an uprooted person. Above all—above all—do not fight for your land. Come to us in Europe, where you'll become helpless people. We'll find a bullshit job for you that nobody any longer wants to do. Come clean up our smelly backyards. You'll be treated like slaves. You'll live a miserable life. Above all, you'll live on your knees. This is what our societies need in order to continue prospering, going away on weekends, and consuming."

---

[3] A non-Muslim living in Muslim lands granted protected status.

Kidnapped in Iraq

There was no humanism in such tactics. Syrian Christians, like the Lebanese Christians before them, only wanted one thing—to stay home. And we, as Europeans, needed to recall something important: before the war, Syrians had done just that. There had never been a mass, willing exodus of Syrian refugees taking leaky lifeboats to Europe. They wanted to remain in their homeland, and we had to help them find a way to do just that.

12

The Church in Syria

Syria was a Christian country at one time. It had even been the ultimate Christian country. Saul, the persecutor of Christians and the future St. Paul, was touched by Christ's grace on the road to Damascus. He was then baptized by a religious man named Ananias in a house in the Bab Sharqi area in what is now Old Damascus.

Likewise, when Peter set up shop in Antioch, in northwestern Syria, there had already been a Christian community established. Here the first church was built, and here the name *Christian* came into being. Antioch was Christianity's major center, and it spread out from there. All of Syria soon became Christian, a rapid evangelization that would only be bolstered by the conversion of the rest of the Middle East through the Roman Empire in the coming centuries.

Even after the Arab conquest of Jerusalem in 636, Christians would remain the majority population in the region. The Muslim rulers gave them the status of *dhimmi*, as they thought Christians were "People of the Book" because of their belief in one God. However, this "protection" had a price. It was the *jizya*, which was the tax that non-Muslims had to pay for protection under the law. This tax would become heavier and heavier, eventually forcing Christians to be converted to Islam or to be exiled. As the centuries passed, each new Muslim conquest would intensify the conversion of countries to Islam. Proportionally, true Christians reacquainted themselves with dwindling numbers, dhimmitude, slavery, persecutions, and martyrdom.

The first Arabic Muslim invasions against Byzantines and Persians would be relatively tolerant of the Christian presence—that is to say, they would use it to hold on to the empire, at least administratively. Christians would become a minority in the sixteenth century, starting with occupation from the Umayyad Caliphate to the Abbasid one, and then from the Arabs to the Turkish Seljuks, and up to the Ottomans. They also passed through the hands of the Mamluks, the Mongols, and the Timurids.

Each Christian generation only found peace among the Muslims in the eventual lull that followed the militant clashes of each new empire or caliphate. But this peace was always temporary, as every time a new conquering Islamic wave arose, Christians would be suppressed through new persecutions. Despite all of this, however, Syrian Christianity has survived. Today, the country is home to Greek, Syrian, Armenian, Maronite, Assyrian, Chaldean, and Latin churches, and the patriarchates of the Greek Orthodox, Syrian Orthodox, and Greek Catholics are there.

13

Trip to Jazira

I had been in Syria for a week when Benjamin sent me a long summary of the missions that needed to be organized. He made it clear that first and foremost, to the best of our ability, we needed to contact all of Syria's Christian representatives and ask them what they needed.

We started in Jazira, a region that holds one of the largest concentrations of Syrian Christians. The news I was able to gather from my contacts there wasn't good: the Christians in Jazira were caught between the Kurds and ISIS. *Jazira* means "island" in Arabic. It's on a piece of land between the Tigris and Euphrates Rivers. It's made up of several provinces, including the province of al-Hasakah, the eastern part of the province of Aleppo, the southern part of the province of Raqqa, and the southwestern part of the province of Deir ez-Zor. The Kurds' sacred land is "Kurdistan" or "Rojava," which is "the West" in Kurdish. They believe that this rich and fertile region in Jazira is one of the four pieces of the big Kurdish puzzle that stretches from Iran's Zagros Mountains to the center of Asia Minor, while passing through all of northern Iraq. This is a region, however, that exists only in the Kurds' hearts.

The concentration of Christians in this area isn't new. They are the direct descendants of the Assyrians and Arameans. Three millennia ago, Mesopotamia's native Assyrians conquered all of the Fertile Crescent, transforming the Aramean kingdoms that were further west into Assyrian provinces. When the Arameans converted to Christianity, they started being known as Syrians. In 1915, this population was joined by the survivors of the Armenian Genocide, the crime that had been perpetrated by the Turks against the Armenians, the Assyro-Chaldeans, and the Syrians (which we discussed in chapter 10). This atrocity was not limited to a "simple" genocide; the victims were also forced into the *safer barlek*, or "the great march." Hundreds of thousands of men, women, children, and elderly people died as they were pushed by the Turks across the desert that went from Raqqa to Deir ez-Zor. And when war struck Jazira in 2012, almost a century later, the Turks, Arabs, and Kurds returned to finish the work of persecuting the same populations.

The trip to Jazira meant taking a plane from Damascus to Qamishli. There was only one drawback with this plan: it meant flying over ISIS territory, as they held northeast Syria from Turkey to Southern Kurdistan. Knowing that I'd be in that air zone for an hour and a half didn't thrill me. I'd heard too many stories about commercial planes that had been shot down in this airspace. And the authorities at Damascus International Airport, taking things seriously, were supremely unimpressed by my official church documents that were supposed to allow me to fly on this side of the country. The security manager, little, round, and mustachioed, made a face when he saw my passport. Grimacing, he told me to wait while he went to make some phone calls. Thirty minutes later, he came back, returned my documents, and irritably let me pass. But that wasn't the end of it: the flight was also delayed by several hours. Air traffic control was clearly worried about what was happening in the eastern part of the country, on the Deir ez-Zor side. After we got through security, one of the other passengers explained to me that the "airways were occupied and divided between the Americans working to the east of the Euphrates River and the Syrians and Russians flying to the west of the river."

The Free Syrian Army had besieged Deir ez-Zor for three years, but it had gradually lost ground to the Islamists. ISIS had given the al-Nusra Islamists two choices: either they could fight under Baghdadi's orders, or they could abandon their positions. Anyone who had refused was mercilessly executed, while the rest fled toward Aleppo, where al-Nusra still held sway.

I could tell from the way the other travelers stared at me that I stood out in the crowd. It wasn't just the extra scrutiny and the delay with the airport authorities that had attracted their attention — I was dressed differently. As I took in all their appearances, I could recognize the Kurds' square features and the big eyebrows of their wives, who had Indo-European features. The Arabs, who were Bedouins in this part of the country, were also recognizable by their look. Some of them were stretched out on the ground, sleeping, while others talked with each other. Most of the passengers were rural people — the men wore djellaba jackets and red keffiyehs. A few of them had canes, mustaches, and round stomachs. And the women, veiled and dressed in black, looked strong and had faces decorated by the old, traditional Syrian tattoos, some of which showed their tribal affiliations. These women had taken the opportunity to stock up on various goods while they were in the city, and the carry-on compartments on the plane were full of shopping bags from Damascus.

Before I had started this leg of my journey, I had contacted the Syrian Orthodox Church in Qamishli through their patriarchate in Damascus to let them know when they should expect me. When I arrived, I saw they had sent a priest and a driver to get me. Abouna Saliba (*Abouna* is the Arabic word for "Father") was very austere, though cordial, and he didn't talk much. He was tall and had a long beard, and when he looked at me, I felt like his eyes were directly examining my soul. He politely asked if I'd had a good trip, but I could tell that Abouna didn't seem to know why I was here, or what I hoped to accomplish by visiting them.

14

Qamishli

We left the airport, heading for downtown. As we approached each barricade, Abouna Saliba's greetings to soldiers of the Syrian Army—men who were ensuring our security—allowed us to pass through easily. Generally, men of God were respected in all of Syria, regardless of their religion. We even avoided the worst of the traffic jams, as other drivers would see him and courteously wave him forward, saying, "*Faddal abouna, ahlen!* Please, Father, come ahead!"

We came to the heart of Qamishli, and I saw the Armenian, Catholic, Chaldean, and Syrian Orthodox churches all lined up in a row on the same street. With them right next to each other, it was amazing to see the uniqueness of each rite reflected in the architectural details of the buildings. We arrived in the Syrian Orthodox church a little before Mass, and I followed Abouna Saliba into the sacristy. The men who worked alongside the parish priests greeted me, offered me a drink, and asked me dozens of polite questions, clearly curious about my background. They wanted to know who I was, where I came from, what I wanted to do here in Jazira, what organization I belonged to, if I had come from Damascus or Iraq, and if I was helping Christians to stay or migrate.

Though their conversation wasn't hostile, I could sense a bit of mistrust mixed in with their curiosity. I tried to reassure them as I talked about who I was and then moved on to explain the foundation, identity, and mission of SOS Chrétiens d'Orient. But they focused on something else. Some very visible scars on my forearms—the stigma of a troubled past—attracted their attention. I could feel in the way they looked at me that these scars told a different story: they didn't fit with the character I was supposed to represent, and the undercurrent of hesitation in the men was palpable. But, at the same time, they kept asking new questions, and I kept being myself, answering everything as openly and honestly as I could.

Westerners often come illegally to this part of the country, both journalists and humanitarian aid workers. They'd come over the border from Iraqi Kurdistan, crossing into "Syrian Kurdistan" through the border town of Faysh Khabur, where they could get in even without a visa. This was, of course, in the best interests of the Kurds, who had political motivations for getting Westerners into the country. The Syrians did not look kindly on these illegal visitors, as they showed such little respect for the national sovereignty of Syria. Similarly, the Church, regardless of the rite, was faithful and loyal to the government and frowned on such tactics of foreign visitors. One thing was clear: any connection with a foreigner who did not respect the rules of the game in Syria was a very bad thing. Naturally, given the context, I tried to demonstrate my respect for their country however I could.

After celebrating Mass, Abouna Saliba invited me to come with him to a big gathering room in the building just next to the main church. The walls were a clean, bright white, standing out in contrast against the dark blue chairs positioned in a large circle in the middle of the room. The priests all sat together in the center, with the first seat going to Father Abdallah. Abouna Saliba showed me where I should sit, on his right side. The parishioners came in, one after the other, and moved forward to greet and kiss each one of the priests, who gave them each a blessing, a familiar ritual for all of them. Some of them had to leave quickly, but others sat down to talk to the priests, many of them with quite serious troubles. Abouna Saliba considerately tried to translate for me and to explain what was going on. Many of the fathers in the community were angry and distressed, and it was the job of the priests to take care of them in all things, helping them manage all of the intensities that life in this region brought them, no matter how varied. They of course helped with religious matters, but they also supervised children's education and even worked to help their parishioners navigate any legal difficulties they ran into with their immediate community, local authorities, and the state.

"Abouna," one man said, "they took my oldest son! They are demanding a ransom, Abouna, or else they'll make him serve in the Kurdish military." His eyes were rimmed with grief and anger, and he was on the edge of tears. His son had been kidnapped by the Kurds in retribution for his fidelity and loyalty to the Syrian Republic. He had been imprisoned for not joining the ranks of the YPG (People's Protection Units), the branch of the PKK (Kurdistan Workers' Party) in Syria. While the father continued to explain the situation, wiping his eyes, the faces of the priests darkened, but they did not look surprised. It was a scenario they had all seen before, one in which there was little they could do to help.

As Abouna continued to faithfully translate everything for me, his face grew rigid and hard, but he didn't add anything to the conversation beyond translating for me, letting me know in his singsong English (the language we had in common) just how serious the situation was. I was surprised by what I heard, as I hadn't imagined that the Kurdish forces would do something like this.

After the parishioners left, Abouna Saliba spoke a little more freely about what we had just learned. "The Kurds are making a regrettable mistake," he said. "And they will surely pay for it later. The rest of us, who are Christians, have always been faithful to Syria. We give it the best of who we are, as we have done in the past. Syria isn't Bashar al-Assad. Syria is eternal and has proven it more than once. Our people brought knowledge and literature to the conquering Arabs, which led to a golden age, but they have credited themselves with that contribution to civilization. Even so, it is because of this contribution that we have survived. While the Kurds want to impose their struggle against the different regional states on us and make us pay the price for our loyalty to the president, they forget that it was our grandparents who taught their families to read and write. They forget that we have lived together for a long time. Soon enough, with tactics such as these, they will bring down retribution on their own heads and lose the little they have."

We talked for another two hours about history, geopolitics, languages, and civilizations. Father Saliba was cultured, and he loved the identity and culture of his community. Like many people, he was afraid of seeing it disappear. Jazira's Christians were threatened by ISIS in the south and were continually intimidated by the Kurdish independents who lived among them. They could choose to run away from the jihadists, or they could stay and accept the ever-growing oppression of the Democratic Union Party (PYD), the offshoot of the PKK in Syria, and its YPG and YPJ (Women's Protection Units) branches. As Christians, they were loyal to the government, which meant that they were increasingly victims of arrests and kidnappings by the Kurdish separatists, who forced them to leave the Syrian Army, or their support of it, and join the Kurdish ranks.

It was an economic, political, and cultural problem. Christian culture was rooted in and fostered by the Church. Without the Church, the preservation of the identity and heritage of Jazira's Christians was threatened, a fact especially apparent in the realm of education. If it was impossible to provide a Christian education for their children — and this was indeed increasingly difficult — the continuity of the centuries of understanding, beauty, and faith, which collectively informed and defined the identity of their community, could be lost in a single generation.

Even the Kurds themselves suffer from the PYD's policy of strength. Many of them prefer to cross the Iraqi border to live under the much more liberal authority of Barzani's KDP.

Around 9:00 the next morning, I left the hotel and went back to Father Saliba's parish. After everything I had heard the previous evening, my desire to do something concrete to help these people was even stronger, but I didn't know how to really begin. When I found Abouna Saliba, we greeted each other and then sat to discuss it all, to get into some of the concrete details of what I hoped to accomplish. I explained once again this mission of our association: to help Christians wherever they were and to assist them however we could. As Abouna thought long and hard, pondering silently, I sat waiting for his response and advice. While I was somewhat ill at ease in the silence, I also felt proud of what we might accomplish and humbled by the immensity of our task and the reality of our limitations. I could also see that Abouna didn't want to ask me for anything.

Finally, he stood. "Let's go visit the city," he said.

He showed me all of Qamishli in a car, even taking me through both Syrian and Kurdish barricades. As we passed through one neighborhood to another, in just the space of a few meters, we went from territory under Syrian authority straight into territory under Kurdish authority. Driving through the city, he became more expansive, telling me the history of the place and discussing current tensions, interrupting himself now and again to point out specific things or people I should notice.

"Did you know that Qamishli is a French creation?" he asked me, laughing a bit. "It was built up by the French in 1926 at the Turkish border, right in front of the Turkish city of Nusaybin. But, even before that, Christian refugees had started settling here, looking for shelter from the massacres of the 1915 genocide. And after that, Kurdish people began to move here as well, adding to the growth of the city. Eventually, in 1933, they'd be followed by the Assyrians and Chaldeans, who were fleeing from a horrific massacre in Simele, a town about two hundred kilometers east of Qamishli."

He paused here. "Look straight ahead. Do you see the cars driving by the buildings over there? They're in Turkey. We're that close."

The Turks were only a few hundred meters away—behind a wire fence.

"The Kurdish schemes do not scare us," he continued. "What we fear the most is the Turks' reaction to whatever the Kurds decide to do. They won't hesitate to make us pay the consequences of Kurdish stubbornness. Neither will they accept the PKK trying to use Syria as its support base. Just as in the past, we'll get caught in the middle of their strife. Enduring unearned retaliation from both the Turks and Kurds is something we've suffered many times over in the past."

As we drove, I noticed on a main road that the old Arabic street names on Qamishli's road signs had been erased, replaced with names to honor Kurdish martyrs.

Father took me by the Syrian Orthodox church's school. He explained that the country's private schools had two principals, one connected to the church and the other to the state. I supposed that this was a way for the government to supervise church matters, but, even so, Father Saliba remained very attentive to the education and cultivation of his young flock. Knowing that their identity and spirituality depended on it, he worked hard to ensure that the traditions of the countless generations preceding them were passed on to his students. His primary concern was the education of Christian youth, with the sure and certain knowledge that the country's future depended on them. However, because of emigration—and for lack of financial resources—the number of students enrolled in Qamishli's Syrian Orthodox schools noticeably dropped, year after year.

After three days of listening and watching, I sat down and took stock of everything I had learned about the education system there.

At the beginning of the conflict, in 2012, the members of the PYD had threatened to close the public schools unless they all switched to teaching in the Northern Kurdish language, a dialect spoken by most Kurds. The government, however, had made it perfectly clear to the heads of these schools that their teachers would get no salaries if they fell in line with this Kurdish blackmail. And so the Kurds went ahead and forced the school closures. In a mass exodus, all of the public school teachers went to find work at private schools, which were quickly overstaffed; the Kurds hadn't dared to take them on yet.

These private schools, which were connected to the churches, were the last defense against the Kurdish language mandates in education and, consequently, the last chance for the youth in northeast Syria to continue being educated. But unlike the public schools, they were not free. Many of the families forced out of the public schools simply couldn't afford them, and so they stopped sending their children to school. Even so, I visited some classrooms where five children shared benches that had been designed for two, where the overall number of children in a classroom had more than doubled, from twenty to fifty. And, not surprisingly, there weren't just Christian children in these schools: there were Christians, Arabs, and Kurds, all mixed together.

The education "front" was just one piece of the puzzle. More and more of Jazira's residents rose up against the local Syrian administration's "Kurdization," including Syrians and Christians of Syrian and Chaldean descent, Muslim Arabs, and even some Kurds. Some of these people did not hesitate to speak out when I asked them about it, and in fact some became quite angry, confiding their frustrations in me: "The Syrian state's authority in this region is in tatters. If you get stopped and asked for a license when you're driving, the police ask you for your Kurdish driver's license—the national license isn't recognized by the local authorities. So now Jazira's residents have to go through two military services, have two driver's licenses, learn a language that is foreign to them.... Where will it end?"

Meanwhile, the Syrian state took the public stance that everything was fine and all were united, saying that the Kurds were a part of the entire Syrian nation, living and working in the region of Jazira. In reality, the Kurds took advantage of a Syrian state that was weakened by civil war and so was incapable of ensuring the safety of its people. The Kurds were seizing the moment, actively working on moving closer to the creation of a Kurdistan.

While I prepared to head south toward al-Hasakah, the next stop on my journey, I knew I needed to sit down one more time with Father Saliba. He'd had a chance to get to know me a bit better, and I had gotten a better sense of his character. I hoped we could have a frank conversation about what our association could do to help them.

"Abouna," I told him, "I haven't come to Jazira to sightsee. I have come to help you. People in France have already made financial contributions to support your needs, and I'm here only as an intermediary between them and the poor Christians that you represent. And if our help can contribute to the needs of the non-Christians who are also suffering, whether from the hands of ISIS or the Kurds, we are more than happy to help them too."

After listening to me, Abouna left to get something and then came back holding a sheaf of paper with both hands. It was a thick stack of charts, full of the names and ages of all the children who had been admitted into their school for the upcoming year. His request was straightforward: "We need help with this. Can you help us ensure that all of these children can go to school this year? Some are Christians, yes, but most of them are Muslims, from the public schools that were closed."

From the Qamishli area of Jazira, I traveled on for a brief stay in al-Hasakah, and from there on to Damascus. I had only just left al-Hasakah when I heard that ISIS had launched an attack against it. There were two violent explosions, one after the other, in the city's outskirts, and forty hours later, they attacked two al-Hasakah neighborhoods, eventually seizing them. For ten days, the Syrian Army fought against them on their own. Eventually, they were joined by Kurdish forces, but the Kurds would only fight against the jihadists on their own terms—by themselves and under their own flags. Accepting that some help was better than none in such a situation, the Syrian Army agreed to the conditions, and both forces moved to counter ISIS individually.

I got a phone call from my friend, Nadia, an al-Hasakah native. Her voice was oddly calm and came through my cell phone clearly. "They attacked us," she said. "They've taken over our neighborhood, and we've left everything behind."

Nadia had been a close friend of the association since its beginning. In 2013, she met with the first people who had participated in its humanitarian actions. Since then, she'd been supportive and enthusiastic about the arrival of these foreigners in her country, wanting to do anything to help the association mitigate the troubles her war-torn homeland had suffered. I had asked for her help during my trip to Jazira, especially in al-Hasakah.

On the phone today, she was somber as she explained that her family had to run out of their building before the attack. "We stayed for two days, watching them set everything up on the other side of our neighborhood. Do you remember that old drained river that's across from the apartment?"

"I remember. They were in the riverbed?"

"Yes, they were there for those two days, and we could see them from the apartment balconies, getting themselves organized. Everyone in our building was watching them, worried, not able to do anything. When we saw them start setting up mortars in the direction of our homes, we knew we had to get out. And we did get out in time, but we saw them attacking our buildings with bombs and mortar. It was just awful."

While Nadia and her family had fled just in time, ISIS crossed over the river, completing their invasion.

"As of now, we're in a camp for displaced families, a little ways out of the city. We're hoping to make it to Damascus as soon as possible, but even by car, that's a nine- or ten-hour trip. But, I mean, we can't go back home. This is definitely not going to resolve any time soon. And if there is any resolution, who knows if it'll be days or weeks till it gets there."

Nadia and her family—her parents and three brothers—did eventually make it to Damascus. Their home neighborhood in al-Hasakah was now completely controlled by ISIS, and they knew there was no going back. Like thousands of other refugees who had come before them, they resigned themselves to finding a way to get settled in the Syrian capital.

15

First Time in Aleppo—The Road to Death

After getting settled in Damascus, I heard from Benjamin again. He had forwarded me an e-mail from a priest in Aleppo and then called to follow up and make sure I had seen it:

"Hello, Benjamin. We don't know each other. I'm Abouna Fadi from Aleppo. For three years, we've been experiencing some very difficult times without water, electricity, or food, and our young people are leaving the country. Even so, we're doing what we can for the Christian community's survival here, and we wanted to get in touch with you because we've heard about the remarkable work that you've done in Maaloula.

"Last night, there were battles on my street. I don't know how long the city will last. We don't know if we'll still be here tomorrow. Please help us!"

The short, powerful message of this Melkite priest from Aleppo made a big impression on both of us, and it was clear as I listened to Benjamin's voicemail that he knew exactly what should happen. "Alexandre, did you see Abouna Fadi's e-mail? It would be good if you could go to Aleppo as soon as possible!"

I finished listening to his message and then read the e-mail again. It couldn't be more clear: they needed help, and I needed to go to Aleppo.

Kidnapped in Iraq

When I shared the news with Nadia, she was flummoxed and not entirely encouraging. "Go to *Aleppo*? Oh yes, that'll be very simple. It's a straight road, and you'll get there in about ten hours—if you don't get yourself killed along the way."

I laughed a little unwillingly, trying to make light of the situation, but she wasn't kidding. It was in fact quite a dangerous road.

"More precisely," she continued, returning to the map spread out in front of us and tracing the route with her finger, "when you leave from Damascus via the highway, you'll have twelve hours of travel time due north. Once you get past Homs, just a bit further on from there, you'll be on a long, bad stretch of eight uncertain hours in the desert. Jabhat al-Nusra will be less than a kilometer to your left, and ISIS will be less than a kilometer to your right."

Danger or no, we both knew this was the next step I was supposed to take, and I made preparations to leave early the following morning. Anxious as I was, it was a short night. I thought of little else but the certain dangers waiting for me the next day. It was a notoriously terrible—and sometimes lethal—road. Anyone making this trip had to really want it. And so I got out of bed, left Damascus before the sun was up, and made it to the bus terminal by 5:00. It was a makeshift bus station on Adaoui Autostrad, but there were buses that left here for every destination—even for Raqqa, which was effectively the capital of ISIS. I watched as the ticket counter opened, then I bought my ticket and sat to wait while the sky brightened.

After an hour of shifting and nerves, it was almost time to go. At 6:00, a crowd of passengers began to gather by the bus to Aleppo. As I stood, waiting to board, I took in the battered appearance of the bus. There were bullet holes on the large windshield—we had no illusions of safety for this trip.

I could feel the other travelers watching me, sizing me up, some even turning around to stare at me. Unlike in Western countries, such behavior is not considered impolite. Some of them were whispering and smiling, while others looked impassive, but one thing was clear: I would be the oddity on this bus. Any time I happened to meet someone's glance, I tried to nod and smile politely, wanting to let them all know that I wasn't there to do any harm.

As the sun rose behind us over Damascus, the engine started, and the bus slowly shook before picking up speed. I was fearful of the journey that lay ahead, but I was also excited to be discovering the great capital of northern Syria. I tried to focus on the more positive elements of my trip, but the people on the bus were telling terrible stories to each other—about terrorists pretending to be soldiers and setting up fake checkpoints, kidnapping travelers, and murdering some of them. If they got me, I told myself, they'd hit the jackpot. Each time the bus stopped, the people got up to look out the windows at the soldiers standing below, talking about them as they summed them up. I realized that they were trying to find out if they were real soldiers or terrorists.

After the restless night I'd had, I was tired, and the gentle swaying of the bus lulled me to sleep in just a few minutes. But it was not a peaceful sleep. I kept jerking awake as we drove over potholes on the rough road, and the frequent roadblocks made me nervous. At each one, the bus shuddered painfully to a halt, and then getting it going again took a long time. It moved ponderously, like a tired animal, and I knew it would never be able to outrun any attackers we might meet on the road. I wished we could just reach a good speed, keep moving fast, and not stop for anything. I began to pray for our safety.

While we were waved through some of the roadblocks with comparative ease, the soldiers at the major checkpoints required us to identify ourselves. The driver's assistant would move through the rows, collecting our IDs individually and passing them on to be examined by the army's security personnel. My French passport looked out of place, and my neighbors noticed it.

"Where are you from?" the assistant asked me, but in a friendly enough way.

"From France," I responded, as softly as I could, not wanting to advertise the fact. If one of the other passengers overheard and decided to make some easy money by calling the wrong people, I could meet with some serious trouble at the next stop. This was a time to play it safe, by any means possible.

About two hours out from Damascus, I realized I could see Homs coming up ahead of us. We went through the large round-about in the al-Zahra neighborhood before going into the city. The line for this checkpoint was long, and it was a favorite spot for suicide car bombers, but eventually we got through with no incidents. The main road through the city had a branch that went off to the right that would allow us to get around by the outskirts instead of going through the busy city center. As the bus turned off to the east, picking up speed after the checkpoint, I saw a blue road sign for Raqqa, and my nerves ramped up again. What if the bus driver turned out to be treacherous and was planning on delivering the lot of us into the hands of ISIS?

Sensing my anxiety, my neighbor, who had been reciting some surahs (chapters in the Koran), smiled and said to me in Arabic, "We're going toward Raqqa until Ithriyah, but then we'll turn off to the left toward Khanasir. It's dangerous, but it's the only road. *Inshallah kheir.* God willing, everything will go well!"

The highway that connected Homs to Aleppo through Maarat al-Naaman and Saraqib had been cut off at the start of the fighting because it went right through the middle of Idlib. There was a makeshift little road in the desert now that provided access to the country's second largest city through Ithriyah and Khanasir. It was the lifeline that ensured the city's daily supply of raw materials and ammunition.

A few kilometers outside of Homs, the road became even more frightening. I watched the endless steppes through the window as I tried to stay calm. After three hours, at Ithriyah, we turned on a different road. The intersection here was commonly used by different military groups, and I could see a blue Arabic sign that one of them had left as they passed through: *Al mout li Amrika. Al mout li Israil.* "Death to America. Death to Israel." This was a favorite slogan of the Islamic Republic of Iran.

As we continued forward, we started seeing yellow flags along the side of the road. They bore the symbol of the Fatemiyouns, who are Afghan Shiite militiamen under Iran's orders. There were dozens of them, similar to the flags of the Lebanese Hezbollah, and there were also black, green, and yellow flags with names written on them: Hasan and Husayn, the second and third imams and martyrs of Shiite Islam.

The bus took a left turn, toward Khanasir, as we approached Aleppo from the south. The road along this stretch was littered with burned-out car frames and old buses, all destroyed by rockets and IEDs and peppered with machine-gun fire. They were like grisly tombstones along our path, an omen of what might well befall us.

"There are still four more hours," my neighbor said. "Four hours by bus to get through the steppes and the desert, in the middle of the jihadists."

Aleppo, Syria's cultural capital, was just thirty kilometers south of the border from Turkey. At this point, it had been besieged by Islamist groups for almost three years; the fighting had started in July 2012. Aleppo has about two million residents and is the real economic heart of northern Syria, but given its location, it was caught directly between two opposing forces: the Victory Front, and Jabhat al-Nusra and ISIS.

I recalled the dozens of articles I'd read and people I'd heard speaking about how these rebel groups were "moderate and democratic Islamists," even praising them for their temperate stance. But, unfortunately, the truth was very different. While they may have started out as seeming allies to democracy, that had been a long time ago. The Islamist Hydra had swallowed them, and within one short year, their slogans, such as "For freedom and democracy!" had given way to "*Allahu Akbar!*"

We passed Khanasir, but all buses stopped in Safira before proceeding on to Ramouseh, the industrial zone that had become Aleppo's southern gateway. This would be the last place after Homs where we could take a break to find a bathroom or eat, but I elected to discover Ramouseh only through the window. I stayed on the bus, and, as I surveyed the endless wreckage of the war zone around me, I found myself thinking of Dante's *Inferno*.

Finally, we were approaching Aleppo. As we stopped at the various checkpoints leading into the city, we saw the army, but the soldiers looked worn out and stretched thin. As I took in the buildings with holes in them, the sandbags, the empty oil barrels, and the torn flags, I understood that they were regularly under fire. The daily bombings had left a hard look on their faces.

Our bus driver was celebrating. "Aleppo! Aleppo!" he cheered, seemingly at least a little astounded at the trip we had just made without injury. After twelve hours of being on this bus, at 6:00 p.m., I stepped into the city.

I'd only been off the bus for a moment when Abouna Fadi, who was waiting for me, recognized me and stepped forward to greet me.

Abouna Fadi was in charge of a group called *jeunesse étudiante chrétienne*, or JEC—in English, the Young Christian Students, or

YCS. "There aren't as many people in the group as there used to be. A lot of young people have left the country for fear of dying. It's heartbreaking to see the empty streets in the neighborhoods where they grew up. Almost everyone has emigrated, and it leaves little hope for those who have stayed behind."

And yet he himself did stay behind. Abouna Fadi was one of the resistance fighters—the precious few people who worked to make life worth living for the rising generation, trying to keep them meaningfully occupied with activities and projects that would build their communities and help them look to their own futures, in their own homeland. He shared some of this with me as he took me to his parish, the Church of St. Michael.

There were a few young men and women in the church base-ment, putting things together for an activity for the little ones of the parish. They made it clear that they thought I was at least a little crazy to have come there.

"What on earth would bring you all the way to Aleppo, with all our death and destruction?" asked one young woman, though she smiled at me.

Someone else continued, "Yes, why would you come here? We want to leave. We'd rather be in France than here."

Other people from the group chimed in, saying similar things, dreaming of different places. A few of them had picked Canada, while others were thinking about Sweden. But they all agreed on one thing: there was nothing left for them here, and they wanted to know why I'd come.

I smiled, then calmly responded, "I came here for you."

Abouna Fadi beckoned, gesturing for me to join him at the other end of the room. I saluted the young people as I turned to go, and they got right back to their work. Father invited me to sit down and have something to eat in the kitchen.

Kidnapped in Iraq

"You must be hungry after this long trip, and you're probably feeling the need to get cleaned up too," he said. "I'm sorry to say you'll have to excuse us—we no longer have any running water. You'll have to go outside and get a pail to wash yourself. The jihadists are entrenched in the city's eastern neighborhoods, and so they have control of the water stations. They make us thirsty by cutting the water off. The government opened the city's underground tank valves for us, but they went dry several months ago. We use the groundwater for a lot, but it's no good for drinking. The state has started allowing us to purify the water that comes from wells under the city's churches and mosques."

I would learn that the city of Aleppo was full of water. But it was underground, so new wells had been dug below the mosques and churches, turning them into water stations and dividing their precious stores among the people.

Abouna Fadi went with me to St. Matilda's Church, home to a community of Salesians, where I'd be staying that night. As we went, I shared some of the things I'd heard from the YCS group at his church. He looked very sad, replying simply, "I need you precisely because of that. I need you to restore hope to our young people. What will our country become if they all leave us?"

The Salesians' home was a Latin Christian community that opened its doors to Christian children from every Eastern rite, offering them summer activities. It had always been a good mission, but it had become especially important since all of these young people were really suffering from the war. They lived surrounded by the sounds of bombs and sirens. And almost every day, one of them would lose a friend. Sometimes they moved away, looking for shelter after being displaced, but just as frequently they were killed.

Abouna Fadi introduced me to the Salesian priests—Fathers George, Monir, and Luciano, as well as the future Father Peter—and we went directly to dinner. As we ate, they told me more about what it was like to live in Aleppo at such a time and what the last few years had been like. They also wanted to hear stories of my travels, especially about the bus ride up from Damascus. I was genuinely touched when I realized how much it meant to them that I had made such a journey to try to help them, and I was also reassured by the courageous and peaceful way they talked about the troubles in Aleppo. Their sense of calm made me think that maybe things weren't so bad after all. That's when I heard the first dull, heavy sound in the distance, a noise that made my stomach turn over. I knew all at once that I was hearing bombs dropping, that they were falling one after the other, and that they were getting closer. But the priests kept sitting around the table, acting as if nothing had happened, calmly eating their dinner.

When the noises finally stopped, one priest paused and turned his head to listen. "That must be coming from the Bani Zeyd area," he said, as if he were talking about a rainstorm.

Father George, the superior of their community, looked at my face and laughed. "It has been like this every night for three years. Welcome to Aleppo, Mr. Alexandre!"

It didn't take long to finish our meager dinner. Father George got up to show me around their home a bit, then led me to my room.

"Tomorrow," he said, "I'll show you the city. Or, rather, what remains of it."

It was a hot night, and the heat made the air feel heavy. I slid between the humid, sticky sheets and tried to fall asleep, but I kept listening. As I started to close my eyes, an explosion burst just off our street. Then there was a second one, coming this time with machine-gun fire. I leapt out of bed and ran into the hallway, but no one else was there. Were they all still sleeping?

Why wasn't anyone else worried, and how could they possibly be sleeping through all of this?

The explosions seemed to be coming closer, and I watched as the windowsills in the hallway shook, throwing dust into the air with each impact. I was petrified. Surely people were firing weapons just on the other side of my wall, directly in front of the monastery. I was horrified, and I was certain that the jihadists were moments away from bursting through the doors, coming in to execute us. My mind raced and my heart pounded, but despite everything, the hallway remained quiet. I was the only one who had gotten up, and I was wandering around in my underwear all by myself. Not knowing what else to do, I turned back to my room, still trembling, sure that we were all going to die before anyone else woke up or got out of his bed.

It was a truly abominable night. Early the next morning, my eyes reddened from lack of sleep, I came into the dining room and found the priests around the breakfast table. I was astonished to see that they all looked well-rested, perfectly fine, not troubled in the least.

When Father George asked me how I slept, I didn't even try to be polite about it. "It was hell!"

The priests all started to chuckle in unison, as if this were some kind of joke.

I continued, dumbfounded: "Didn't you hear the bombings?"

"It has been our background noise for three years," explained Father George. "We don't pay any more attention to it, you know."

He found a piece of paper and a pencil, gestured for me to come sit with him, and started drawing a map. He started with one small dot, then drew a circle around it, roughly the shape of an apple.

"That's where we are," he said. "And that's Aleppo around us."

Then he drew a little triangle coming out from the middle of the circle, like he was making a pie chart.

"That's us – Christian neighborhoods that are still being held by the army. All the rest – almost seventy percent – is in the hands of the jihadists, whom your newspapers call 'the rebels.'"

He sadly shook his head.

"They harass the people of Aleppo. They cut off our water, yes, but they don't stop there, not by any means. It's lethal to be near the eastern part of the downtown area, and also by the western suburbs. ISIS is in the eastern rural areas, while al-Nusra is in the western outskirts. The human toll is heavy. There are thousands of displaced people, refugees, missing persons, people who have been wounded and killed, and countless homeless, including widows and orphans."

He explained that there was only one main road connecting the southern and western parts of the city. This was the route that kept the Syrian economic capital alive, allowing its businesses to operate, to import and export. But more often than not it was cut off by the jihadists, who were only a few kilometers away, sometimes only a few hundred meters away, both to the west and to the east. Most of the people in Aleppo who could afford it had left the city already, taking refuge in the safer regions of the country. Some had left altogether, going to settle in Europe or elsewhere, never to return. Those who couldn't afford it or simply didn't want to leave stayed where they were, steeling themselves to confront the dangers – and sometimes to suffer the ultimate price for their devotion.

Abouna Monir picked up the conversation. "Today, because of so many kidnappings that have already happened, Aleppo's residents are afraid to take a taxi after five in the afternoon. The Christians in particular know they are targets simply because there's this fantasy that Christians are wealthy. We've been living in this horror for three years."

I asked what our association could do for them, and their answer was simple: Get out and support Aleppo's young people. They went on to talk in particular about a place called the Valley of Christians, a peaceful haven where young people could go and experience what it was like to live in safety for just two weeks at a time.

"The Valley of Christians has hardly been affected," said Father George. "It's an ideal place for children who are used to living only in the midst of death. If there were a way to get all of the children, of all ages, out of this city to experience a peaceful moment in a safe place, just for a brief window of time, that would be marvelous."

His eyes grew a little damp as he said this, and I turned the idea over and over in my head as the priests got up from the table to continue with their day. It would be so wonderful to do such a thing for the children, but I knew the risks were substantial. If anything happened to them, I'd never forgive myself.

Even in these early morning hours, before the sun was fully up, the air outside was still heavy with heat as Father and I left the monastery to walk through the city. The neighborhoods seemed dead, and the streets looked deserted. One lone silhouette was hurrying along. I heard some shots in the distance, and I fell back against a wall, trying to take shelter, but the shell fell much further away than I had expected. Everything in the city seemed crooked and haywire, especially in the gray light.

Aleppo had become a city of fleeing shadows, murky silhouettes sliding along the dilapidated façades. With so much darkness, theft and other delinquencies had become commonplace. The city lay in stark contrast to what my memories brought to mind: when I visited Aleppo in 2007, Syria had been one of the world's safest countries.

But despite everything, life went on, such as it was. The businesses that could open up were opening up. Those who could buy were buying. The people who had the luxury of having a meal in a restaurant and of going into the few open cafeterias to smoke hookah were doing it. Despite all the death and destruction, a little voice somewhere in the hearts of these people insisted that they must continue living.

On the day I left Aleppo, I was able to tell Father George that we had arranged things with the association. We would advance the necessary amount in order for Father George to set up some rolling funds, giving the Salesians the ability to allow the greatest number of children possible to leave the city for a week or two at a time. They would enjoy the Valley's peace before returning to the hell of Aleppo, and they would learn that another life was possible.

A different project we'd be supporting was making water more accessible. Mr. Nounou, an engineer whom I'd met there, suggested that SOS Chrétiens d'Orient could supply better management of the already existing wells in two simple ways: by providing pumps to install in them and by purifying the water with the help of filters from the four parishes—St. Matilda, St. George, St. Dimitri, and St. Thérèse. Getting a home water distribution service in place would also be hugely helpful. It would mean the parishes could load big tanks of water onto vans to fill containers that would be distributed among people who couldn't come to get the water for themselves. Most of these people were isolated because of handicaps or infirmities that came with age, or they simply didn't have a car, and carrying large amounts of water over great distances wasn't feasible.

Mr. Nounou had another project that we could support: electricity. The jihadists had blown up all the power plants supplying the city, except for one, and that one had been destroyed by the Americans in 2015. A whole system of generators had been put in place throughout the city, but they needed support to keep it going.

As I prepared to leave the Salesian monastery, each priest gave me a fond farewell, letting me know that this was not goodbye.

Abouna Fadi took me back to the bus terminal, and I could see all of the world's distress in his eyes. "You know, Alexandre, Aleppo won't hold up. The Syrian Army tries to hold back the jihadists every night, but we don't know how long they'll be able to keep them at bay. Who knows when you might be able to return here ... but thank you for coming."

His words moved me deeply, and I tried to tell him so as I said farewell.

I got on the bus and prepared myself for the drive back on "the road of death" to Damascus. As I watched Aleppo slip away, I felt a great strength rising in me. I knew I was going to come back to this city.

16

Kessab

I hadn't been back in Damascus for long when I left on a brief trip to Latakia, a town on the Syrian coast about four hours north of Damascus. I was traveling with Nadia and with Charlotte d'Ornellas, one of the founders of SOS Chrétiens d'Orient, and I looked forward to meeting Archbishop Nicolas Sawaf, the Melkite Church's bishop.

One afternoon, as we were working at the Melkite church, distributing baskets of some simple necessities to displaced people who had come there from Qamishli and Aleppo, I ended up talking with one of the men who had come to collect a basket.

"You must go to Kessab," Agop said. He was an Armenian who had brought his family to the relative safety of Latakia, leaving Aleppo behind them. "What happened there is beyond comprehension. The Turks attacked the city in person!"

I turned to the priest who was working with us, and he confirmed what Agop was saying, shaking his head and looking away momentarily, clearly upset about it.

He then took the time to explain it to me. "Kessab has been forgotten because it's too close to the Turkish border. It's a strictly Armenian village in the historic sense of the word. Long ago, the Armenians paid the Ottoman Turks to preserve the city of Kessab.

In Arabic, *Kessab* means 'to win.' The Armenians had won the right to keep Kessab by this payment. At least," he concluded, "that was the way it was at the time."

I had heard a bit about Kessab before and knew something of the tragedy that had struck its five thousand residents a year earlier—Turkish forces had supported rebel fighters coming from al-Nusra, letting them in to attack the town in 2014—but I was ready to learn more. The general consensus was that this was just one more forced and violent deportation at the hands of the Turks.

Kessab is on the border with Turkey—halfway between Latakia in Syria and Antioch in Turkey. It is surrounded by Turkish mountains, which border it on the north, east, and west sides. The area, which had been retaken by the Syrian Army after being in the hands of the rebels for almost three months, was not easily accessible; they don't make it easy for visitors to get in. Nevertheless, after talking to Agop about it, I wanted to find a way.

Nadia frowned when I asked her about getting us an authorization. "With all the restrictions they have in place, this is not going to be easy. But we can try. Let me talk to the political leaders in the Latakia province. They might have a way for us to take the road from here to there, and they might know how we can arrange to stay there for a bit."

Remarkably, just two days later, we had a special travel document that outlined the name of our association, its manager, our passport numbers, a brief description of our planned activities—and it included written permission that allowed us to stay in Kessab for forty-eight hours. I'd never been to that part of Syria before and was glad for more reasons than one to be allowed to make the trip.

Kessab was sixty-five kilometers north of Latakia, roughly an hour and fifteen minutes by car. As we started our trip, stopping at the major checkpoints on the way out of the city, I was glad for the long, straight road that brought us up along the coast toward the Sanjak of Alexandretta. On the coastline side, we could easily see the mountain that marked the separation between Syria and Turkey. The closer we got to Kessab, the more magnificent the landscapes were. We followed the Bloudan Dam on our right while the Mediterranean Sea was on our left. Trees, tall grass, and mountains surrounded us. The landscape was incredible, lush and green, with everything surrounded by the blue sea and sky.

When we got to Badrousieh, we turned right off the main road, heading up into the mountains. We climbed higher and higher, with the twists and turns getting steeper and longer and the curves tighter. The car started struggling as it worked up the sharp slopes. We took a break and climbed out to look while the car rested. It was gorgeous from up here, with a wide, clear view straight down to the Mediterranean Sea behind us.

It was just beyond this stop that we finally cleared the mountain hiding Kessab and Turkey. We came around a final curve, and Kessab appeared, resting below us. Ramez, our driver, kept slowing as we came into the city—every time he saw a burned-out church or a charred building, and there were many of them. Some places in the city seemed to be completely abandoned and deserted, as if the community had never returned.

In the midst of this gloomy atmosphere, a man came to welcome us, wanting to shake our hands.

"My name is Garo," he said cheerfully, in broken French. "I'm the Armenian community's manager." His French was fairly good, though his Armenian accent was very strong.

Garo clearly loved his city. "If you had known Kessab before the war. . . . It was the best tourist spot in all of Syria. People came from far away to rest here. Now they don't dare do it anymore. What happened here left its mark on them, as it did on all of us. People are scared."

Kidnapped in Iraq

Before the war, Kessab lived on tourism and agriculture. Garo grabbed an apple and offered it to me. He was so enthusiastic and so eager to share that I couldn't possibly refuse it. According to him, these were the best apples in the whole country. "The famous Kessab apples!" he told me, with a big smile.

After a brief time chatting and visiting with Garo, we got down to business. We had come to evaluate the situation, which meant we needed to visit the churches that had been burned by the Islamists last year. We also stopped to looked at the Armenian cultural center that had been destroyed by fire. We could no longer make out its original red color; everything had been darkened by ash and soot.

As Garo led us to the village's heights, in the section that was closer to the bare mountain, he pointed out the Armenian Apostolic church. He showed us the bell lying on the ground in front of the church. Apparently, the Islamists had fired on it from below and eventually climbed up to cut the ropes that held it, letting the bell crash to the ground.

It was one more mark of the Islamists' obsession with silencing the Christians. I had already seen it in the villages in Qalamoun where they had taken over Christian churches. In addition to the destruction and theft of precious artwork, and the desecration of the holy things, they always stripped the churches of their bells.

"You know," said Garo, "the Algerian privateers from the Ottoman Empire, whom you refer to as the Barbarians from Barbary, worked for their sultans and acted in this same way for many centuries. Kidnapping Europeans on their ships wasn't enough for them. They accosted the whole European coastline, kidnapping men and women, plundering the villages, and stealing the church bells."

He explained that the population in Kessab is 60 percent Armenian. A little over 30 percent is Alawite, and there is also a small number of Sunnites. Kessab is the easternmost Armenian city of what was once Greater Armenia. There had been an Armenian Kingdom of Cilicia south of Anatolia in the twelfth to the four-teenth centuries. It had been founded by Armenian refugees who were fleeing the Seljuk invasions and persecutions. The most recent invasion of Kessab was perpetrated by Islamists who were members of the al-Nusra Front, the Ansar al-Sham, the Ahrar al-Sham, the Harakat Sham al-Islam, and the Free Syrian Army.

In the early afternoon, following our visit to the Armenian Apostolic church, Garo brought us to the grade school where the Islamists had previously set up their quarters. A man came toward us. He was small, stocky, and bright-eyed. He looked right at us and spoke in perfect French. It wasn't the formal, stilted French that's learned in books but real spoken French—street French. Hovsep (Armenian for Joseph) introduced himself to us as a "former soldier of the Foreign Legion," where he had served for fifteen years. He had lived in France for almost twenty years before going back to Syria.

"Come," he said, "let me show you the buildings."

The school was next to another building that had been a hotel before the war. As we went up its terrace, we could see Turkey perfectly in front of us and below us. As I walked, I felt some hard objects under my feet. There were thousands of cartridges, cartridge cases, bullets, and used rockets on the schoolyard grounds. Mortar caps were scattered around, and I even saw the tracks from a caterpillar tank.

"These are the killers' tracks," Hovsep told me, gesturing to-ward all the ammunition detritus. "On March 21, around five thirty to six in the morning, we were awakened by the sound of '*Allahu Akbar*.' The bombing of Kessab started that day. But it was strange: the shells never actually touched the houses. They would just explode in the air two feet from the ground. The intensity and rapidity of the strike's rhythm was unheard of. It was quicker than a Kalashnikov rifle that fires automatically; the strike rained everywhere without stopping. Kessab's entire population cleared out in just a few minutes."

"Were you here in the school?"

"Yes, I stayed because I'm the head of the school. I waited for my bosses to come pick up the important documents and order me to leave."

I looked at him, and suddenly I no longer saw a school caretaker in the countryside but the legionnaire who was waiting under fire for his superiors' directives.

He went on. "Turkey was bombing us with its tanks. They were positioned four or five kilometers away and made a barrage of artillery fire, forcing people to run away and clear out. And then they launched their troops on foot. They came hurtling down the mountain. It was hard for me to believe such a thing could happen in this bucolic place, and without warning."

"Nobody saw it coming?"

"There's no army here—only two police stations, one for the National Security Bureau and the other for the secret police. There are only about ten men in each station. There are no soldiers in Kessab," he said, shrugging his shoulders. "But I had at least warned the police. I had seen what was coming."

"What do you mean?"

"If you go to Sakhra, which is one town over from Kessab, you can see into Turkey much better. I had been there several days before the attack, and I saw that they were starting to place tanks along the hills on the Turkish side of the border."

His breath caught a little, but he swallowed and went on. "A few weeks before the attack, the Turks had started to build some observation and surveillance posts just above Kessab, where the mountain is bare and rocky on the top. I could see them from this side of the mountain, and I watched them carefully. There were two or three orange construction trucks that came through each day or two, and I could see them heading toward the Turkish building operations. I couldn't seem to get anyone else to pay attention. And then there were the Turkmen from the nearby village."

He was silent for a moment before he continued.

"They started talking among themselves. You know, Mr. Alexandre, we Armenians understand Turkish. These guys were talking about weapons that would soon be in the hands of the Turkmen near Rabia—around thirty kilometers from Kessab. When I heard this, I immediately warned the soldiers who were stationed at the nearest roadblocks and barriers, but they looked at me as though I were foolish. I couldn't seem to get through to them, try as I might to make them understand that, if something were to happen, there weren't nearly enough of them to help us hold any ground. They shrugged and replied, 'Hovsep, sure we understand, but what can we do about it right now?'

"A few days later, I learned that in that very spot near Rabia, where I'd warned the Syrian soldiers that the Turkmen would be well-stocked with new weapons, two jeeps with fourteen Syrian soldiers, on a simple patrol, had fallen in an ambush. It had been set up by the jihadists, who massacred them. The killers also fired some missiles and rockets on Kessab from Rabia. They were aiming for the security and information stations and satellite dishes in the days leading up to March 21, when they finally descended on us from the surrounding woods and mountains."

Hundreds of guys had started to come down, shouting "*Allahu Akbar!*" and spraying the air with bullets. The village's peasants fled before them. The few police officers there had returned fire, but they were vastly outnumbered and had quickly been killed. The officers who were assigned up at the two or three security stations in the heights immediately had their throats slit. Kevork, a seventeen-year-old boy, was executed. He had tried to save the people in Kessab with his motorcycle, running multiple trips to bring them to safety in the nearby village of al-Nabaein. The poor kid had shoes that looked like soldiers' shoes, and so he was accused of being one of Assad's soldiers.

Other Armenians had been killed by snipers. Some people were kidnapped, even one elderly couple. The old man had almost lost his mind. He told Hovsep later that they had shut themselves in their house before the bastards machine-gunned the front door, burst through, and found the old husband and wife fearfully hugging each other. They had been taken as hostages into Damma, a village near Jisr al-Shughur, and put in a henhouse. They said that on that first day, there were maybe only four hundred Islamists at their camp. After two days, there were between eight thousand and twelve thousand. It's only four kilometers from Kessab to the Turkish border, but there were enough Islamists that they could build a human chain all the way from Turkey to Kessab.

"Look, Mr. Alexandre." Hovsep pointed to a division running down the middle of the schoolyard. "They cut the playground in half. Their officers had one side, and their simple soldiers had the other."

He also showed me the bars of the enclosure that surrounded the facility. "They set their targets up here. They'd make crosses out of wood and shoot at them."

He had worked hard to clean out the school and clean up the grounds, and he had clearly made progress. He showed us bags he'd completely filled just with the old bullets from their target practice. But the amount of work still to do was immense.

"In your country, revolutionaries are seen as something noble, but in our society, they are the lowest of the low. They have sold themselves to the highest bidder. They are simply killers and their country's traitors."

17

The Russians Arrive – The Bear's Paw

After our visit to Kessab, our driver, Ramez, began the trip to take us back to Damascus. Hailing from Maaloula, Ramez was the only full-time driver for our association. In order to feed his wife and four children, he now traveled on the country's most dangerous roads with me. He was a discreet and silent man, a calm and confident pilot behind the wheel of his car.

Even so, on this trip, he did not immediately see a huge caravan coming up behind us, and he turned in some surprise when he heard a horn blast. First one truck passed us, and then another, with a whole crowd following along behind them. It was like some impressive, enormous, and majestic dragon moving along the road, lifting tons of dust in its wake. We realized what it was. What everyone for several months had hoped for and expected was there before our eyes: the Russian task force was on its way.

They were greeted as heroes during their entire trip. All the other drivers on the roads opened their windows to salute them, cheer for them, honk their horns in celebration, and signal victory to them, buoyed up by this brute force that was on the move.

Their tanks — beige, like the uniforms of the soldiers seated on the vehicles' roofs — were impressive and brand-new. They made up one long beige column, each soldier shrouded in a dusty halo from his helmet to his boots, glowing in the light of the sun. They moved without stopping, and they were followed by trucks loaded with tanks. I asked Ramez if he knew where they were going.

"To the north, toward the remote areas in the provinces of Latakia and Idlib. Tonight," he said, a fatalistic tone in his voice, "these people will die."

Like many Syrians, Ramez was conflicted and divided even in his own heart by this war that was killing so many of his fellow Syrians. "Except for the Islamists," he would say. "I don't feel conflicted about them being killed. I don't want to be whipped into going to a mosque."

I laughed a little darkly. We had all heard the stories about what the Taliban did in Afghanistan. "You're a Christian. Why would you go to a mosque?"

"That may be," he replied. "But you know as well as I that, if they win, they'll try to force 'conversion' and the mosque on every last one of us."

18

More Volunteers

I was back in Damascus. I was the only one here who managed the administration of our association, its publications and accounting, as well as the necessary meetings with different members of the clergy. It was an intense life, and I felt like I was living in a way that I hadn't for a long time. Serving other Christians in such a manner filled me with joy.

We had encouraging news coming from France. The word of our efforts had spread in Christian circles, and more and more volunteers wanted to join us, to help us, and to prove something to themselves. They were eager to participate in this story. They wanted to come, to push their limits, to meet other people who were doing the same work, and to learn more fully who they themselves were. This was a mission and a cause that they could not find in France. As I interviewed various volunteers, I sensed their desire to leave a stagnant and increasingly lifeless country, a country becoming suited more and more to its retirees than to its rising generations, a country content with sitting endlessly in this muffled and prevalent mediocrity.

All these young people who came to me were motivated by a desire to serve the cause of Christianity, which was under attack everywhere in the world. Where could such a desire be put to better use than in places like Syria, where the Christians—like the Lebanese and the Armenians before them—were the target of so much hellishness in their everyday lives? "Here, being Christian means something," a young person told me. "Here, they are really in solidarity with each other."

Most of these volunteers came during their school vacations and, as such, would only stay for a month or two. But in September, people started arriving who were ready to stay for much longer. They had all started their journey in Paris, where, just as I had, they sat down with Benjamin to learn about the mission of our association. After these interviews, Benjamin would make an assessment of their abilities and send them out to wherever their skills could be put to best use. He did send a lot of them to Syria, and I was the person who welcomed them to this country when they would first arrive in Damascus. All sorts of people came knocking at the door.

Alf was a former infantry regiment marine of Polish descent. He was about thirty years old, and he was nervous and energetic. He only obeyed the person in charge and didn't exactly mesh well with the rest of the crew, especially when he didn't agree with the orders that were given. He saw his time in Syria as a way to heal and to be reconciled with a war zone, since he was coming as a humanitarian aid worker this time and not as a soldier. I would learn, after a number of confidences, about painful moments that he had endured in Afghanistan: suffering the loss of friends, witnessing gruesome deaths, and struggling with despair. He came to work with the association because he wanted to be in a place where he could confront these same demons again but in the role of a healer, not as a soldier—he hoped to find healing for himself while he worked to provide it for the Syrians.

Others tried to take advantage of the situation, like Patrick and Pawel. Unlike Alf, they had volunteered with an ulterior motive — they wanted to travel under the guise of volunteering missionaries to get to the Kurdish zones so they could join forces with the Kurds. Once I learned what was going on, I sent the two of them to different places: Patrick went to Maaloula and Pawel to Kessab. As it turned out, both of them ended up doing wonderful work for us, taking their roles quite seriously and really investing themselves in the tasks we entrusted to them.

Some of our volunteers were the sons or daughters of soldiers, people who wanted to give themselves to a similar life of such meaningful commitment but who desired to work on the humanitarian side of things, approaching it all somewhat differently than their parents had done. Pierre-Augustin, at twenty-two years old, was one of these young people. He had decided it was time to stop being a spectator of the tragedy occurring in the Middle East, and that was when he got in touch with Benjamin. He was the son of a soldier, and it was his father who told him about these regions in the Middle East that had some long-standing relationships with France. Pierre-Augustin could be nervous, but he was ultimately a courageous young man.

Béatrice and Maylis were young women who worked with nurses in the French hospital in Damascus. They assisted with maternity and neonatal care, and they helped with the children's activities in the Salesians' home. They were both the oldest of many siblings; they knew how to take charge of a big group of kids, and they were good at leading teams and coming up with games and activities for the youngest children. But in working here they were motivated, as never before, by a context that imbued their creativity with a meaning, purpose, and satisfaction that they had not previously felt.

Olivier was a different sort than some of the others. In sharp contrast to some volunteers, who had the exaggerated profile of the model Versailles resident, he was working class and definitely hadn't grown up steeped in the French Catholic tradition. I would even say that it bored him a little bit. Yet because of the tragedies facing Syria, Olivier and the rest of the volunteers found themselves united in their desire to help; back home in France, their paths never would have crossed. He was a builder, a mason, but despite his more secular background and lack of familiarity with our Catholicism, he wasn't insensitive to our mission's rhythm of prayer in our daily life. Olivier was in a place where he was seeking something that he knew was missing. Many Frenchmen of our time were deprived of their roots and their historical identity, based on two thousand years of Christianity, but, though they didn't know exactly what they were missing, they were still in some way cognizant of the lack of it in their lives. For Olivier, it was this ardent desire for something deeper, and a thirst for justice, that brought him this far.

Olivier, Béatrice, and Maylis; Pierre-Augustine, Patrick, and Pawel; Alf, and dozens of others like them had remained faithful to St. Louis's promise and Francis I's commitment, with or without this knowledge of French history. Whether it was through ideology or common sense, through a spirit of zeal or curiosity, they had come from all over France—and sometimes from all over Europe and beyond—to try to alleviate the suffering of the Syrian people.

I hadn't been back to Jazira since my first visit in 2015. I knew that the situation in the region had stabilized to the Kurds' advantage, with the region divided in half. The Kurdish-Syrian armed groups that grew out of a new alliance, the Syrian Democratic Forces (SDF), developed under the guardianship of Western forces. As ISIS's land was retaken through one victory after another, it became clear that the Kurds were in the process of realizing their dream—that is to say, the creation of their own state.

I was sitting in our office, thinking on all of this and trying to decide what our next step should be. I decided to talk to Nadia. I sat down with her and asked if she'd like to come with me back to her home in al-Hasakah. We needed to speak with the people there and find out what they needed, and she would be exactly the right person to talk to them. I anticipated that it would be a difficult decision for her, and not surprisingly, all manner of emotions briefly crossed her face when I first proposed the plan to her. But ultimately, and also not surprisingly, she said yes, that she wanted to come with me; she wouldn't pass up this chance to see and help her friends who had managed to survive the ISIS occupation. Good humor and joy came naturally to her, and they were present in this conversation as always, though I knew her smiling face hid a great deal of apprehension. Nonetheless, we made our plans to leave the very next day.

As usually happened when traveling in this region, our flights were delayed for hours the next day, over and over, while we sat at the airport trying to maintain our patience. We made it there by the early afternoon, already worn out from all the complications of the trip but glad that at least al-Hasakah was not quite so warm as it was during the height of the summer months.

When we passed some huge silos painted in the colors of the PYD, I heard Nadia whisper from the back seat where she sat, "Oh my God, this isn't Jazira anymore. They've turned it into Rojava." She didn't say anything else, but her lips were pulled tight, and I saw she fought back tears.

As I mentioned earlier, Rojava is the region in the north of Syria that the Kurdish PYD see as one of the four parts of their ancestral land. Clearly, with their colors so prominent this far into the Jazira region, they had made a lot of progress in the fight to establish themselves here. They were not slow in taking charge and felt themselves protected by the blood of the Kurdish martyrs who had died in this conflict before them. Their mark was everywhere, crying out to us that the city belonged to them: their colors, flags, and giant signs with the effigy of their martyrs, their checkpoints, barriers, and vehicles, their inscriptions on the walls. Nadia lowered her head, as if unable to bear all these visible proofs of their dominance.

Sitting next to the driver, I realized I was dazed. I didn't say a word. All I could think was that I couldn't believe this was reality, not some bad dream. Eventually I learned that portraits of their fallen fighters had been set up in the city's four corners so that no matter which way people were coming or going, they would be sure to see these "martyrs" and their accompanying yellow triangular flags (for the YPG) and green flags (for the YPJ). When we finally arrived at the Syrian Orthodox church, we greeted Father Gabriel warmly and then got right down to business, talking about how things stood with the different factions in their city. The situation differed from one neighborhood of al-Hasakah to another. The Syrian Army had fought to take over Nashwa, and the Kurds had fought to take over Ghuwayran. Both of these neighborhoods had been held by the Islamists for the past several weeks.

Father sadly shook his head as he got to talking about the ever-expanding role of the Kurds. "Because of their success in fighting back against ISIS, they're exerting their presence and their power over us like never before. Their victory has enabled them to become increasingly discriminatory against anyone who supports the Syrian government. What this means for us day-to-day is that life is becoming more and more difficult economically, that Kurdish areas of the city are almost impossible to access, and that we can never escape the patent reminders of their cultural identity, which, with inscriptions to their martyrs on every public surface of the city, they try to assert over all of us."

Father said the cultural heritage they were trying to impose on everyone in the city was far-reaching. Some of the martyrs they publicly honored were from the days of the Nahda, the cultural renaissance of the nineteenth and twentieth centuries, but others were from as far back as the Umayyad dynasty of the seventh and eighth centuries—the first great Muslim caliphate.

What he shared confirmed what we had seen in the streets as we drove to see him. The Kurds were "protecting and sanctifying" all of Jazira with portraits of their martyrs that were regularly positioned all along the streets and boulevards and in the middle of every intersection.

We supposed there were around six thousand Kurdish martyrs. One of the men sitting and talking with us shook his head sadly at this number and asked, "What about the million and a half Christian Syrians, Assyrians, Chaldeans, and Armenians who died at the hand of the Kurds in the last century? This whole region should bear our names."

I silently agreed. The memory of the genocide of the Armenians, Assyro-Chaldeans, and Syrians by the Turks in 1915 was still very present. They weren't about to simply forget 1.5 million of their own people who had been murdered, especially when it was the grandparents of these same aggressive Kurds who had killed them.

19

The Cellar

February 5, 2020, somewhere in Iraq, not far from Baghdad.

The days went by. We had disappeared sixteen days ago, and we had spent the last eight days in this metal cage.

We thought about starting a hunger strike, if only to gain some sort of leverage against our captors.

I found myself thinking about my friend Lad, who used to talk to me with great passion about the power of the Rosary. And then I thought of my mother, who often told me that whole wars had been stopped through the power of praying the Rosary and the sacrifice of fasting. I realized I needed to really start believing that true strength comes through the surrender of prayer and sacrifice. Up until this point, we hadn't done a good job of accepting this trial; we needed to shift our whole mindset, to offer it up, and to trust. During the first two weeks of our captivity, it had been impossible to see past the fear, doubt, misunderstanding, and anger that overwhelmed and blinded us, but somehow I was seeing more clearly now.

Later that same day, a guard took me by the arm when I was going to the shower and barked at me in broken English, "Alexandre! Do you see something?"

"No," I answered, startled. "I don't see anything."

But he was looking at the ski goggles I had on, and I could tell he was unconvinced by my protestation. "Yes ... you see everything!"

When we got back to the cell, he ordered Abou Dany to gather all the ski goggles and hand them over. He was going to add another layer of paint to the lenses to try to make sure we really wouldn't be able to see anything once we put them back on.

An hour later, our guard returned and had us face the wall as he came in. Making us keep our faces to the wall, he put our goggles back on over our eyes and noses. The goggles reeked of paint. At the same time, he tied our arms behind our backs, squeezing them tightly and triggering a sharp pain in my shoulders. Other guards came in and grabbed us by the arms, one by one, taking us out to what I guessed was another GMC.

As we left, the one guard who had seemed more kind than the others asked me to remember him. He told Julien not to forget him when he was playing cards — and that he'd always remember Julien when he played cards. As he said goodbye, he stated that he was sorry this had been difficult for us. Did that mean we were about to be released? It was hard not to hope. He seemed jovial, kissed me, and even danced the *dabke*, taking our arms and singing. His mood was catching, and for a moment, I even felt happy. For a moment, I thought this was the end of our captivity and that we were about to be free.

But it was only a moment. The other guards shoved us into the trunk of the car and shut the door on us. We sat there, cramped and increasingly nervous, for twenty minutes, the car not moving. When we finally heard some of the men climbing into the car and starting the engine, my level of panic rose sharply again. I told myself to breathe, to calm down, that I just had to hold on as long as the car was driving.

The feel of the road changed several times during that hour of driving. Between the smoothness of some stretches and the bumpiness of others, I could tell we were moving from asphalt to dirt roads, with incomprehensible gaps between them. We sped up, we slowed down, and as we grew hotter and sweatier in our small, cramped trunk, my ski goggles slipped down my face, making it even harder to breathe.

Later, Abou Dany told us he could tell we were close to Baghdad from the noise of other cars going past on the highway. "I could hear going over the speed bumps. Those particular speed bumps are only on the highways close to the capital—nowhere else."

When we finally slowed to a stop, we listened as the men got out of the car. We thought we had been left alone there, but then a phone rang in the front seat, and we heard one of our guards answer it.

After about twenty minutes of waiting, they opened the trunk, untied us, and gave us each a lit cigarette. Rarely have I felt so relieved and so grateful. That trunk was barely big enough for two people, let alone four.

They got us out one by one and led us into a basement that was down a long flight of stairs, probably four meters underground. The air was damp and cool, and in my mind, the questions started again. Where were we going? Was this just a landing zone before they brought us back to an embassy? What was this place? They had brought me down first, and I tried to make out my surroundings as best I could while they went back for the rest of us. I thought I saw a bed, and maybe some pipes. I saw colors and what I thought was food on a table.

I thanked God that we weren't in that shipping container anymore, and I prayed with gratitude and hope: "Thank you, Lord! Please, let this be coming to an end."

Our guards led my companions to the nearby beds, then turned to tell us we'd be staying here for the time being, but they didn't say how long that might be, or what might be coming next.

Before they left us, one of them came up quietly beside me and suddenly moved his hand right next to my face, like he was about to strike me. When I flinched, his suspicions were confirmed, and he lost his temper. "This one can still see!" he shouted. "*Ichouf hadda!* He's looking!"

The "comedian," the man with the strange, funny voice, was also here, and he responded to this guard who had just betrayed my secret. "*Min? Aledsander?* Who? Alexandre?"

But they didn't do anything to punish me and instead just shook their heads and started walking to the door. As they were leaving, they shouted back, "Abou Dany, let no one get closer than one meter to the door! Tell that troublesome Frenchman. Don't let him get near the door."

We were having trouble with Abou Dany. His subservience toward our jailers exasperated us. In their view, we were all slaves, but he was the chief slave—the one who translated to us and gave us the directions. And because he knew that as an Iraqi he would be the first one to die, he tried to do everything he could to make good with them when they were interacting, but then, when they were gone, he always fell into largely noncommunicative despair. He went to bed with two blankets, covering his body and his head. We looked at each other after watching him cocoon himself, and we all silently understood that he was letting himself die. His attitude was a confirmation of our worst fears, but we did our best to shake it off, to find some hope to cling to.

Able to really see again, we looked around and took stock of our new arrangement. I realized that I hadn't seen water pipes; those had been the legs of a table that had cans of food, cookies, and cream cheese on it. We saw bubble cameras in each of the room's four corners, and there was one in the bathroom too.

Again, the days began to go by. Much to our dismay, we eventually accepted that this wouldn't be ending anytime soon. There was no exit, no release, no freedom—no way out. For how much longer? It had already been more than two weeks. Only two weeks? Surely it must have been at least two months ago; our families certainly felt that far away.

This basement was dark and very cold, and it didn't smell great; the toilet plumbing was definitely close by. Eventually we realized the door was bulletproof, and every time they opened or closed it, we heard multiple locks sliding across the iron, reminding us that we'd never be able to escape. But at least they slid meal trays in to us through a small door.

One day, as a guard was leaving, he turned and teasingly asked Abou Dany, "Who are you? Why are you here?"

"We are humanitarian aid workers."

"Ah, right. You mean you are spies! Well, the Frenchmen may get out of here, but you surely won't." He laughed unkindly, then turned and left.

This had the desired effect on Abou Dany, who didn't translate anything to those of us who couldn't already understand. He wrapped himself in his blanket and turned his back to us, leaning against the wall, as if he wanted to disappear into it.

The days went by slowly, each minute stretching out like an hour. We faced reality and tried to accept that we would be here for an undetermined length of time. That cheerful guard had made us think we'd be getting out soon, but there was no exit here.

We all started to pray the Rosary regularly and then began fasting, eating only bread and water every Wednesday and Friday.

We found that this gave a rhythm to our lives, and we clung to it, building our waking hours around it. And, in my mind, I was traveling in Syria. I kept returning there, where I could think of my wife, Fimy, and our baby. I wondered what they were doing right now.

20

Fimy

September 10, 2015

It was summertime in Syria, and I decided to go to Aleppo. I had
a pattern built where, once a month, I'd hit the road to go visit
the Salesians and see what we could do to respond to the needs
of Abouna Fadi and the local Melkite church. Aleppo's young
people were the main concern of all these priests—the war that
had already been raging for three years was slowly killing the city's
youth, either directly or by driving them out as refugees.

Abouna Fadi had needed financial aid not just to organize his
camps but also to bring them to life. If the camps that this priest
organized offered no entertainment or, more importantly, spirituality—both of which could help the youth momentarily forget the
atrocities they lived with every day, and so give them the strength
they needed to bring a light and purpose to their daily lives—these
young people would gradually let go of the Church and, in the end,
Syria. Many of them had already packed up and left.

In early September, I met Father and the young people in the
"Holy Land," which belonged to the Franciscans in Aleppo. The
place was huge, and it was far from the center of the rest of the
city's Christian areas, near the districts that separated us from

the jihadists. They were never far away, but for here and now, our gathering was warm and joyful. A lot of the young people who had come were excited to see me there too, and they asked me to take pictures with them to remember the day. The brothers had organized a pastry contest, and everyone was getting involved. Ingredients for chocolate cake in war-torn Aleppo might have been hard to come by, but what they lacked in supplies they made up for in enthusiasm.

As I was getting settled, preparing to jump in and help the participants, I felt someone staring at me. I turned around and saw a pair of large, black eyes in the face of a small, young woman with long hair, dressed all in black. There was something in her gaze that was cold and dismissive, and yet her friends whispered to her, looking at me. It didn't take a genius to figure out they were talking to her about me.

When I went back to Damascus, I realized the picture of her face had stayed in my mind. And yet I didn't even know her name. More and more, I would catch myself thinking about her, and each month when I went to Aleppo, I found myself hoping to see her again. I told myself I had developed a fraternal affection for her and that I wanted to look out for my little sister. Eventually I found out that her name was Fimy, and I heard that she was an architecture student who dressed all in black to mourn the loss of her father.

Each month, I came to visit her at the Young Christian Students' Association. Even if Abouna Fadi didn't request me, I came to see her. I sometimes surprised her by waiting for her on a street corner or on the first floor of her home. If she recognized me coming, she would run and jump into my arms.

While she had also started out telling herself that we shared an affection of siblings, over time, without us realizing it, we began to feel quite differently about each other. One day, when we began to speak of it, I finally got up the nerve to ask her if she'd like to marry me. Understandably, she needed a little time before she could say yes. So I asked her if she could introduce me to her family, with Abouna Fadi there with us, so that everything would be proper and transparent.

I didn't want anything to be underhanded. I had a strong desire to protect her from myself, from what people would think of her if they saw us spending time together without any formal arrangement in place. The possibility of slander and gossip was real, and I didn't want her to be hurt; Middle Easterners don't always assume the best of intentions when it comes to Frenchmen. I wanted to make our relationship official, to place it under God's eyes, and to receive her family's blessing.

In the Syrian tradition, this is what's called a "pre-engagement." On June 28, 2016, while Aleppo was still being bombed, we, along with Abouna Fadi and Ramez, went to see Fimy's family. They were expecting us; her mother, brother, sister, two paternal uncles, and her maternal aunts were all there.

Everyone in the room waited for me to talk, but I didn't know how to begin. Abouna's voice broke the silence, explaining the reason for our visit to our hosts. Then he invited me to express my intentions.

I cleared my throat and, trying to keep my nerves at bay, addressed Fimy's mother. "Ma'am, I come to ask you, in Abouna Fadi's presence, to allow me to visit your daughter. I would like your blessing. I'm doing this because I want to marry her."

Fimy's mother, who was as uncomfortable as I was, granted us her permission. Abouna Fadi stood and prayed for us a prayer of blessing, asking for the protection of our relationship.

After this day, Fimy and I could walk in public alone, go out to have a drink, or sit to eat in one of the few open restaurants without worrying about the way this could be perceived. We had been open before God and her family, and we could move forward with all grace, approval, and freedom without risking her reputation by leaving anything unspoken.

One day, as we were walking together, I asked her about her father. I knew that she had been wearing her black mourning clothes for a year, but she had never told me about him. She turned and looked at me, then decided to entrust me with the story of her grief.

Her father had been from al-Darbasiyah, she said, not far from Qamishli, on the Turkish border. Her mother was from Jisr al-Shughur in the province of Idlib. Her father's lands—those he had worked for forty years—had been confiscated by the PYD men to fuel their war efforts in the creation of a Kurdistan. All of his agricultural equipment had gone to the Turks, who had sold it, and the profits were given to the PKK. On her mother's side, the Turkmen who had been employed by Erdogan, the Turkish president, had seized their olive tree crops. These were the same men who had taken over Hovsep's home in Kessab. The sad reality was that, like thousands of Syrians, Fimy's parents had lost everything.

She had little faith that there could be any meaningful reconciliation between the two sides after they had treated her family and so many others in such a way. "A reconciliation with these Muslims, who wake up one day and simply strip away what little you have—never!" She didn't make any attempt to disguise the passionate anger such an idea provoked in her.

She summed up the situation eloquently and completely: their entire country had been developed through decades of hard work undertaken by a minority of honest workers. And, in the space of a few weeks, their whole society had been dismantled by raiders equipped with Bedouin morals.

Fimy's father, who suffered from Parkinson's disease, was dependent on medications. He had been sick well before the war but, up until then, had received good care through regular visits to Lebanon. That care kept him alive. But after the violence started in 2012, it was no longer possible to supply the medications he needed. Violence aside, the economic restrictions that the United States and many European countries imposed on the region had many consequences, some of them very negative for ordinary civilians.

Fimy had gone into a mad rage after she learned about the number of European NGOs helping the fighters and civilians in areas held by the jihadists, when her family, still at that time on the side controlled by the Syrian government, had received no help. Then she watched her father slowly fade away, powerless in the midst of a war with incomprehensible stakes.

As we grew closer to each other, she shared this and many other things with me, including some funny or sweet stories of her childhood, and I began to fall more deeply in love with her. A mutual friend of ours, Elias, always wanted to hear how we were doing and was pleased to see us so happy together. He had introduced us, after all! I knew he was also looking to meet his own soulmate, and Fimy and I would occasionally talk about one young woman or another who we thought would get on well with him. But Elias would never have the chance. One day, as he was going to get his hair cut in the Sulaymaniyah neighborhood, he was killed by missile shrapnel.

March through Old Aleppo to celebrate the victory against
Islamist terrorists. In the background, the citadel of Aleppo.

Examining the scale
of the destruction of
the Great Mosque
of Aleppo.

A heavyweight
carrying a Syrian
army tank on the
road of death between
Ithriyah and Khanasir.

Map of the Syrian Conflict, August 15, 2015

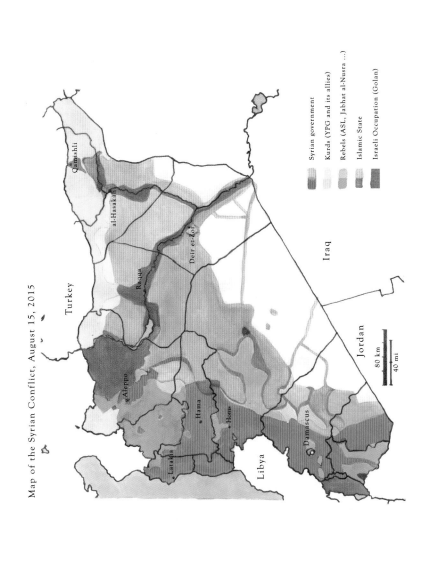

Turkey

Qamishli

al-Hasakah

Raqqa

Deir ez-Zor

Aleppo

Hama

Homs

Latakia

Libya

Damascus

Iraq

Jordan

80 km
40 mi

Syrian government
Kurds (YPG and its allies)
Rebels (ASL, Jabhat al-Nusra ...)
Islamic State
Israeli Occupation (Golan)

On the front line of Mhardeh with Simon al-Wakeel,
after rocket fire from jihadists in the Idlib province.

Alexis and I straighten the cross, full of bullet holes
and lying in debris, on the roof of the Syrian Orthodox
church of Deir ez-Zor, on Cinema Fouad Street.

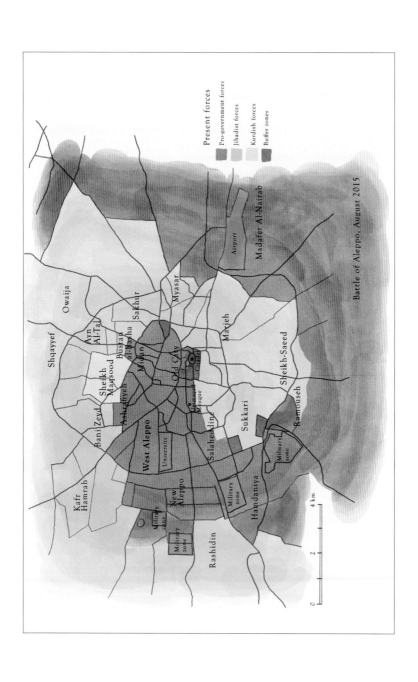

Present forces

Pro-government forces
Jihadist forces
Kurdish forces
Buffer zones

Kafr
Hamrah

Shqayyef

Owaija

Ayn
Al-Tal

Sheikh
Maqsood

Bani Zeyd

Bustan
Al-Basha

Ashrafiyeh

Midan

Sakhur

Myasar

Rashidin

Military
zone

New
Aleppo

West Aleppo

University

Old City

Citadel

Mosque

Marjeh

Military
zone

Salaheddine

Sukkari

Sheikh-Saeed

Handaruiya

Military
zone

Ramouseh

Airport

Madafer Al-Nairab

0   2   4 km

Battle of Aleppo, August 2015

Al-Waer, a neighborhood in the suburbs of Homs. A couple of jihadists are exfiltrated with their weapons of war in front of Syrian army soldiers. They will face each other again in Idlib.

A father and daughter with the Shahada (Muslim profession of faith) inscribed on their foreheads during the exfiltration of the jihadists in al-Waer.

Broken and charred statues and icons in the churches of Yabroud.

Father Aubry and the entire SOS Chrétiens d'Orient team
for the month of July 2017, after celebrating the Holy
Mass in the chapel of the Fortress of the Kurds.

Mass on the heights of Kessab, celebrated by Father Hervé. The
jiahdists from Turkey desecrated the place by inscribing on the wall.

Modern slaves in a brickyard in Punjab, Pakistan.

Arrival at Vélizy-Villacoublay military airport on March 29, 2020, after sixty-six days of captivity. From left to right: Benjamin Blanchard, Julien Dittmar, Alexandre Goodarzy, Antoine Brochon, and François-Xavier Gicquel.

21

The Feast of the Holy Cross

I climbed up the steep mountain to the village of Maaloula. I had started to do this every year on September 13 in honor of the special feast day: this was the vigil of the Feast of the Holy Cross. This year, however, was even more special. It was the first time the villagers were having a full celebration of the day since the end of the occupation of their town by the Free Syrian Army jihadists and Jabhat al-Nusra. Each time I came back, I was in awe all over again at the unique beauty of this place, where the cave dwellings, built into the mountain, formed an exceptional architecture.

When Vespers finished that evening, everyone gathered in the little village square, tightly packed into two groups that faced each other, waiting. I watched as the cantor, or spokesman, of each side was hoisted up above the crowd, carried on the shoulders of several men. They took turns speaking and singing back and forth, putting on a show for the whole square. First one would sing out a poem, and then the other had to respond in prose. All the while, the crowd cheered them on, and, in between each match, everyone would sing and toast and drink a glass of arak. In Old Maaloula, the smell of the spirit hung heavy on the summer air, and the women smiled at their men. Somewhere, a man started beating a drum and singing in a deep, powerful voice, and I soon heard the sound of what had become a new tradition: villagers firing Kalashnikov rifles as they sang.

The literary sparring went on for a good half hour, and then half the crowd went to the Orthodox mountain, while the rest went to the Catholic mountain.

There were two immense crosses set up on top of each mountain, impossible to miss. After the village had been freed from Islamist control on April 14, 2014, the Feast of the Holy Cross became even more meaningful. The villagers didn't erect just these two large crosses; all over the town, they had put small, bright crosses on numerous roofs, proudly displaying their Christian identity and their faith. It had only been a year and a half since they'd been freed, and though the village was gradually reviving, many of the people who fled were still in Damascus.

As I climbed up with the crowd to the Catholic mountain, I watched some of the children run and leap from rock to rock while the older villagers took their time and stayed on the path. Even for the young and agile, who practically ran up the mountain without stopping, ascending the mountain was no easy feat. I could hear them breathing harder as they went along. I climbed with a group of teenagers and young adults, who were all excited to have a stranger there to celebrate with them. I was one of the few French civilians in the whole country, and certainly the only one in the village.

The sun had set, casting the small village below us into shadows, and the night was already dark. At the top of the mountain, people had lit tires on fire as impromptu fireworks; they burst into flame, illuminating the night sky. They had also found some old logs to light on fire, which they rolled down the hill together with the tires. As the objects rolled, they shot out sparks, sending dizzying showers of minute flaming particles in brilliant revolutions. The tires disintegrated as they spun, leaving incandescent firepits on the rocky mountain's side.

Everyone cheered and yelled as the fireballs rolled, and I got as close to the top of the mountain as possible, wanting to watch from a perch high up. While some of the tires and logs broke into thousands of tiny pieces on the mountainside, or hit a fir tree, which was illuminated in turn, others rolled all the way down the streets of Maaloula, sometimes even onto a villager's front porch. But no one was upset; all of the townspeople, and their numerous guests who had come to join in the fun, were celebrating on the rooftops and decks of the Old Maaloula homes, built into the rock just below the Catholic mountain.

The fiery suns and circles threw out sparks in all directions, some even landing on us. The young people took advantage of the freely flowing sparks and the general air of liberality to be more flirtatious with each other than they would on any other night. As the night wore on, the sound of chanting and poetry rang off our mountainside, coming from the celebrations on the Orthodox mountain, calling across the divide to rouse an equal reaction from us. The Catholics responded in turn, with fireworks and singing, until the small hours of the morning, when calm and silence enfolded the village that was finally asleep.

22

Displaced People

October 2015

"It would be good for you to talk to them and tell them they're not alone."

I nodded my head in agreement. I had been invited by the Syrian Catholic church in suburban Homs—in Zaidal—to come speak to Qaryatayn's displaced communities. Fathers Barakat and Naumann were hosting me.

"You must support them," they kept telling me. "They have lost everything."

The villagers of Qaryatayn, which is in the middle of the desert between Homs and Palmyra, had fled just days before ISIS took over their town. They arrived in Homs by the thousands.

They were huddled up in front of me, looking tense. I didn't know what the priests had promised them, or what they had said we could do for them. But I did know that there was some animosity emanating from this group. The husbands and fathers were angry, the wives and mothers terrified, and they all knew winter was coming—and they had no homes.

The two priests calmly talked to the group, explaining how they saw things and what they could do to help. And then they turned the floor over to me. As the refugees swiveled their heads toward me, I knew I would have to find a way, through our association, to help and support them. Though I had been an instrument for humanitarian aid many times over by this point, I had never found myself in a situation quite like this. All of their hurt, angry, sad, and hopeless faces pierced me, and I tried to gather myself to speak the words they needed to hear. I had to say something to restore hope in them, and part of that meant finding practical solutions to help them survive day to day.

Our means were modest; all I could do at the moment was give them some bare necessities—clothes, food, blankets, and oil-burning stoves. One of the men stood up, ready to speak and looking mistrustful. He peppered me with questions, one after another, voicing demands and insisting that they needed ways to improve their own economic situation; short-term handouts, though helpful in the moment, were not enough. I understood where he was coming from, but at the same time no one expected them to be here for any length of time. They were in makeshift, temporary homes and would be forced to move on again before long. What long-term solutions could we realistically set up for them when they almost certainly wouldn't be here that long? Frustrated as they were, they did understand what I was saying, and their overall mood of incendiary irritation abated to a dull anger.

"I'm sorry," I told them. "But we just don't have the means to provide you with things that even your own government cannot. There are things that I can help you with, like the blankets and stoves, and I'll bring more of them. But for these larger questions, we'll have to find a way for you to communicate with the Syrian government."

23

A Return to France

November 2015

During all these travels, I found that I didn't miss France too much, except for my family. That said, I did need to return for at least a few weeks to meet with the association's leaders and give them a proper update about how things were on the ground. There had been dozens of requests for help pouring in, and the work of the association had expanded exponentially since its early days. I got plane tickets for the end of October—I'd been away from home for nine months.

As I flew home, my mind was full of ideas, and I realized I was more eager than I had expected to see familiar places, eat favorite foods, and of course spend time with my family and good friends. I couldn't wait to share all the stories of the people and places I had come to know, not to mention hear from them about what had happened since I'd left. As far as the work I'd do with the association while I was home, we had set up a conference cycle for Father Toufic. It was a terrific opportunity for us to share the realities of life for Christians in the Middle East, a way to raise awareness about many things that Westerners too easily never saw. The association had invited me to speak with Father in some cities in western France; specifically, they wanted me to talk about the jihadist invasion in Maaloula.

Kidnapped in Iraq

One night, November 13, 2015, after coming back from one of the conferences, I met up with some childhood friends in Cholet, planning on spending the evening with them. Raphaël and Johnny were brothers whom I'd known ever since we were kids in Cholet. This was my last night before going to Brussels, where I'd be staying with the Franciscans at St. Anthony's Monastery while I delivered another talk on the work of our association. As I walked that evening with Raphaël and Johnny, eventually settling in their apartment, we talked about everything and nothing, about our plans to change the world, about things we'd done as children—until our conversation was abruptly interrupted by Johnny's phone ringing.

"Damn it!" he yelled. "Guys, there's something crazy going on. It's happening right now.... There's an attack in Paris at the Bataclan nightclub! It's all over Twitter. Raf, turn on the TV!"

Every news reporter on TV was talking about it, some of them saying that accounts were already coming in of forty-five people killed.

"Wait, what's the Bataclan?" Raphaël asked.

"A theater in Paris," said Johnny.

"But wait," I broke in. "I don't understand. It looks like something is happening in Saint-Denis too?" I was checking my phone, looking over messages friends had sent from Paris. Saint-Denis is a northern suburb of Paris, and it looked like people were being attacked and killed there too.

As the story came together, it was hard to make sense of it. There were already reports coming out that some of the attackers had yelled "*Allahu Akbar*" as they shot people down and self-detonated. Raphaël, who had converted to Islam in 2001, was worried about the negative impact this would have on French Muslims.

As more details came out, we learned that one group of terrorists had gotten into the concert hall we'd first heard about, while another terrorist had tried to enter the Stade de France during a football match. And in Saint-Denis, people were sprayed with bullets on café and restaurant terraces. ISIS was already claiming responsibility for the tripart attack, and, together with the rest of our countrymen, we were stunned and overwhelmed that such things could happen in our capital city. The *Charlie Hebdo* attacks had been only eleven months earlier, but here we were again, and on a much larger scale.

A strange sensation took hold of me, almost of déjà vu. I had just come from Syria, which was in the middle of a war. Things like this happened there every day, but I had never expected to come home to France and be met with such atrocities. It was as if the war had followed me home. I felt almost dizzy with the weight of it all, and I thought back to people I'd met in Iraq and Syria, people who warned me, "What is affecting us here at home today will strike you tomorrow!" I had agreed every time, knowing intellectually how quickly and forcefully evil and violence can spread. But it was one thing to take it as an intellectual hypothesis and an entirely different thing to accept that it was actually happening. I had told myself that when I came home from Damascus, from Syria, that when I came back to France, I would be safe. Clearly, I had been wrong.

In the hours following the attacks, I started receiving messages from friends in Damascus and Aleppo. Despite the conditions they lived in every day—being bombed, not able to sleep, not able to get enough food, risking their lives almost every minute of every day—they wanted to know how I was doing. I was deeply touched and unable to communicate with them what it meant to me that they knew what was happening, that they were looking out for me and praying for me. In all fairness, they could have said they'd warned us, that it was our turn, that we should have seen it coming. And, even more understandably, they could have been indifferent, seeing that this sort of thing was normal for them. But no, they were kind, concerned, worried for us, and ready to empathize with us.

President François Hollande and the French government had considered ISIS a terrorist organization but didn't think of it as threatening enough to take seriously, or to warrant any significant response or efforts at deterrence. To justify his nonintervention on the issue, Hollande had simply said that destroying ISIS in Syria would amount to supporting Bashar al-Assad, helping him remain in power. He was merely echoing the unbelievable Laurent Fabius, his minister of foreign affairs, who could always be relied on to say something idiotic. While the United States had gone ahead and put ISIS on the list of terrorist organizations, Fabius had dared to broadcast that Jabhat al-Nusra, the militant Islamist group with ties to al-Qaeda, was "doing a good job on the ground." His "brilliance" left people astounded, and he was quickly enshrined as the most devoted al-Qaeda fan in history. The events of this night cemented him in that position.

It was a short night, full of wakefulness and sorrow. I met three friends in the early morning, as planned, to travel to Brussels. The weather was gray, and a light rain fell. When we arrived at the border, the road narrowed, merging into one lane. Cars idled, waiting their turn before going through the checkpoint. Police were conducting a thorough search of each car.

"What's going on?" Camille asked.

"It's because of the attacks that just happened," I told her. One of the news stories I'd seen talked about how some of the terrorists had come from Belgium. "The cops are looking for them, trying to intercept them if they make an attempt to get back across the border."

We watched as they checked the several dozen cars in line ahead of us. When we rolled up, one of the officers gestured for us to pull off on the side of the road; they hadn't done this with the other cars. Damien, who was driving, rolled down his window so he could hear their orders. One officer went around to look in our trunk, while the other instructed Damien to turn off the engine and asked to see his ID and the car registration.

As Damien handed everything over, the police officer looked back at me and politely asked to see my documents as well.

I started to get nervous. Everyone knew that, in all likelihood, some of the perpetrators of these attacks had been connected to Syria, and here I was with my passport, full of stamps and visas from my many trips to Syria, Lebanon, and Iraq. But he didn't seem too concerned. He checked all of our papers, flipped through my passport, and casually handed the stack of documents back to Damien.

"Have a good day," he said. "Drive safe!"

I was astonished and horrified. There had been 130 deaths and over 400 wounded just on this one night, and this was how the police were handling people who had connections to the Middle East? It would have been better if they had detained me once they'd seen what my passport looked like. How on earth did they expect to catch these guys on their way to Belgium if they were so lackadaisical about these checkpoints? I sat back in my seat, stunned.

During the following days, I found myself just as flabbergasted at the overall reaction of my countrymen to what had happened. There was no ... anger. There was only a limpid response, as if our whole country were too tired and close to extinction to put up a fight, to rouse the aggression that allows for survival.

"You will not have my hate." That became the catchphrase of all we were capable of saying to these cold-blooded murderers. The sentiment originated from one man whose wife had been killed at the Bataclan. In the days immediately following the attack, he wrote an open letter on Facebook to the organizers of the attack, in which he talked about how he and his infant son would move on with their ordinary, daily lives and would not waste time or energy hating or thinking about the people who had taken his wife away so brutally. He would eventually write a book with the same title.

It was a mind-numbingly inhuman response to what had just happened; it would have been comical if it hadn't been so tragic. It was not natural to respond with so little vim and vigor to such an event, and yet that is what the entire French nation did. I was embarrassed for my country, which had clearly lost its national pride, and I couldn't help but think of what the response would have been if one of the ancient and beleaguered Christian communities I had grown to know and love in Syria had been so attacked—as they often were.

Those Syrian Christians fought so as not to disappear, and their villages had courageously arisen as one man to resist elimination. I imagined them asking me what our country was planning to do in response, what the people of Paris would do in reaction to such an attack, and I practically squirmed as I thought about what my response would have to be: "We've written some books, spoken a lot on TV, had some demonstrations, gone on silent marches, lit candles, and released balloons. That's about it." I caught myself laughing an ugly laugh. None of them would understand why or how the courage to cope, to remain standing, to handle moments like these with respectable strength, decision, and execution were no longer traits and abilities that France could claim. When had such virtues been abandoned by our national consciousness? When had we rejected the historical legacy that had been built on fortitude, honor, and bravery? When had cowardice invaded our country?

That's a huge question.

24

Caught in the Battle

I flew back to Beirut on November 20 and then took the road to Damascus. The France I left behind was in mourning, stuck between amazement and bewilderment. But my displaced people from Qaryatayn were waiting for me, and I hadn't forgotten my promise; I had to do my best to keep my word at all times—even when it was difficult (*especially* when it was difficult, Father Toufic would have added).

While I was in Damascus, I made inquiries about blanket sets and oil-burning stoves to set up a delivery to Homs. The supplies would go to the Feyrouze district, where the displaced people from Qaryatayn were staying. We'd organized donations like this before, with volunteers helping us set up the orders, sort them all out, and ship the merchandise from Damascus to Homs in pickup trucks. But we'd never had an order this large before, and we realized we'd need a total of three trucks. Blankets would go into one, stoves into another, and then they'd meet a third truck, a larger one, at an exit outside Damascus, near Jobar. Everything would get loaded together onto the larger truck, which would take the risky road to Homs on its own. The drivers of the smaller trucks refused to go on that route; too many truck drivers had been kidnapped or killed along that road.

Kidnapped in Iraq

Qaryatayn had been taken over almost two months before. As ISIS moved forward across the region, its fighters' next targets would probably be Sadad and Hmein, which were just to the east of this road that connected Damascus to Homs. If the Syrian government lost this essential transportation route, the Syrian state's survival would be in serious jeopardy. It wasn't hard to predict that this was exactly what the Islamists were planning.

My phone rang. It was Talal, one of the drivers, calling to let me know that his truck with the blankets was arriving at the meeting point and that the large truck from Homs would be getting there soon.

I was with the driver in the truck with the oil-burning stoves. We moved to park about a dozen meters in front of Qaboun, a dangerous area at the capital's exit that led to Ghouta's entrance. We had just left the highway when a guard on the exit ramp motioned for us to pull off on the shoulder. We sat waiting for a few minutes, then a tall man on a motorized bicycle gestured for us to move forward. I was confused about what was happening and couldn't tell from what this guy was wearing who he was. I asked the driver if he was a security guard, and he shrugged nonchalantly, looking remarkably blasé, I thought, for such a situation.

Moving slowly, the bike rider opened up a side road that went off to the right, and we pulled along behind him, our truck advancing slowly in concert with the motorcycle. We crossed over some safety barriers and drove into an area that, up until then, had been completely closed off to any other drivers. I thought we were stopping there, but he continued leading us forward, deeper into this zone that had been badly damaged by the violence.

The streets were empty, except for fighters sitting here and there behind sandbags, some on the ground floor of various buildings, others higher up in larger buildings that were still standing.

Gradually, I realized it was a huge mistake for us to be there—nobody, except for the soldiers, should have been there. Strangely, this didn't seem to occur to anyone else, and I managed not to panic about it. As we continued moving forward and I saw one scene of destruction after another, I started hearing sounds of fighting close by, and I realized danger was just around the corner; this whole area would be destroyed.

We pulled to a stop, and as I stepped out, I realized instantly that there was a problem. Immediately ahead of me, men had started firing Kalashnikov rifles into the buildings across the street. Two men were heading back in my direction, and I saw at once that they had been wounded; both had blood flowing freely from their temples. They quickly ran to take cover and find bandages for their head wounds. The shots of the skirmish continued to ring out in the early morning, and then I spotted the men firing from the building across the street. As I took cover behind our car, I counted about ten of them, shooting out into the street, peppering everything in their path.

"These militiamen are reinforcements!" our driver shouted, and I tried to make sense of what was happening.

I thought fast. I had just realized that our ill-chosen meeting place was on the front line that separated the Syrian Army men from Ghouta's terrorists. I talked to the petrified driver in the cab. He was back behind the steering wheel, and he wanted to get out, now. But during a cessation in the shooting, the militiamen immediately surrounded us, wanting to know what we were transporting. We showed them the stoves, and they told us to pull them all out and put them under a tarp. Not thrilled about this order, but not sure what else to do, I turned to the driver and asked him where the larger truck was.

He just shook his head. "All I'm supposed to do is drop these stoves off—I'm not responsible for anything else!"

His fear was catching, and I started to get nervous. It was clear he just wanted to leave the stoves and go. I looked around and realized that our blankets had already been unloaded in this same spot; our other small-truck driver had already come and gone, not sticking around to ask any questions or make sure his cargo got on the truck to Homs. This had not been the plan, and I felt frustration brewing alongside my nervousness. And where was the Homs truck?

The soldiers from the Syrian Army started to get irritated at my stalling. They wanted some straight answers, and I realized I must look fairly foolish to them. What was I doing, they wanted to know, driving into a war zone with a bunch of blankets and stoves? What was I, some kind of idiot? Truth be told, I didn't know why I was in this spot either. Why had we followed that biker?

I tried to explain what I could. "I'm a humanitarian aid worker. I'm bringing blankets and heating equipment for the displaced people in Qaryatayn who live in Homs."

"Qaryatayn's residents are terrorists. They're all terrorists! Is this what you're trying to do? To give equipment to terrorists?"

"No, you don't understand. I—"

"Documents!" one of the officers barked at me.

I felt that I was irritating everyone, and I knew that they were irritating me, not letting me finish any explanations. I handed over my Iranian passport and told myself that surely they'd calm down after that. And they did. The officer immediately relented and turned to his friends. He nodded his head in my direction, and I heard him say "*asidiqa*," which means "friends" in Syrian.

With a much more patient and gentle tone, he asked me again what I was doing here, and none of them interrupted this time as I talked through it all. I even asked if a large truck had come from Homs, and while they hadn't seen one, they did show me a place where I could relatively safely make a phone call to try to figure out what was going on. I managed to get ahold of Nadia, and she said the driver had been stopped on the road, that he was facing questions about why he was traveling to Damascus. Well, at least now I knew what was happening. Most likely it would only be a temporary delay, and I decided that I should stay put for the time being and hope that the Syrian soldiers' position held at least until the transport truck arrived. I'd just need to be patient.

As I sat waiting, I noticed some of the men around me had multiple long scars along their arms, starting at their shoulders and streaking their skin all the way down to their forearms. My Iranian cousins had scars like this; Shiites make them during religious celebrations like those of Ashura as a kind of physical mortification. The most zealous Shiites also strike their heads and bodies with blades as a tribute to a martyr named Husayn who'd been cut up in pieces by the Umayyads. Sometimes these scars are also used to intimidate enemies. Men mutilate themselves before fighting in order to appear more fierce and gruesome. I saw such things often in Tehran's southern neighborhoods, and I myself even have some scars like this, but not nearly so many.

In case there was any doubt, now I knew that they were Shiites. They also had some tattoos that I was trying to make out. One of them had a large sword on his forearm, which I recognized as Ali's sword, Zulfiqar, by its two-edged blade. The good news for me was that while I knew the Syrian Army considered Iranians to be their friends, the Shiites were even more friendly with Iranians. Some of these guys asked me to take pictures of them with their war weapons, and then they posed proudly holding their machine guns, with huge cartridge belts around their waists. Afterward, to my amusement and delight, they asked to take some selfies with me, and we leaned in close for pictures. They all wanted to see the images and asked to pass my phone around. I was glad when they wanted to see some of the other pictures too; I was able to show them scenes from recent trips to Yabroud and Maaloula, where the destruction of the churches was clearly evident.

All at once, shots rang out again, and I could see the faces of men in the upper windows across the street, glaring as they shot at us. Littering the ground between us were UNHCR tarps, sandbags, and empty gas cans emblazoned with the colors of the Syrian Arab Republic. Together, they formed a chaotic setting in this field of concrete ruins that was full of bullet holes.

The barrage of gunfire became continual, and I watched as men passed in front of us in groups of ten and twenty. Some of them were recently wounded, and I noticed an increasing number of head wounds with makeshift bandages wrapped around them. One man was limping, and another had a bandage on his calf. I sometimes heard men shouting to each other, and it sounded like they were on walkie-talkies or calling for reinforcements. Suddenly, one man ran toward the end of the street. He lifted up his Kalashnikov rifle, waving it and then firing at something on his right before he himself ran in that direction, shouting all the while as he disappeared from view.

I couldn't believe where I was, what I was seeing. These guys were going to war with each other right in front of me. Damn. What a mess I'd gotten myself into.

I asked one of the men who'd wanted pictures what this neighborhood was called. He pointed at the street with distaste and said, "This is Qaboun. Ghouta is just behind that building."

No wonder things were so bad right here—we were sitting just feet from the border. And that damn truck still hadn't gotten here!

The shots got louder and closer. One of the soldiers right next to me motioned for me to follow him inside a nearby building. "Boom, boom!" he said, and he was laughing.

The machine guns gave way to mortar fire, which was indescribable and deafening. I couldn't tell which direction the explosive shells came from, but I was pretty sure they were being fired on us and by us, flying in both directions. A soldier took me to an empty storeroom in the building, telling me I should shelter there until the situation eased. All my time in the Middle East and I still didn't know how much damage these war machines could cause.

While I sat there, waiting and listening to the sounds of war raining down all around me, my phone rang. I saw a French number, and I thought that it might be the Parisian office of the SOS Chrétiens d'Orient, so I answered. But to my surprise, I heard the voice of my mother.

"Hello? Alexandre?"

In answer, she heard a bang that shook the walls and momentarily deafened me. Dust fell from the ceiling, and the walls crackled as the vibrations peeled away the paint.

"Alexandre! What was that? Where are you?"

I tried to respond in an even voice, not wanting her to know how hard it was for me to stay calm. I told her everything was fine. "Don't worry, Mom."

"But where are you?"

"Well, you know, somewhere in suburban Damascus." I tried to reassure her, clarifying that I wouldn't be here long and that I'd never planned on being in such a place to begin with. I didn't want her to think I made a habit of getting myself into situations like this. I told her I loved her and that I'd call her again soon, once we could talk more easily.

After we said goodbye, it was only a few more minutes until someone came back looking for me. He brought news that our truck driver had finally arrived. As I came back to a spot where I could see the street again, I saw a mass of people arriving from the left. This was a new round of militiamen, coming to help bring the fight to a finish. Maybe that guy I'd seen running up the street with the rifle a little earlier had called them in.

A stocky man with beige-colored battle fatigues led them. His square appearance and small size made him look like a grizzly bear. He had close-cut brown hair and a square face, and he didn't smile. He led his men in hand-to-hand combat; this was the infantry on the warpath. The many men around him, dressed in black, had a withered but indomitable appearance, with striking eyes. They knew death might well be waiting for them, and they walked forward, uncowed, to face it down. As they walked, one of the aides to the commander seemed to be reporting to him on the situation that lay ahead.

I'd never seen anything like this. It was hard to believe it was real and not some movie set. I pulled my phone out to take a picture, and suddenly a fist swung directly toward my face. I dodged it, but the young soldier who had tried to hit me grabbed the phone from my hands. Looking at the crew ahead of me, I knew this was not the moment to put up a fight. I dropped my hands and just waited as thirty of the men surrounded me. They grabbed me and pushed me forward, and suddenly I stood nose to nose with the commander I'd watched just moments ago. Apparently, it was my turn to present a report for his review.

The young soldier who snatched my phone and handed it over was proud of himself. As their leader scrolled through the photos, the kid commented on them, boasting about what he thought was a trophy. He kept glancing at their leader as he spoke, clearly trying to catch his attention and receive some mark of approval for his work. I was not in a hurry to try to burst his bubble and waited as calmly as I could for them to decide what would happen next.

With most of the rest of the men there, I watched the commander as he scrolled through my pictures. He stopped on the one I had just taken. I could see from where I stood that this kid had been staring straight at me the moment I'd snapped the shot, that he was the only one who had seen it. He must have moved quickly to get it out of my hand just after.

As the commander looked at the picture, the kid said to him, "I heard him talking to the others earlier. He says he's Iranian!"

The commander looked up from my phone and fixed his gaze squarely on me. Between that and all his men around me, I was firmly surrounded.

"Are you Iranian?" he calmly asked me, in Persian.

I replied in the same language, "Yes, I'm Iranian."

"What did you come to do here?"

"I'm working for a French humanitarian association. I'm responsible for bringing the equipment that you see under the tarps here to the refugees who have fled the violence in Qaryatayn."

The men who surrounded us, as far as I knew, didn't speak Persian and so didn't understand a word of what was said. But I could see them watching our looks and movements very closely, trying to understand what they could.

He looked back at my phone and scrolled through more pictures, trying to get a better sense of me. When he got to the ones of me posing with the soldiers in the selfies they'd asked for, holding their weapons, he slowed, finally stopping on a particular one. I caught a glimpse of the photo, and realizing what was happening, I tried not to smile. The soldier standing next to me in that picture was the very same soldier who had just stolen my phone, who was shamelessly preening for approval in front of his superior. The commander turned to him, witheringly looked him up and down with evident dislike, and, to the laughter of the surrounding men, crumpled his ego with a few short words: "I see you're a fan of selfies."

Then he turned back to me, his tone suddenly serious again. "Do you know there are Iranians fighting on the other side? Some of them hire themselves out to the terrorist camp a few kilometers from here. Irrational idiots, acting like the People's Mujahideen!"

I quickly understood what he was getting at. The People's Mujahideen was a political and military group in Iran that sought to overthrow the government and set up their own state. In short, he was letting me know that being Iranian wasn't enough to prove my innocence. There were plenty of Iranians doing terrible things, fighting against these very soldiers.

Trying to get a better sense of where he was coming from, hoping for some common ground, I told him that he spoke Persian well, and I asked him if he was a Syrian Iranian. Truthfully, he obscured the beauty of the language and generally didn't speak it very well; he often had to pause to find the right word, and it was clear he was no master of it, even though he could speak well enough to communicate. The particular way he spoke made me think of Dari, which is Afghan Persian. I asked if he was a militiaman from over there.

"I am Syro-Persian," he responded. "My grandfather was an Iranian from Herat, Afghanistan. He came here a long time ago and married a woman from Syria. Where do you come from?"

"From France. My father is Iranian, and my mother is French."

He was continuing to look through pictures as we spoke, and he had reached the collection from Yabroud; the images showed disfigured and burned icons, broken gravestones, and crosses from its churches. Another series of pictures testified to the violent destruction that had reduced Qalamoun's villages to ruins.

The young soldier who had received such a put-down reinserted himself into the conversation. "He says he's a Christian!"

Here again, I knew what he was doing. It was an unlikely story, after all, sure to make me seem suspicious. What was an Iranian who claimed to be from France doing in Syria on a Christian humanitarian mission? It wouldn't be the first time someone stopped to wonder about my background and if it all added up.

Their leader asked me in Persian, "You're a Christian?"

"Yes, I'm a Christian."

He looked at me for a long moment, then said, "Okay, not a problem."

He turned his head toward his men, his gaze resting specifically on the young soldier, and said with emphasis, "There's no problem here." He nodded at me courteously, turned on his heel, and strode away.

25

Aleppo, or the Great Cold

My next visit was to Aleppo. I'd never been there in the winter before, and I was anxious to see how some of the infrastructure projects we'd helped establish were surviving during those cold months of 2015–2016.

Aleppo was an oven in the summer and a freezer in the winter. After three years without electricity, the cold had taken solid root in the buildings, and living conditions were not great for the residents. Moreover, with daylight fading as early as 4:00 p.m., students could only do homework by candlelight, no one could relax around a television, and the sinister spectacle of their daily life became the only source of entertainment for the people caught in the siege.

The good news was that the Iranian wells' filtration systems were working without a hitch. But we'd received other requests for help in sourcing both electricity and food. As the cold set in, the requests became more urgent. My first morning back, I stopped in at each spot where our association had people working on the ground in the city, checking on how well they were managing to provide consistent support to their immediate communities and taking note of what they needed, looking for practical ways to provide improvements. For one thing, there were large, noisy generators everywhere on the streets, protected by steel wire mesh, providing limited electricity to those who could afford to pay for it and get the right equipment to access it. A multitude of wires ran out from the generators, connecting them to nearby buildings. Amp batteries were needed for this. Without amp batteries, hundreds of the most impoverished residents couldn't get any electricity. So SOS Chrétiens d'Orient found the funds to supply approximately 250 families a month with amp batteries; each battery allowed a family to have a power supply for ten hours of 220 volts of electricity.

On this visit, I had decided to stay in a hotel. There were only two in all of Aleppo still open to Western visitors: the Basha, which was being used to billet officials and some troops as they passed through, and the marble Park Hotel. The Park was in a strategic location, overlooking the public park in Aleppo's city center, offering a breathtaking view of the entire old city from the top floor's deck. Unfortunately, the very qualities that made it so lovely had also made it a dangerous spot ever since the fighting had begun. It was a favorite place for snipers to set up, and any unsuspecting guests enjoying the view were easy targets for assassins on the ground. Situated as it was on the front line, the place had become wretched, and over time it gradually emptied to the grisly rhythm of attacks and counterattacks. The Armenian Christians who ran it lived in the basement, waiting for better days.

Not surprisingly, I had no trouble finding a room, but it was freezing cold and had no light. The sheets at least were clean, and despite signs of destruction and all, I could still appreciate the sight of the city behind the curtains. I took a flashlight up to the deck on the top floor that first night. Making sure I had a sheltered spot behind a parapet, I looked at the streets stretching out below me. The fighting in the streets continued into the night, strangely grandiose and certainly frightening. I could see the flash of every bullet, the fireworks of every explosion, as the opposing sides took turns striking back and forth at each other, each one lighting up its corner of the night, one instant at a time.

Some Aleppo residents—the ones who were the most well off—had left the city for various safe havens: Tartus on the west coast; the Valley of Christians in Beirut, Lebanon; Erbil in Iraqi Kurdistan; or all the way to Germany, France, Sweden, Australia, or even Canada. Others were not so lucky. Some died in their homes, which collapsed on them in the midst of the fighting, leveled by all manner of explosives. Some met their end on the street, torn apart by gas canisters flying through the air. Perhaps worse, other families slowly died in silence, either from thirst because their water had been cut off, or from freezing to death because there was no money for heating.

It was incredible to me that there was so little coverage of these conditions in the international press. On the rare occasion that the overarching situation was covered at all, journalists didn't discuss the siege of the city from the point of view of the civilians suffering through it—they always approached it from the point of view of the "moderate rebels." Meanwhile, a million and a half residents had lived in lockdown for four years, under constant threat of mortar fire, rockets, gas canisters full of nails, and homemade missiles in cast-iron pipes. And as if this barrage of munitions weren't enough to contend with, they also had to be wary of snipers' bullets in the western section of the city.

I visited Aleppo once a month, making the rounds of our clergy and volunteers each time. And every single month there would be new faces missing: someone I had known either killed or who fled in despair. It was the unwelcome question I asked myself on every trip. Who had died, and who was still alive, in this endless siege?

The epicenter with which I was most concerned was the Sulaymaniyah area, where all of the Christians lived in close quarters in the besieged city center. There were tens of thousands of them, many convinced it was only a matter of time before the city fell into the waiting hands of the jihadists. Each time I wrapped up a trip, promising to return the next month with more resources and support, there were always some friends who said goodbye to me as though they did not expect to see me again. They could feel the vice grip of the jihadists tightening around them, and they knew the Syrian Army had to concentrate its forces on what it could still save. Increasingly, this did not seem likely to include them.

26

The Kurdish Betrayal

One young man I came to know in Aleppo was called Joseph. Ever since July 2012, thousands of people in Aleppo had been forced to flee their neighborhoods as the battlefront approached. Joseph was one of them. Only in his twenties, Joseph bore on his face the scars of a gas canister that had exploded close to his eyes during some of the fighting in his native district. Any closer and he likely would not have survived, as he well knew.

His home neighborhood, Jebel Sayed, was north of Aleppo. In English, it was called the Virgin Mary Mountain—in Arabic, Sheikh Maqsood. Christians and Kurds had lived there in harmony until Easter Sunday of 2013, when everyone was forced to flee the Islamists' advance. Like so many other Christians, Joseph had taken refuge in Sulaymaniyah.

One day, late in the afternoon, he and five of his friends, all of whom had fled Jebel Sayed together, set up some chairs on a street corner, and as they sat smoking hookah, they told me their story. The sweet, warm, apple-scented smoke from the hookah hung in the dry air.

To the north of the city, he explained, straddling the western and eastern sections that divided it, Sheikh Maqsood ran along the city districts already occupied by the jihadists: Bustan al-Basha, 'Ayn at Tall, Abou Shuqayif, Bani Zeyd, and Ashrafieh. All these areas had fallen quickly to the Islamists, and together they surrounded Sheikh Maqsood. The only gap in their chokehold was through Midan, the Armenian neighborhood at its southern end that met the western area in Aleppo controlled by the Syrian Army.

In March of 2013, the jihadists made their move. The al-Nusra Front advanced into Sheikh Maqsood through Bustan al-Basha on a Friday morning. After two hours, the Syrian Army entered the fray, fought back the Islamists, took over Sheikh Maqsood, and gave it back to the Kurds, who, fooling everyone, initially ensured its security.

But it was only a matter of weeks before the truth started to come out. In April, Joseph and his friends starting hearing rumors that the Islamists from the al-Nusra Front were going to come back. They tried to alert the Syrian Army, but no one took their warnings seriously, and then it all came to a head on Good Friday that April, two days before Easter. Initially, nobody offered any resistance, and it took the Syrian Army four or five hours to respond and show up. But when they arrived, there weren't enough of them, and the soldiers who had come didn't have enough ammunition. They put up a poor fight for two hours, then turned around and left, abandoning Sheikh Maqsood to the Islamists.

"It was only after the fact that we found out what exactly had happened," Joseph said. "We had never had problems with the Kurds before; our Christian community had always gotten along rather well with them, living side by side for so many years. But in the end they decided to sell our neighborhood. We learned that some of the emirs from the al-Nusra Front had offered them money to hand over our homes, and so they stood back and let them come right in, telling them everything they needed to know to move with speed and efficiency."

The other guys nodded their heads in agreement.

"Yes, that's exactly what they did. It was like they wanted us gone but had no stomach for the fight themselves, so they farmed it out. But their new alliance wouldn't last long."

The others all laughed, and I asked what had happened.

"Well, people say that the money the Kurds received for their betrayal was counterfeit."

Another jumped in. "They got so angry at being tricked that they felt impelled to attack the Islamists and take the area back."

Naively, I asked, "So if your homes are back in Kurdish hands, if the Islamists are gone again, why not return?"

An older man shook his head wearily. "It's more complicated than that. The Christians are too afraid. They no longer feel confident in any agreements. These Kurds might do anything, and I'm not alone in saying that I can never forget their betrayal. I'm fed up with all these lies. Even the government lies—the politicians say we're all Syrians, that there are no differences among us, blah, blah, blah. But their platitudes ignore the fact that the Sunnites slit our throats for the caliphate. The Kurds hand us over to the same swine for their Kurdistan. The state claims that it's merely the fault of foreigners. And on it goes. Yet everything that's happening to us today has already happened at least once before, in our grandparents' time. This is nothing new, and there's no reasonable way to expect to build any sort of trust with these people."

I realized I was beginning to feel as fatigued as he sounded. Thinking this over, trying to find a solution with them, felt like chewing on a clod of rancid dirt that I couldn't spit out.

27

Palmyra

"It would be good for you to come with us, Alexandre. We'll be going to Palmyra tomorrow with the patriarch."

I was speaking with Philippe Barakat, who would one day be the Syrian Catholic bishop in Homs. We had gotten connected through one of our deliveries of blankets and stoves, the one for the Qaryatayn refugees during the battle of Qaboun. The Syrian Catholic patriarch he spoke of, Ignatius Joseph III Yonan, had come directly from Lebanon, bringing with him an entire delegation from his church. They all wanted to visit Palmyra to take note of the destruction of the churches there and to see what their fellow Christian community was facing.

Palmyra is a town in central Syria, rich in the history of ancient architecture. It changed hands many times during the civil war, and many sites that used to house priceless treasures had been reduced to rubble.

"We'll leave at seven tomorrow," Philippe was saying. "I'm a little afraid of what we'll discover."

The next morning, we appeared at the meeting point. We'd be traveling in a convoy that was under strict regulations from the local government, all arranged in an effort to ensure our safety. Ramez, driving our Kia, sat at the steering wheel, waiting for the signal to drive. Sebastiano, an Italian journalist who focused on the Middle East, was riding with me. As we got underway, our escort was impressive, including, in the front and back of the convoy, pickup trucks loaded with heavily armed men carrying submachine guns. Along the road, we saw dozens of bombed-out car frames, both military and civilian. There were also long trenches dug along the road, providing cover to any would-be armed attackers. At one point, we even saw some Russian fighter jets in the distant sky, some of them firing as they flew. We realized there must be a Russian military base in that direction, but we had no idea how far it might be.

On our way, we stopped to visit Qaryatayn, specifically the site of the Monastery of Saint Elian. It was a fourth-century building ISIS destroyed with a bulldozer; they wanted to be sure that people couldn't worship a god who was not their god. It was a brief visit and a sobering harbinger of what lay ahead of us.

As we got closer to Palmyra, deeper into the desert, I thought back on memories of my visit before the war. In the 1930s, the city had been cleared out and all of its inhabitants moved to a nearby town, allowing the entirety of Palmyra to be converted into an archaeological site; it became known as the Lost City. It is a desert oasis, an ancient city at the foot of a mountain, where a citadel, the Palmyra Castle, had been erected.

On my earlier visit, I had spent more time at this fortress than in the rest of the ancient city. For one thing, standing up at the castle parapets, I could see the entire ancient city below me — all its colonnades, the arch of triumph, tetrapylons, theater, and temples — in one grand view. I could stay there for hours, trying to absorb the infinite horizon, the endless mountains. In the evenings, when the sun faded, the entire desert glowed pink. Walking through the ancient city was of course enjoyable, but looking down at it from such a vantage point was somehow even more lovely.

ISIS attacked Palmyra in May 2015, and the entire city fell to their control by the end of that month. They sought to destroy everything in their path—stones and men—that held a memory for the people of that place.

One of the more horrific stories that came out of their occupation was the execution of Khaled al-Asaad, a historian who was more than eighty years old, in August of 2015. He was the head archaeologist of Palmyra, which is a UNESCO World Heritage Site. Despite threats and torture, he refused to tell ISIS where his team had hidden some of the most priceless treasures of the site, Greco-Roman antiquities of untold value. After weeks of imprisonment and torture, none of which broke his resolve, they cut off his head in a public execution, left it on the ground by his feet, and hung his body from a traffic light. The video of his execution was put online, spreading fear and horror.

His execution was not the only one perpetrated there. When ISIS arrived, they took over one of the historical sites, the Roman Theater of Palmyra, and transformed it into a new Colosseum: an arena for public executions, routinely filling it and forcing unwilling spectators to witness their grisly massacres.

As we neared the end of our drive, Ramez's little car started shaking. After a few more turns, I finally made out, through the dust of our caravan, the shape of the ancient castle above the city. I was relieved to see that it was still standing.

At first glance, nothing in the city seemed to have changed. People said that "only" 20 percent of the site had been destroyed, but it was a crucial 20 percent. In fact, the Lion of Athena, the Temple of Baalshamin, the Temple of Bel, the city's funerary towers, and the Arch of Triumph no longer existed. Huge piles of stones and rubble had taken their place. When the city was first under attack, the local tourist guides and history lovers had been terrified by the idea of the destruction that might erase so many of their artifacts and ancient buildings; ISIS had already wreaked havoc on such sites in Iraq, particularly in Nimrud and, to a lesser extent, Hatra.

As we looked around, we noticed a lot of Russian soldiers about the place. Father Philippe explained that they had fought like lions to free the site of ISIS soldiers, and the troops we now saw were bomb disposal experts, cleaning up the mines that the Islamists had left behind as they'd been forced out. We noticed warning signs posted frequently around the town, under the authority of the Syrian Army, threatening loss of life if we did not stay on the paths that had been cleared for foot traffic.

The Russian troops had arrived in Palmyra in early October 2015. From a distance, my volunteers and I followed their advance, which went hand-in-hand with that of the Syrian forces and their allies, all of whom were working together to push back the ISIS troops, forcing them into retreat. As the months went by, the Syrians seemed to get back on top, many times aided by valorous actions on the part of some of the Russian forces.

One of my journalist friends told me specifically about a young soldier named Alexander Prokhorenko, a twenty-five-year-old man from the Russian special forces who gave his life for the city. He was a ground flying guide; his job was to mark out targets with laser guidance, showing the Russian Air Force where they should direct their bombings. On March 17, 2016, he was on the ground and realized he was being rushed by a group of ISIS militants. Refusing to be taken prisoner and knowing that a strike on his exact location could take out a large number of enemy combatants, he called in to his leadership and insisted they strike right where he stood. They followed his guidance, and he was killed in the hit. Just ten days later, supported by Russians, Iranians, and militiamen, Syria took back the entire city.

Young Prokhorenko's death moved even the Americans, who praised his courage on social networks, despite long-standing and ongoing military tensions between Russia and the United States. Some French people expressed their indignation at the silence of the media, upset that such an act of heroism was largely ignored. As it happened, the most beautiful tribute would come from a couple in southern France, Jean-Claude and Micheline Mague. They decided to donate military medals that had belonged to their grandfather, won during World War II, to thank the young soldier's family. They traveled to Russia in order to hand deliver the Knight's Cross of the Legion of Honor and the Croix de Guerre with a bronze palm. Another Frenchman would follow in their steps; Daniel Couture, from Hérault, offered Prokhorenko's family his own father's Legion of Honor medal, "thanking them for what they were doing over there to defend us."

In the end, the Russians did not "just" offer heroism; they also helped to restore culture to Palmyra as the community sought to restore a sense of culture after the occupation and destruction of ISIS. The Roman Theater, which had been used for public executions, was rededicated to its original purpose by welcoming a Russian philharmonic orchestra. It performed a memorable concert entitled "Prayer for Palmyra: Music Brings Ancient Walls Back to Life." While knowing that nothing could ever erase the memory of the atrocities that had been perpetrated in that spot, the musicians sought to mark the end of that horrific era, to remind that space—and the audience, far and near, that listened—that the reign of terror to which ISIS had subjected it was no longer. Only a few weeks later, Father Zahlaoui brought his Joy Choir from Our Lady of Damascus Church to that same space, where they sang with the same purpose of rededication.

But, as happened all too often, the liberation of Palmyra proved to be no certain and immutable fact. Late that same year, as Aleppo was on the cusp of freedom, ISIS carried out a new offensive and retook Palmyra on December 11, 2016. This painful event happened at the same time that the Battle of Mosul in Iraq led the coalition's forces to leave a corridor in the western part of the city, providing the opportunity for the ISIS fighters to withdraw through Syria.

We knew ISIS would reappear somewhere in Syria, but we didn't know where, and we didn't know when. It was anyone's guess. Many people thought it would be in Aleppo, despite the fact that the city was so close to being back in the hands of the Syrian government. Others thought the ISIS deserters, who scattered wide as their forces were defeated at various fronts, would regather to swell their ranks in Deir ez-Zor, bringing that entire region completely back under their control.

But as we saw that December, they chose to reappear in Palmyra. To our horror, after only three days of fighting, the ancient city fell back into their claws, and we heard from afar as they picked up where they had left off, bent on destruction of the ancient beauties and architecture that had been treasured and preserved for centuries before them. They exploded the city's Tetrapylon and reduced the façade of the Roman Theater to rubble.

Ultimately, however, the winds of fortune changed yet again; just three months later, Palmyra was wrested back from them, and ISIS fled.

28

Death on Bastille Day

In all of the countries where SOS Chrétiens d'Orient worked, it had become a tradition for volunteers to gather at the local French embassy to celebrate Bastille Day on July 14 each year. But in Syria, this presented a problem: the embassy in Damascus had been closed since 2011, when France severed relations with Syria. Given our circumstances in 2016, we knew we'd have to modify our celebration of the national holiday, but we did not anticipate just how bleakly different that day would turn out to be.

At 8:00 p.m. on July 14, 2016, the first messages arrived on our cell phones: "Islamic terrorist rams truck—attack in Nice. More than eighty deaths and four hundred wounded on the Promenade des Anglais."

I turned on the TV in the office. Filling the screen were images of Nice at night with flashing police lights and law enforcement cordons. A terrorist with a truck had just driven for almost two kilometers on the sidewalk, crushing people who had come out to watch the fireworks from the Promenade des Anglais. The vehicle's driver had been killed by the police, but not before killing eighty-six people, including women and children, and wounding 458 more. ISIS had claimed responsibility for the attack.

Kidnapped in Iraq

The talking heads on the news stations, as always, spoke in ignorant platitudes in the aftermath of the attack, adopting warlike attitudes and grand theories of explanation. Meanwhile, as we were told to hug our neighbors and families, since we knew neither the day nor the hour the terrorists might strike again, our uninspired and uninspiring Prime Minister Manuel Valls advised us all to "get used to living with terrorism." I thought with annoyance of the contrasting response that Putin had offered when speaking of dealing with such terrorists; he hadn't asked his people to accept it. Rather, he had vowed that Russian soldiers would hunt down any such attackers, "tracking the terrorists down to the toilet" if need be. Once again, I was ashamed by the weak and lackluster response of my own government.

My Syrian friends, however, just as they had after the terrorist attacks in Paris on November 13, 2015, impressed me with their heartfelt and immediate care and concern. I received more messages than I could keep track of, asking how we were all doing, what things were like in France, and promising prayers and sympathies, not just for me but for all of France and all of our people. Their tears and love, their support and empathetic outrage at the injustice of it all, were genuine and unstinted. Our political leaders could have learned a thing or two from these foreigners about what was appropriate.

Our government had let Syrians suffer and die at the hands of terrorists, time and again, when it could have stepped in and offered real help and resolution. But despite such treatment, these people loved us and mourned our dead. The Syrians prayed for us, even while factions of the French population called for the fall of al-Assad, "the tyrant," which would of course usher the entire Syrian people into a state of domination and violence under the reign of the madmen who were eager for power.

One friend, amid his sympathies, was also not afraid to offer a criticism of my country and the way our leaders responded to these terrorist attacks: "It would seem that France isn't up to facing this kind of phenomenon. It's starting to happen to you too often. When we prepare a cake for other people, we have to expect someday to have to taste it."

The sentiment among some of our former volunteers, while not surprising to me, surely would have shocked many citizens in our mainstream culture. They called me, saying on the phone that they wanted to go back to Syria, not just to continue the good work against terrorists there but because they felt safer there than they did in France. In Syria, they said, at least the lines between foe and friend were discernable.

In the days after the attack, as I knew would happen, there was crying, talking, lighting of candles, peace marches, and a temporary dimming of the lights on the Eiffel Tower. I had seen this all before, in the aftermath of the Bataclan attacks the previous year, and I found it just as unedifying and disproportionate. With each passing year, I understood my country less and less. Surely her citizens realized that these thousand cowardly acts of grieving without a single move toward retribution could never equal an ounce of courage. There was no pursuit of justice, only a surrender to grief. By contrast, in Syria, they had been battling for five years against the worst kind of killers, whose roots were scattered over ninety countries. In France, we had been attacked multiple times in a year by these same murderers, with hundreds killed, but we had no stomach for the battle that should have been fought against them in defense of our homeland.

Shortly after the Bastille Day attack, still in Damascus, we were providing a news commentary for France 24 in front of the headquarters of SOS Chrétiens d'Orient. Suddenly, in the middle of our interview, the night around us erupted into gunfire, and a chorus of Kalashnikov rifles echoed through Damascus. I couldn't see what was happening from my unobstructed view inside the interior courtyard, so I climbed the staircase to the top floor and went out to the roof. I could see the red sparks from the bullets spraying in all directions, and I realized it wasn't a skirmish; there was a party going on in Damascus. The residents were celebrating an attempted coup underway in Ankara, the capital city of Turkey.

29

Aleppo's Blockade

The Aleppo winter of 2015–2016 went by, and the intense heat of the following summer settled into the buildings and rubble that surrounded us. Our association's plans in the besieged city could only be developed and implemented at the pace that the fighting—and the conditions necessarily accompanying it—would allow. The locals were exhausted by these last four years of war, but while they so often suffered in silence, they still found ways to resist, even as the siege tightened around them. Two-thirds of the city had fallen into the jihadists' hands, and many of the people I met no longer had any hope; they simply awaited death. They were convinced that if the falling bombs didn't kill them, the heat would. As the August sun raged down, it did terrible damage, forcing Aleppo's residents to hide in their homes, in their basements or staircases.

A few weeks earlier, in July, the Syrian Army had succeeded in freeing the Bani Zeyd district. This area was strategically located, overlooking the rest of the city, and the Islamists had used it as a staging ground to launch their mortars and rockets on Aleppo's civilian neighborhoods for the past four years. Winning it back was a great success, but it also came at quite a cost. In the process of the fight, the only access road connecting Aleppo to the rest of the world was cut off. While this had the positive result of cutting off supply routes for the jihadists, it also cut off supplies to all of the civilians in the city. This road had been built in 2013, and for all intents and purposes, it was an umbilical cord for the city, connecting it to Homs and, from there, to everywhere else. It was through this route that Aleppo received its entire supply of food and every product: gas, fuel oil, fresh produce, meat, cheese, bread, groceries, dry goods, and so forth.

The real anxiety was caused by the fact that the private generators and well pumps needed fuel: without fuel, there was no water, and it was 105 degrees — in the shade. Words failed me when I tried to contemplate such a situation. There were a million and a half people trapped in this heat with no water. Was it a war crime or a crime against humanity? In the end, it didn't matter what you called it. Quite simply, it was an atrocity.

The only good news was strategic, and it was coming from all around the country. The Russian Air Force was making real progress against the Islamists, and day after day, we heard of more jihadist strongholds falling apart. But unfortunately for the people of Aleppo, they seemed to be the ones paying for it. Every time the Russian Army struck the jihadists, loosening their grip elsewhere, the terrorists responded by tightening their hold on Aleppo even more. The blockade of the last few months had intensified, and each time I visited, I discovered a population that was on edge, exhausted by the last five years of deprivations and bombings.

Though it wasn't exactly direct or convenient, there was at least another route into the city now. I noted in my journal the date this route opened: "September 10, 2016: Temporary ceasefire in Aleppo. Demilitarization of the Castello Road." The Castello Road went off to the northeast of the city before looping back around to grant access from an alternative route. It was longer and more dangerous than the road from Homs had been, but at least it was a way in.

At the end of September 2016, once I made my way back into the city, I met Jean-Clément Jeanbart, the archbishop of Aleppo's Melkite Greek church. I took the opportunity to ask him what he thought about the fate of Syrian Christians. Not surprisingly, he had much to say on the subject, all of it spoken with great decision and seriousness. I let him talk, not wanting to interrupt the flow of his words.

"Our society needs Christians," he began, "because they selflessly work to have people live in harmony, to accept each other. Here, Christians have often been at the leading edge of medicine, science, and town planning, in particular. Syria was of course Christianity's birthplace, and so, naturally, as the culture advanced, much of that advancement, in many fields, was made thanks to the millions of Christians who contributed to its edification. Today, Syria is my land as much as it is the land of those who hold other beliefs that have been passed down through the ages. We all have to stay here because we are all rooted here—both religiously and socially.

"But, as Christians, we have accomplished remarkable things in such drastic times. In less than two years, we have restored 250 homes, making it possible for their families to stay in them. We have provided free loans to seventy young people. We have offered scholarships for twelve hundred students. We have created a training center for the building trades and another one for women. We've built a food cooperative, and we've started a movement called 'To Build in Order to Stay.' We hold on to the hope of peace, and we continue to take what practical steps we can to ensure it and to build a world that will be ready for it, no matter how bleak our daily conditions might be. We know that that peace will be the whole world's salvation. To that end, one day just this month, we gathered more than a thousand seven-to-twelve-year-old Christian and Muslim children to pray together for reconciliation and peace."

He continued in a different vein. "We do manage to stock up on some essentials, thanks to humanitarian organizations. But we have no electricity. The water is often shut off, and the work becomes impossible. There are no more jobs. We're terrorized by what's happening. The situation has never been so worrisome. The respite that we were hoping for with the last truce has, unfortunately, not taken place. What will become of us? We have been living under bombs for five years. Our city was once prosperous, busy, and cosmopolitan. Everyone could live together hand in hand here. And now? All that has been reduced to nothing. It looks as if Aleppo has undergone the same fate as Hiroshima or Nagasaki. We hope that we'll be able to rebuild all of this someday, but who really knows?"

As I listened to him, I thought back over the last year. It had now been more than twelve months since I first settled in Syria, and I was proud of what our association had accomplished in that time. In addition to the many more practical things we had done, over the past summer, we had organized regular youth camps, making it possible for more than three thousand children to get out of Aleppo. However temporary these camping trips were, they showed the kids what life could be like and gave them hope for a brighter future. There were often French volunteers on-site to assist in running the camps, pitching in as the supervisory staff directed.

Despite the war, there were many organizations in addition to ours that did excellent work in Syria. But SOS Chrétiens d'Orient was one of the rare associations present in the field every day. I knew it was appreciated by the Syrians — they told us as much. They were very grateful to see us experience the difficult daily life with them — especially in Aleppo, where each one of our visits was welcomed with a lot of fanfare. Nothing could match the value of our actually being there on the ground with them. And, of course, it had its practical administrative benefits as well, helping us to make sure our resources were being put in the right places, that projects were progressing as we planned, and that our association was accomplishing the work that our Syrian friends most needed.

30

Mhardeh, a City of Resistance Fighters

A few weeks earlier, in August 2016, we had visited a small Christian city that was about two hours southwest of Aleppo. I had first learned about the state of affairs in Mhardeh when a woman in Aleppo saw me talking with some of our volunteers, going over the progress of some of our projects, and approached me. She was well-dressed, in her mid-forties, and spoke impeccable French. It turned out Mrs. Reem, as she introduced herself, was in fact a French teacher at the university, but her foreign language school had been bombed and destroyed when the city was taken over. She wanted to know where we were from and what we were doing there. When we told her, she didn't hesitate an instant to tell us, first, that we should rebuild the foreign language school and, second, that we needed to visit her hometown of Mhardeh. The situation was not good there, she said, and if we could help, we should.

So here we were on the road, two weeks later, making the best of the horrible driving conditions. "If the terrorists don't kill us with their bombs, our fellow Syrians will kill us with their driving." Our driver Ramez was laughing as he swerved around obstacles — mostly other cars on the road.

Anytime we didn't feel in danger because of the speeding cars, the poor physical condition of the road itself became a problem.

Between the tanks and trucks that drove on the road each day, repair crews simply couldn't keep up with the maintenance. There were frequent accidents, some caused by shoddy driving, some occasioned by the broken road, and others of course by terrorists. No matter their cause, they were almost always fatal.

There were six of us driving that day: Benjamin, Charlotte, Anne-Lise, Henri, and Damien were on their summer break and had come to visit me and see how our work was going. Despite the heat of the unrelenting, dry summer, the car chugged along, with all of us crammed inside. As we made it past the city of Hama without stopping and then crossed the Orontes River, managing to finish the last short leg of journey without any delays, I thought back to what this woman had told me of her hometown: "Mhardeh is a completely Christian city, and the way things are now, the Christians are besieged and totally surrounded." I asked Ramez what he knew of it.

He shook his head in distaste and spat out the window. "It's the Muslim Brotherhood's former fiefdom. Bashar's father, Hafez al-Assad, crushed them during their revolt in 1982 but clearly not hard enough. And now they're back, thirty years later."

I looked up at the mountain range ahead of us, stretching out as far as I could see, standing there like a gigantic bastion. Mhardeh is situated along the river that runs through the mountains, which means it is surrounded above and below by little mountain villages. In a way, it was protected by its mountainous location, which served as a natural fortress, but small attacks could always advance stealthily through the little hidden villages that encircled it.

As we arrived in town, something about it made me think of an old American Western. A long main street crossed the whole town, but the buildings were mostly small. There were no highrises. Mrs. Reem had preceded us here and was waiting for us at the city's aid station.

"I'll be taking you to Mr. Simon's home," she said after greeting us. "You have to see him first. He's the one who has saved this city more than once."

Simon al-Wakeel, in his sixties, was big, strong, and happy. He was the National Defense boss. Since 2012, he had been in charge of organizing Mhardeh's defenses against the jihadists. He carried multiple cell phones and walkie-talkies, and he was constantly and politely excusing himself to respond to the frequent calls he received. It didn't take us long to get right to the heart of the matter; he knew everything there was to know about the state of affairs in his town, and he settled himself in his kitchen chair, looking out the window as he spoke to us.

"When the revolution started, the residents of the surrounding villages began sneaking in and out of Mhardeh. They came to rob our homes at night—especially the ones that were more isolated on the city outskirts. They took anything they could at gunpoint—jewels and money—everything they could take. From there, they moved on to kidnapping our residents on the highways of Hama and Masyaf. And then, arguably even worse, they got enough organization and backing to go openly into Mhardeh to impose the *jizya* on people. This is the tax that a *kafir*, an 'infidel,' must pay to the Muslims. They even sent me a message asking me to 'financially support' the revolution. Naturally, I refused."

He hadn't been alone in his refusal. Some members of the National Defense worked in silent agreement with him. When the war broke out, Mr. Simon had been a successful entrepreneur just recovering from cancer. He and his company had been building roads all through Syria. But when he got sick, in the middle of a contract with an Iranian company in Abu Kamal on the Iraqi border, he couldn't do anything but go back to Mhardeh for a whole year, resting and waiting to get well again.

"It turned out I wasn't the right man to lead this fight," he told us. "Quite simply, I didn't have the strength."

During our visit with him, he took us out in his big black pickup truck to see the city. He kept an AKS-74U assault rifle on the passenger seat, within easy reach of his spot behind the steering wheel. There was also a National Defense volunteer in the truck, carrying a Kalashnikov rifle, wearing a combat vest, and packing extra ammo, just in case. In such a setting, we could be under no illusions about what might meet us on our brief exploration.

"We still stayed on the outskirts of the city," Mr. Simon told us, "as the crisis spots near the city center are too much trouble for just the two of us officers. There are no politicians in Mhardeh, and the only soldiers we have are just the ones doing their military service, not battle-hardened bears to defend us here. We used to have an intelligence service, but these so-called revolutionaries started to attack it, and in the end there wasn't anything we could do, despite our best efforts to mediate peacefully. If these bastards want to overthrow their president, let them demonstrate in Damascus, not here in Mhardeh. There's no real army, no real power for them to protest here!"

We gradually moved away from the city's main roads and then arrived at a roadblock. There were a few huts on the right, constructed from wood and sheet metal. A man came out with a gun strapped over his shoulder. He recognized Mr. Simon's vehicle and instantly moved to lift the big metal roadblock, waving his hand in greeting as he did so. As we climbed out of the truck, someone else greeted us and granted us access to their secure area. In this spot, the National Defense had some Russian tanks that looked like they'd been rescued from the 1950s, a BMP vehicle, a Russian military vehicle, some Grad missile launching ramps, and some big barrels, all aimed at Idlib. We overlooked the front line from Mhardeh's war arsenal, realizing that this place was like a watch tower that dominated the horizon.

There were many young volunteers in battle fatigues all around us. They were curious about why we had come to visit, and they asked us a number of questions as they could. Meanwhile, prompted by one of these volunteers, Mr. Simon turned to tell us the details of some of the encounters they had recently faced, including one that had cost them the life of one of their own.

A few days previously, two of Mr. Simon's young volunteers, Tariq and Eli, had been hit in their tank by a TOW missile. It had immediately knocked them out. When they were hit, the inside of their tank heated up like an oven. Tariq, who was stunned, had just enough time to come to his senses and get out of the tank, not even realizing his friend was still inside, burned and motionless.

Mr. Simon shook his head at the tragedy of it all. "Life is strange," he said. "That very same day, Tariq's wife gave birth to a little boy. When, in the aftermath of it all, they realized that they had lost their friend Eli, they named their newborn son for him."

Pointing to a spot up in the mountains, he explained where the enemy missile had come from. "The Islamists targeted them from the crest line behind the castle, up on the heights of Shaizar."

He went on to tell us how all the Muslims of their villages had welcomed "the bearded men" — that is, the violent extremists — cheering and calling out their support as they approached. Thanks to the willing collusion of these villagers, the extremists were situated at the base of the castle, directly in front of Mhardeh's gates, perfectly poised to offer serious threat to Mr. Simon's National Defense team.

As he spoke, another strong-looking man, with fine hair and a medium build, joined our circle. Mr. Simon introduced him. "This is Assad. He's the man who makes the Grad launch pads and sends them to the Islamists on the other side. He was a building engineer before the war."

As Assad began chatting with us, telling us a bit about his background and his role in the current conflict, I was very surprised to hear that he was receiving regular training in Iran.

He nodded. "Yes, every four months the Iranians who are fighting in the country take some of us to an unknown place over there. They train us for several weeks, safe in the undisclosed location, to make and use these devices before sending us back to Syria."

Assad and I did not share a common language, but another young Syrian soldier there, Salem, translated for us. Salem had a perfect mastery of French and Italian.

Another volunteer broke in at this point, as if to answer me indirectly. "Is he so surprised that we receive help from the Iranians? Yes, Iran actually helps us. And what does France do? All they can seem to figure out is how to finance and arm the jihadists who want to wipe us out."

It was obvious Salem was not happy about translating these remarks. He looked quite uncomfortable, but he went on translating. From everything he related, it was clear the Syrians here had not forgotten that France had promised to provide protection to Christians in the Middle East—even if, as it seemed by France's mainstream inaction, France itself had forgotten its promise.

Salem continued, "We know France. We love and respect it. We remember what it was, but we no longer understand what it is. The Islamic Republic of Iran, which is Shiite, is taking care of Christians in a way that France should, according to its promises. If France no longer wants to meddle abroad, that's one thing. But it's not just that it's not being active in the fray here; it's supporting these monsters. In a way, we are fighting them for you. Why mourn the lives that these killers took in the terrorist attacks in your country and, at the same time, encourage them to take ours over here?"

I didn't know how to respond. I had nothing to say. I knew, and agreed with, all the accusations of hypocrisy and betrayal he had leveled at my country's doorstep. I looked at the faces of all of these young people around me. They weren't warriors. Speaking for himself, Salem explained that most of them were in fact students. All of them had chosen to study in Hama in the morning and fight in Mhardeh in the afternoon.

"So much for their diplomas and professional future," he said. "Now they are soldiers and social workers. Whole families volunteer their time, as they are able, whether it's to help with handicapped people, older people, orphans, in emergency rooms, health centers, or the military. The Rescue Brigade is charged with going to the scene of a blast to remove the dead and wounded. They work closely with the city's two hospitals. Meanwhile, the National Defense acts as a backup for the Syrian Army, and it works closely with the Syrian and Russian Armies and with the Iranian militia. They all fight the Islamists in Idlib."

As we made our way back to the truck and returned to the city, Mr. Simon told us about a day that the Islamists had entered the city. He showed us the way they'd gotten in, terrorizing the city's residents.

"It was on July 30, 2011," he said. "I remember it well. They entered Mhardeh from the west, from the Sunnite villages of Tell Malah, Jdeide, and Tremse. They went into Mhardeh's industrial zone on the pretext of demonstrating against the government. There hadn't been any weapons in Mhardeh until then. The city's residents didn't have any interest in participating in such a demonstration, arguing that protests against the government surely wouldn't get much notice in a little place like this. But when they refused to join, the Islamists started burning their stores and destroying everything in them.

"Fifteen days later, they entered from the east, via Halfaya. By then, the Syrian Army had sent two tanks and fifteen soldiers to the monastery in Mhardeh. This of course was entirely insufficient. What could such a little group of men do against this army of jihadists? When the Islamists entered from the east, they kidnapped eighteen people, including women and children. One of the kidnapped, Zyad al Frashe, was killed shortly after being taken. No doubt the jihadists wanted to use him as an example to scare the rest of us, and it worked, though perhaps not in the way they'd been hoping.

"We were motivated to get ourselves organized, to work for our own defense, since clearly the Syrian Army was lacking either the means or the interest to give us the help we needed. With ransom money, we managed to get back the children who had been kidnapped, and then that very day, we started setting up barriers to protect our city. These thieves, seeing our city as easy prey with no real defense, had attacked us for no reason. And from then on, everything rapidly deteriorated.

"The Alawites who were working in our intelligence centers started to flee the city; as the favored group of the ruling Assads, they knew what fate awaited them if they fell into the hands of these jihadists. And then the police officers were Sunnites. While perhaps officially they were on the side of the state and the government, when push came to shove, the Sunnites' hearts lay with the cause of the jihadists. It wasn't long before they began to abuse the people whom they were supposed to protect. And it wasn't as though anyone could arrest them.

"So people started forming popular civilian groups and organized messages to be sent out to our attackers, warning retribution if they continued their encroachment of our city. But they were past taking messages seriously, already committed to violence, and our missives received only bullets in response, courtesy of their Kalashnikovs. Not knowing what else to do, we turned to the Syrian Army, asking for help.

"We got together to evaluate the situation, and we decided to establish guard towers in the streets and patrols in Mhardeh. We checked in with the Greek Orthodox church, and they were on board. We got ahold of some walkie-talkies to make communication easier. All of this was something, at least, but I wasn't satisfied with it. I told my companions, 'Look, if we really want to protect ourselves, we need to do it from outside our home, not directly from our city streets.' I said we needed to have checkpoints outside Mhardeh, and eventually everyone agreed.

"Despite our limited resources and manpower, we decided on seventeen spots where we needed coverage. Nature and geography defend Mhardeh to the north, and hills also protect it to the west. The weaknesses were to the south and east, and they stretched for six kilometers. At first, we only carried weapons at night to protect the city. We continued to be kind of civilian guards, not wearing any uniform, out of respect for the residents; we didn't want any implication that we were pro-government. We didn't take up arms to defend President Bashar al-Assad—this was for our homes, for our families. For four months, we were able to keep things going like this, but on December 12, 2012, they kidnapped my son at the infantry barracks in Aleppo. What followed changed everything.

"Before the war, the neighborhood knew I had been a mediator between the Sunnite villagers and the Alawite intelligence services. In this role, I had actually saved the life of the uncle of Sami Rahmon, one of the jihadists. He was a doctor who had been kidnapped by the Alawites, and I negotiated a solution that saved his life and brought him home. When he saw me after his release, he knelt to thank me, striking his own chest. He kissed my hand and said that if I ever needed anything, for the rest of my life, all I had to do was ask him.

"It was only a few weeks later that Sami Rahmon, his nephew, kidnapped my son. Knowing what had just occurred between our families, I was sure there was some misunderstanding and certain that I could talk to this doctor I had just rescued to reach a quick resolution. But when I called him, I was horrified by his response. He said my son had killed a jihadist, and there was nothing he could do to intervene. I never expected such cowardice, such betrayal, after all I had done to save him, and after all his promises of gratitude. 'Is this how you thank me?' I asked him, angry and outraged. And his only response was that if I wanted to keep my son alive, I should send them ten million Syrian pounds. And if I wanted him released, the ransom would be one hundred million. I swore at him through the walkie-talkie, and in my anger, I made terrible threats. 'If you touch a hair on my son Fahed's head, I will kill all of the babies in the wombs of the mothers in the Rahmon family, and in all of Halfaya!' At this point, I heard another voice coming through: 'We will cut off his head.' And then they stopped responding."

He stopped, and we could see that it was still too troubling for him to continue talking about. He suddenly looked tired, deadly tired.

Salem looked at him, then picked up where he had left off, sharing the end of the story. "I had been kidnapped, too, and Mr. Simon was able to pull together the ransom money for both of us. We were both eventually released, relatively unharmed, but from that day forward, it has been total and uncompromised war between Mr. Simon and the jihadists. No more mediation, no more trying to work things out."

We were curious to know how Salem had come to be friends with Mr. Simon's son—apparently, they had both been at the barracks in Aleppo before its fall.

"Well, I started out as a translator," Salem said, "studying languages while I was in university. In 2010, I also got to spend a year in a Salesian university in Rome as a psychology student. When I returned to Syria in January 2011, life was normal, and I began my work as a translator, primarily for foreign merchants—some Swiss ones, in particular. At the same time, I taught French classes. I really like to teach and know other people. It opens up horizons and increases your understanding.

"I studied French literature for four years in Damascus, and translation for a year. Now, it's true that we had heard about political demonstrations in Egypt, some of which had reportedly gotten violent, and this news seemed strange to us. It seemed unimaginable that such a thing could happen in our own country. Sure, we had some disagreements, but we thought that, as a whole, Syria was a united country. Our people got along well, and we didn't have problems like that—except, occasionally, with the Muslim Brotherhood. But the president's father had taught them a lesson, years ago, and we thought that was the end of it.

"But of course we were wrong. On March 15, 2011, the demonstrations started here. We told ourselves, 'They're only kids, it's nothing.' We continued to trust in peace, and in the Syria that we knew. But in reality, we were sitting on top of a volcano that had just woken up. Today, five years later, the fire of that volcano is still raging, raining down on all of us."

After a brief pause, he went on. "There's mandatory military service in Syria that starts at age eighteen. It's postponed if we go to school, but once we've finished studying, there's no getting out of it. This was the dilemma for all of Syria's young people when the war began. Many of them fled the country in order to escape it, if they had money. And those of us without money stayed to defend the homeland that the wealthy had abandoned."

Salem, from a low-income family, began his military service on May 1, 2011. He was sent to the infantry academy in Aleppo, and for the most part, things in the country held steady for his first year. But in July 2012, things started to go downhill quickly, first in the countryside and then, increasingly, closer to Aleppo. Because of the city's proximity to the Turkish border, it was easy for the jihadists to come in from Saudi Arabia, Qatar, and Libya. And once they were in, the violence got worse and worse. Talk of demonstrations was a joke, he said. It wasn't a social revolution but a coup to create a caliphate and return to the time of the prophet Muhammad. Salem said that, in the beginning, the slogans people shouted on the streets had been all about promoting democracy, but within six months they changed to "*Allahu Akbar!*" Their intentions were entirely transparent: they wanted to bring Sunnites to a position of dominance over the whole country and to execute anyone who didn't agree with their agenda.

Salem switched tacks to talk about how all of this had affected his military training. "Life in the barracks fell into disarray as classes and leave were canceled. Morale was very low, and it didn't help when we had to set up watch points on our perimeter, knowing we were vulnerable to attack. Over time, we lost staff, tanks, and soldiers; our strength and numbers dwindled.

"Despite all this, our barracks ended up being tasked with protecting the great city of Aleppo and the surrounding areas, from Saraqib to Azaz. None of the leadership who ordered this seemed to care that, by that time, there were only three hundred of us in barracks designed for three thousand men, and only one man out of six had completed his training. To make matters worse, one hundred soldiers fled at about that time. They were ethnically

Sunnites and had no interest in fighting against the Sunnite jihadists, even if they were supposed to be Syrian soldiers first. There were some Sunnites who remained, but, even so, we had trouble trusting their allegiance, and suspicions and divisions grew within our diminished ranks.

"One day, we received orders to rout a small village nearby, Atarib, because it had become a nest of jihadists. But our attack was a disaster, and we lost a lot of men. When they turned to attack our barracks, we were grossly understaffed. This was the real reason the academy collapsed—this and the fact that most of us there were only students. The special forces and the Syrian Republican Guard were in Homs and Damascus. We didn't even really know how to be soldiers yet.

"When the siege of the academy began, there were jihadists surrounding us in great numbers. They had come from Idlib, Aleppo, Raqqa, Deir ez-Zor, and Hama, and there were fewer than two hundred of us students to stand against them. One day, they managed to break through the exterior walls of the compound, and they set up sniper nests on the perimeter. We had become targets in a fishbowl, cut off from the outside world, with no access to supplies and with all the roads out blocked off to us.

"The Syrian Army tried to support us from the air, dropping canned goods and bread from helicopters. But the jihadists targeted the aircraft, making it increasingly difficult for them to resupply us. And sometimes they would drop the food in the wrong location, feeding the enemy instead of us. Even worse, though, was when one of us would stockpile supplies that he had gotten to before the rest of us, refusing to share, and fighting would break out. The atmosphere among us had become atrocious.

"Strangely, one thing we still had was a working television. We had this one connection to the outside world—we could watch the news. One day, we heard the journalist Shady Hulwe explain on a live broadcast that Aleppo's military academy—our military academy, where we were all imprisoned and starving to death—had been saved by the Syrian Army. He lied right to the camera and said there had been a victory, that the enemy had been pushed back. On that day, we understood we were doomed. We had been abandoned, and nobody would ever know that we were going to die.

"In the end, all we had was hunger, fatigue, and death. If someone was wounded by a sniper, there was nothing we could do to save him. He stayed on the ground, and if he lived or died was in God's hands. We rarely recovered the bodies of the fallen, as snipers would wait for us to try to retrieve them and then kill more of us. Our corpses piled up, and hungry dogs and cats started to devour our dead friends' faces. There was nothing we could do, and the smell of death was everywhere in the barracks.

"The surviving soldiers were exhausted. If someone wanted to smoke a cigarette, since there were none left, the soldiers rolled tea up in a tree leaf. I had a lot of cans stored in my bedroom. I shared them with others, including Fahed. But still, I couldn't feed everyone. So many of them mixed water with grass and fed themselves with it, as if it were a soup. More people died. We buried them, if we could rescue their bodies. Three of us Christians buried the body of a lieutenant, a friend of ours who had fallen. I made sure to bury him with his name, in hopes that one day his friends and family could find and identify him.

"Finally"—he almost sighed in relief at this point—"the jihadists decided we were weak and broken down enough, and they managed to come into our barracks. Many were able to escape in the chaos that ensued, but they ended up in Aleppo's central jail, where they were imprisoned for desertion. And when Aleppo was under siege, they would find themselves in the exact same situation yet again, stuck and going mad for another whole year. The seventy of us who remained were kidnapped and taken to Halloq, near Shaykh Najjar's industrial zone in Aleppo. We were kept in a factory for a few days and then they moved us to the countryside, near Idlib, to a village called Tarmala. At first, jihadists thought, since I was from Damascus, that I must be a Sunni Muslim. But when they found out I was a Christian, the beatings began.

"As it turned out, there were foreign journalists in Tarmala, reporting on the conflict from both sides. The jihadists were eager to share their interpretation of events, and they asked if any of us could translate. I took the chance to try to get a message out and told them I spoke Italian and French. They grabbed me, pulled me forward, and told me to relate what they said as they talked about their glorious revolution and the myriad benefits they had brought to the country. I pretended to translate and asked the journalists to react appropriately. But, in bits and pieces and undercover, I told them the truth of our story—that they had kidnapped us after having killed many of the young men in the academy, that they were barbarians and killers, that they didn't want any freedom and democracy. The journalists played their part beautifully, and I was grateful to them, but in the end I didn't think it would actually make much difference for us. I was sure we would be executed before long."

Salem said that he also wanted freedom and democracy, that in fact all of Syria wanted that. But the jihadists had taken over the revolt right from the start, with entirely different intentions. They didn't want freedom, and they definitely didn't want democracy; they simply wanted to impose Islam and its fanatical ideas everywhere. Each country needs a different sort of democracy, Salem argued. You have to consider the culture of each people and each place.

"Here," he said, "religion is the basis for everything, and in the end, we end up with shit. We have too many different denominations in Syria, and there's no good, moderate solution. If we talk about a democracy via religion, we must deal with secularism, which, unlike so many religions, actually respects differences."

He shook his head, then went back to his story. After the journalists had left, the prisoners were taken to a villa near the barracks, where they stayed for two days. Then, in front of a camera, they were forced to say they had abandoned the Syrian Army to join the revolution. After that, the jihadists threatened, insulted, and separated them. Some of them kept repeating that Christians had to pay a large sum in order to leave or they would be sold. They also said that the Sunnites should fight beside them, but they would have to be punished first for having served in the Syrian Army's ranks. As for all the poor Alawites, the chosen people of Bashar al-Assad, they would be executed, without exception.

"One day, they led us all outside the academy, separated out the Alawites, and beheaded them. They forced us to stand and watch the executions. One of them shouted as he worked, 'Come, come see what's happening to al-Assad's dogs!' They told them they wouldn't waste any bullets for them, that cutting their heads off was cheaper, and, besides, then they could play soccer with their heads, which in fact they did, much to our horror. They seemed happy as they went about their grisly business. 'Who will have this honor?' they shouted. 'Who will be the first one to cut off an Alawite's head?' It was an honor for them, and they even began to squabble over whose turn it was.

"I saw one of them who didn't open his mouth during the whole ordeal. He kept silent up to the last moment. At the end, an emir came closer. He was a sheikh who had come from Libya to distribute money to the fighters. He was happy about what had taken place—to see how the Alawites had been treated. 'They are *kafir*,' he said. 'We must not hesitate to execute them when we have the chance.'

"And then the jihadists pulled me forward, showed me to him, and asked, 'What judgment does this rotten Christian deserve? Surely we must at least cut off his hand, which carried the gun against us.' They dragged me into a room, ready to do it, and I yelled at them that I wasn't afraid, that they could kill me—why stop at my hand? But their leader came up behind me, and I heard him say, 'Calm down, we're not going to do anything to you. This was just a show for the sheikh. You're worth a lot of money, and we're keeping you till your family coughs it up.'"

Salem would remain captive in Aleppo for another five days, receiving one meal a day, before being sent to Idlib. They told him at that point that they had agreed on a ransom sum—500,000 Syrian pounds would buy his release. As long as they kept him, they continued trying to get him to work as a translator whenever they needed it, but after his initial encounter with the journalists, he refused to cooperate.

"And then one day, Fahed, Mr. Simon's son, was released. I didn't know his father was wealthy, but the jihadists told me that Mr. Simon had paid a very large sum to retrieve his son. He turned to me on the day he left, and he told me not to worry, that he would help me, that he wouldn't abandon me. But after he left, I suddenly found myself crying. I was alone and desperate, and I knew I couldn't ask my family for anything. We didn't have money. All at once, I wanted to die rather than wait for some enormous sum of money that I thought would surely never come.

"Little did I know that Fahad wasted no time when he got home to Mhardeh, going around to his old friends and neighbors to raise the funds to help me. My own family was able to send one hundred thousand pounds, and Mhardeh's residents gave the rest of it. On January 21, 2013, I was freed. When the jihadists delivered me to Mhardeh's entrance, Mr. Simon was waiting for me, and he welcomed me by taking me in his arms. Then he brought me to his home so I could call my family to tell them I was alive. When Fahed saw that I was alive, that I was free, he started to cry too. I couldn't believe it. I had lost all hope, and yet hope had found me again."

Salem shook his head. "We were all united before the war," he said. "We all spoke the same language, had the same gestures and the same behavior. We were all united in public, but in the secrets of some of our hearts, this hatred was being nursed all the while—Shiite against Sunnite and Alawite against Sunnite. We Christians have always been on the fringes of this conflict, but the tyranny of the war doesn't spare any of us in the end, no matter how distant we think ourselves from the central conflict. We have been forced to enter into it, if only to defend ourselves, to stay alive. Jesus Himself has told us to be strong, just as He was against the injustice in the Temple. He wasn't weak in front of the robbers and Temple merchants. And our Temple is our religion, our existence. We must defend it—either by dying or by living—but always with dignity. We can't be sheep, paying the *jizya* to these wretched people, waiting for them to slit our throats in the night, stealing our culture, our country, and our whole lives."

31

"Let Them Go Die in Idlib!"

October 19, 2016

We were back on the road, heading to Maaloula. Ramez was happy; we'd need to go up to Aleppo in a few days, but for now we were enjoying life, enjoying not being on that highway to death. As the night fell, we went through the roadblocks, one after another, noticing that the soldiers seemed unusually agitated. Finally, at a stop, Ramez asked one of them what was going on. The soldier seemed nervous as he explained, and I saw him spit on the ground.

I couldn't quite understand what they were talking about, so Ramez turned toward me to explain. "They're transporting captured jihadists from Qudsaya to Idlib, near the Turkish border."

I saw the soldier smile wickedly, and I understood his next sentence perfectly. "They're going to die over there."

Suddenly, we hear another soldier yelling, and we looked over to see him waving his arms in every direction as he came out of the darkness, illuminated by our headlights. He told us we needed to get off the road; this path was being exclusively reserved for the prisoner convoy. We saw probably ten green buses moving out in front of us, following each other bumper to bumper. The soldiers escorting them past us were clearly tense. The green buses of prisoners were surrounded by army and Red Crescent vehicles. Despite the fog on the windows of the buses, I could see the faces of bearded men, the captured jihadists.

This scene would repeat itself in northern Homs a few months later. On that trip, I was accompanied by François-Xavier, our director of operations, and François, the communications manager for SOS Chrétiens d'Orient, who had all of his cameras with him. We had been authorized to go to the site and witness the evacuation. After being defeated and going through negotiations, the jihadists who had controlled the al-Waer district accepted the government's terms—they would leave the district and be taken to Idlib by bus.

I couldn't remember another time in all of history that such an agreement had been made in the negotiations after a surrender. In the model I knew, enemy soldiers lost, surrendered, and were taken as prisoners of war under the care of the Red Cross. But this was nothing like that.

Just as I had seen last time, the army had created a cordon all around the buses. As we approached them, I could see anger and weariness on the faces of the soldiers of the Syrian Army. But however little they might like this arrangement, these were orders. Some nervously puffed on their cigarettes as they glared at the crowd of jihadists boarding the buses. François got closer and started photographing the scene. When the jihadists saw they were being documented by a photographer, they started showing off their handguns and waving their Kalashnikovs. I was appalled. The prisoners were allowed to keep their weapons? This made no sense whatsoever.

Some of them started shouting at us, "Hey, journalists, don't go too far away! You'll be hearing from us again soon!" And then they saw some of the civilians who had come to watch, and they yelled at them, threatening ugly intentions. "Hide your children—you know we'll be coming back to find them, sooner or later!"

I watched as a woman, dressed completely in black and carrying a gas stove in her hand, followed her husband onto one of the buses. He wore a combat vest and carried a Kalashnikov rifle. A father and his two young daughters, about fourteen and seventeen, were in the line just ahead of them. They had headbands with inscriptions of the Shahada—the Muslim's profession of faith—on their foreheads. The men were signaling victory, waving their weapons above their heads.

After I returned to Aleppo, I got a chance to sit down with a young Armenian man, Vahan, whom I'd met at the same time I'd met my Fimy. He was from the Young Christian Students' Association, and I thought he might have some insights about the situation. I didn't understand why the Syrian Army would transport these animals to what was essentially a home base for them, with all their weapons. Surely they would only end up facing them again and likely being killed by them.

Vahan had been very much affected by the war, living on the front line in Midan. He took a slow drag on his cigarette before responding to me. "You see, it's a mixture of pragmatism and reasonable accommodations. The government knows that some people have only been on the opposing side out of financial need, so they invite them to join the Syrian Army ranks or to get a job in the military apparatus that works against the 'terrorism' they were, up until very recently, supporting. For many people, this does actually work. They return to their families, build a new life, and reforge their place in society, mistakes forgotten behind them. As for the others, the diehards who don't want any compromise—let them go die in Idlib. This northwestern region of Syria is back-to-back with northern and northwestern Turkey. It's where all of Syria's terrorists, as well as many foreign fighters, have piled up for months at a time. There have even been ISIS fighters there, like the ones who were fighting in Yarmouk Camp to the south of Damascus.

"It's like this," he said. "Starting in 2013, the Syrian Army has been methodically shutting down these scattered pockets of terrorist activities one by one. Each time they shut another down, they gather up their prisoners and consolidate them in a single spot: Idlib. It's become the dumping ground for all of Syria. They benefit from it because they'd rather surrender and be transported than be killed after long sieges, and our army benefits because it means soldiers and resources are not tied up indefinitely all over the country in endless and sometimes lethal standoffs. The problem, of course, is that as close as it is to Turkey, Turks have now been able to build observation towers in the area of Idlib nearest to them, and the place has predictably become a breeding ground for jihadists and a stronghold of Turkish command in Syrian territory. The Islamists have become almost untouchable, and their numbers have increased. So now we have a war zone emerging, and for all intents and purposes it's in Turkish hands. The Turkish President Erdogan will absolutely use this to his advantage, in any way he can."

Vahan held what was arguably the most interesting piece of the puzzle until the end. "The truth is that the Russians did most of the work," he explained. "They were the ones who suggested this strategy to Bashar al-Assad." Their plan? If Syria gathered all these jihadists in one spot, near the Turkish border, then they could choose the time and circumstances under which to crush them, in one fell swoop. Anyone who fled the attack would cross the border, be picked up as refugees by European countries, and would no longer be Syria's problem. The Europeans, through cowardice disguised as diplomacy, would continue doing nothing concrete to combat the situation.

Vahan finished with a cutting remark: "Diplomatic cowardice is the one thing that most of the world still holds in common."

32

Aleppo, the Unending Siege

That same October, during the same stay in Aleppo, I heard about a man named Dr. Antaki. He was a renowned cardiologist, and he and his wife were very involved in the city's defense. One of my friends told me about him and the macabre records that he kept: a daily tally of deaths in Aleppo, published on his account on Facebook. There were too many political leaders and newscasters who lied about the facts, trying to make things seem better than they were. Dr. Antaki and his wife wanted everyone to know the truth. I checked his account and read the following: a daily count of the city's deaths "so the world doesn't forget and talk nonsense." When I checked on Facebook, I saw these notes, among others:

- Wednesday, September 28: fifteen killed.
- Friday, September 30: seventeen killed.
- Tuesday, October 4: eight killed (including three students who were killed by the shell that fell on the college of agriculture).
- Thursday, October 6: ten killed on al-Jamiliye Street (business district).
- Friday, October 7: four killed (a family) in their apartment in Midan in the morning. Four others killed at night, hit by the shells that fell on several neighborhoods. The terrorists

who control eastern Aleppo fired these shells (and mortars, rockets, and gas canisters) into western Aleppo's populated areas, seriously wounding many civilians in addition to the ones they killed.

I started forwarding these posts to supporters of our association and to any others who wanted to know what was really happening on the ground in the city. Then, on Sunday, October 23, 2016, we saw a post from our friend, Abouna Fadi Najjar. He had shared a photo of a huge shell that had landed in the front yard of the Carmelites sisters' convent, not injuring any of them or destroying any of their home. Under the photo, he wrote the following:

"They said that God's mercy has disappeared. We tell you: look at the picture. God is still with us. They want to persecute Christians in Syria. We tell you: look at the picture. The gates of Hell will not prevail against the Church. They say that what's happening in Aleppo is that the Syrian Army is bombarding *eastern* Aleppo. We tell you: look at the picture—a big missile fired today on the monastery of the religious Carmelites in *western* Aleppo. Thanks be to God, it didn't explode. Look at the face of the sister standing behind it; her gaze reflects the sadness of the merciful God in the face of the missile, and the missile reflects evil and the devil. Each believer who experiences a peace inside his heart knows it because they gaze toward the Cross. And, after the Cross, we believe that there will be a great resurrection."

33

A Helping Hand

On November 1, 2016, we met to assess our mission in Syria, take stock of the progress of our current projects, and ensure that we were upholding the mission state of our association. As we discussed the state of things, one central goal coalesced: we had to find a way to slow down the emigration of Christians. People were fleeing because they no longer saw any reason to stay. We had to find a way to bring them hope. And so that's precisely what we did.

If we were really going to be bringers of hope, the first thing we had to do was rebuild, and quickly. People would come from the villages to Aleppo, using it as a stepping-stone before leaving for Beirut, Lebanon, or if they were lucky, for Europe or Canada. This meant we needed to rebuild in the villages first. While homes were of course a great necessity, the central need in each location was a functioning church, complete with a priest.

We began in Qalamoun. Once a church was there, Christians could rebuild their lives there. Through the leadership of its priest, a church would mean the stability of an entire Christian community. Our reasons for rebuilding the churches were the same reasons the Islamists had destroyed them. The presence of the Christians was rooted in the Masses, prayers, scouting, schools, catechesis, humanitarian work, private hospitals, and so forth that churches could provide. Additionally, the role of the priests in Syria was one of a representative and mediator between the state and the Christian community's residents.

Things were different in Aleppo, however. Here, the focus was on urgent humanitarian work, which included educational and cultural support and material needs. In Jazira, it was different still, isolated as it was in being collectively surrounded by Turkey, Iraq, and the ISIS Islamists. The focus here was primarily on education—school enrollments, scholarships, and home support. We couldn't let the war undermine the quality of education that Christians had always received in Syria; we wanted to ensure the transmission of a multimillennial heritage in spoken education, whether that heritage was Syrian, Armenian, or came from another tradition.

Other concerns we discussed at this November meeting included supporting individual families, offering food, household goods, warm clothes for winter, water, electricity, and the oil-burning stoves. We had plans for food distribution in the large cities of Damascus, Latakia, and Aleppo, as well as in some of the small villages. With the road to Aleppo sometimes cut off, the residents suffered from shortages of basic necessities. The hospitals in Aleppo were also always in need of supplies; we'd deliver containers of medical equipment to the two main hospitals and about fifteen dispensaries, medical centers, and clinics.

Medical supplies, food, and other basic necessities aside, the bulk of our work in Syria was reconstruction, primarily in Maaloula and Sadad, the al-Hamidiye district in Homs, and the Midan district in Aleppo, where the homes had been destroyed by the bombings. We added other locations to our list over time as conditions in various villages deteriorated. If we wanted to build well, we had to start our construction projects in the spring. Currently, about fifteen houses in Maaloula had already been rebuilt or were in the process of being reconstructed. We also helped repair the Melkite cathedral in Homs. Meanwhile, we offered French courses in the Maronite Diocese of Tartus; there were young people there who were preparing to enter the seminary in Lebanon.

34

Engagement

I left Aleppo on October 28 while the whole world was watching it, and I went to meet my mother in Damascus. I was getting formally engaged to Fimy the next day.

Russian forces had arrived to assist the Syrian Army on September 30, and paradoxically, the more victorious their advances were on the ground, the more scarred the city was by the intensified bombings that paved their way. The Islamists ran riot as never before—like wounded animals. With nothing left to lose, they furiously and almost madly dished out everything they could. Shells, missiles, rockets, and bombs exploded on the city every day, the death toll mounted, and the waves of displaced people surged.

Ramez was my driver again. With traffic getting out of the city badly jammed up, we sat in a line of cars tightly packed on the right side of the road; everything was congested with the large military convoys heading into the city. The sight was unforgettable: rows of cars, GMCs, tanks, and trucks, all transporting war equipment, driven by men who seemed strangely determined. The feeling here was different than it had been in the previous few years. I could tell something was happening, and Ramez said what I suspected. "They're here to crush al-Nusra, and they're really going to do it this time!"

Even as we inched past, we saw cannons pointed toward eastern Aleppo and the western periphery, spitting fire from the rear of the pickup trucks that carried them. Mortars exploded every few seconds, and rockets shot off like stars, disappearing into the not-too-distant horizon. Planes rumbled above us, leaving white and black smoke trails behind them, and smoke filled the buildings of the skyline behind us. Once we got past the worst of the congestion, and especially as we really picked up speed, we started hearing the firing of the jihadists' Kalashnikov rifles in the hills that lined the road; we drove like mad, dodging obstacles in the broken road and doing our best to keep clear of stray bullets that pursued our flight.

To put it mildly, I was not confident about bringing my mother back this way. But that was the plan, and we had to find a way to make it happen.

On our return trip, as we got closer to Ramouseh, the city's southern gate that had formerly been the symbol of the industrial center of the Middle East, we realized there was nothing left of it. The jihadists had destroyed everything they could and brought everything else back with them to Turkey. As on our way out, this last long section of the road toward Aleppo was congested with endless, impressive convoys, stretching out across kilometers. Ramez noticed something and pointed it out to me—civilian trucks transporting huge quantities of ammunition. There were Syrian and Russian military convoys further on; they brought in tanks and big guns. It was a sad sight that surrounded us, and the gloomy sky above rumbled as planes set the city ablaze. It felt like we were walking into a dark mouth that would swallow us without a second thought.

I turned to my mother. "This is where we're going—into this blaze. We'll be there soon."

I was trying to reassure her, but the reality of the situation was that we were one of hundreds of vehicles, parked bumper to bumper on the highway, waiting. Passengers sat in the windows of their cars or stood in the beds of their pickup trucks, watching. Many of the younger ones had weapons in their hands, ready and waiting for the moment they might need to use them. It was a striking scene, and these young men were impressive. I felt oddly ridiculous just sitting in my warm car with no intentions of joining the fray, a feeling that got worse when our eyes met: They were going to confront death in a matter of moments, ready to defend all that they were. I, on the other hand, was simply passing by on my way to go get engaged. And my mother, God bless her, was saying her Rosary.

We were close to making it into the city, almost to the gate, and the sounds of war grew louder alongside us. As we passed by a house, its door opened and, just for a moment, I saw the face of the man who came out. He wore a traditional long gown and held a Kalashnikov. He shouted fiercely and waved his weapon in the air, firing it toward the sky. Hundreds of men around us followed suit, and we realized we were moving through an entire tribe whose leader had just given the signal to attack. Bullets sprayed around us, and I felt like an idiot for making such a trip at such a time.

Ramez's face had tensed up. With the road here even worse than usual, he had to concentrate fiercely as he worked his way around all the broken pavement and detritus. He suddenly stopped, steered, accelerated, turned to the left, back to the right, put the vehicle in gear, put his foot on the clutch and brake, and accelerated again.

"They're right there!" he said, gesturing off to the right. "The terrorists have taken back the road we were driving on yesterday. They're just over there, and our army is on the left."

I saw a mound of dirt that was surely hiding a trench and a clutch of jihadists. We were driving down the battlefront, and I felt like we were on death row. I turned to my mother. "I wouldn't mind it if you said an extra ten Hail Marys for me, Mom."

She grimly smiled back at me and nodded—as we reached Aleppo's southern gate. We had finally arrived at Ramouseh.

Our engagement ceremony was at 4:00 p.m., and it was 1:00 p.m. There was just enough time to eat, change, and make it up the street to St. Michael's, the Franciscan church where we'd be betrothed.

By the time we arrived, Fimy was already there with her whole family and Abouna Fadi. The loud explosions of the bombings in the city crashed around us, and the church walls trembled. But even in the midst of a war, the beautiful things that give life its meaning move on, and we were engaged.

After the ceremony, Fimy and I withdrew for a photo session in the Shahba Aleppo Hotel's park, and the explosions followed us. We could hear them all around us, but this was still a good day, and we smiled at each other in the midst of the chaos.

A few hours later, we all met up again at the Wanes Restaurant. The bombings didn't let up, yet we had a wonderful day, and nothing could have disturbed this joyous moment. We danced and laughed all night long in the heart of Aleppo. That day, as in the book of Daniel, we danced in the furnace.

The terrorist lightning fell on us that entire night, and the Russian and Syrian planes responded in turn. The walls of the house in which we slept trembled all night long, not abating until the early hours of the morning.

35

Aleppo Released!

I looked at the calendar hanging on the wall. It was November 18, 2016. It had been a month since I'd moved to Aleppo on a permanent basis. SOS Chrétiens d'Orient had found a house in the Azizieh district for me to live in with about ten other volunteers. Like every other winter since the war had started, there wasn't enough heat to counter the frigid temperatures. The furnace routinely went out, so we stayed bundled up indoors and slept in all of our clothes. It wouldn't have been an enjoyable place to live anyway; bombings still shook the city every day, and we would wake and sleep to the sound of them. The jihadists blindly bombed the western part of the city, and the Russian Air Force returned fire to the eastern neighborhoods. The violence on the ground was constant, and planes flew overhead regularly.

Even though the liberation of Aleppo was still in progress, our Syrian volunteers had started some home reconstruction projects in the Midan neighborhood. The front line had moved back, and this deeply wounded neighborhood could start to come alive again. In addition to the reconstruction work, we continued getting people connected to the generators for electricity and making regular supply runs of food, diapers, water, and oil-burning stoves.

Kidnapped in Iraq

And then it was December 7, 2016. My report on that day was a good one: "The siege in Aleppo ended today."

In the previous forty-eight hours, the Syrian Army had managed to drive the Islamist rebels from the Ancient City of Aleppo. This section of the city was the most difficult to take back because of its topography—namely, a network of alleys and dead-end streets and multiple tunnels. However, eventually the Islamists abandoned the Ancient City to take refuge in southeastern Aleppo. Everyone thought this meant they had lost all hope of resistance. At this point, most of the eastern civilians had taken advantage of the chaos and had managed to get into western Aleppo, which meant the inhumane jihadists could no longer use them as human shields.

Although the five neighborhoods that made up the Ancient City had been taken back and the heart of Aleppo was no longer under occupation, there were still small pockets that had not yet been cleared, such as the neighborhoods of al-Kallaseh, Bustan al-Qasr, and Sheikh Saeed. This meant that Aleppo's citizens weren't yet entirely free of falling rockets and shells, but the end was in sight.

The liberation of Aleppo received a lot of attention in the press, and it became the main topic of conversation for many of the newscasters at that time. But there was a problem in the way the journalists approached the story: they talked about the fall of Aleppo rather than its liberation, and in their praise of the Free Syrian Army, they were clearly on the side of the rebels who had made life hell for years on end. Thanks to social media, these lies flooded the planet. People watching the news on the other end didn't ask who these "journalists" were or what ulterior motives they might have in presenting the story in such a way. In the end, an American cameraman ended up winning a prize for his coverage of the situation; he had done a number of live interviews with various emirs, none of whom were at all moderate in their own viewpoints.

One correspondent from the Qatarian newspaper that was based in Aleppo, *Al-Quds Al-Arabi*, wrote that "the setbacks were also the consequence of the divisions between the terrorist groups." He added that "the groups had forgotten the religious obligation to be united with each other." But how could people manage to distinguish between moderates and terrorists if unity had to do with—in his own words—"the religious obligation"?

I left Aleppo for a brief visit to Homs, Palmyra, and, last of all, Sadad, where I needed to check on a school we were rebuilding. When I returned on December 10, four large mortars had fallen on Azizieh, right next to our house. The jihadists, who now controlled only 5 percent of the territory in the southern section of eastern Aleppo, were hanging on by the skin of their teeth.

Starting on December 12, the general public was allowed to go back into the Ancient City. It was the first time in four years that most were able to see it, and Fimy and I wanted to go too. When we walked through the deserted park, we saw just a few people out, bundled against the cold and moving quickly. As we came up to Clock Tower and the Sheraton Hotel, the Ancient City was just a hundred meters away. Some red-eyed soldiers were stationed in various places along the way, and I could see that even though they were tired, their eyes were shining. Victory was here, within rifle range.

But as we moved forward and took in the scene around us, the chaos was indescribable. Every building had been destroyed. Some had collapsed in on themselves. The Ancient City looked like a film set about the end of the world, with every single street and alley obstructed by piles of rubble. Gigantic holes had been drilled in some of the buildings to let fighters move quickly from one neighborhood to another, avoiding the snipers. I made out what remained of the Great Mosque of Aleppo at the end of the road, and we saw other people walking, on both sides of the streets, dazed and stunned by the destruction. The curtains still hung on many windows, open to the blowing cold air. And, on the ground under our feet, we realized they had left posters of Bashar al-Assad with his eyes gouged out. Everything was incredibly sad. The extent of the ruination left me speechless. The mosque, which was also called Zakariya, had been in the center of numerous battles, and the Islamists had ransacked it, even knocking down a minaret—a mosque's equivalent to a spire or a bell tower—to try to keep the Syrian Army from being able to get into the courtyard.

A man sat on the ground, curled in the fetal position, with his head in his hands. He was grieving and repeated over and over, to anyone who would listen, "Zachary's bones have been stolen and taken to Turkey!"

As we stepped over the rubble that used to be part of the walls of the mosque, we found ourselves in the bazaar right behind it. There were clothes left behind by the rebels, some flags, and some empty food boxes; they had gotten food from dozens of places, including Turkey, Qatar, and Saudi Arabia. There were also empty oil barrels piled up on each other, supported by sandbags, that had been used as ramparts around the mosque, watch spots for snipers. One of the Syrian Army soldiers who was there now, guarding the mosque from further destruction, gave me a beautiful white tasbih as a souvenir. It was one of a few objects still here in the mosque that had been spared.

As we left the Ancient City and headed back downtown, we heard eruptions of gunfire on both sides of the street. But we realized, upon listening, that these were joyful shots announcing an almost complete victory—only 2 percent of the city still needed to be cleared out!

Some frightened but supposedly well-informed news reporters stressed that the Syrian Army was proceeding "with the brief execution of the last 'resistance fighters,' but this information can't be verified." These were the same sort of resistance fighters who terrified France in 2015 and 2016, and I knew the reporters were spewing out the same unreliable, slanted nonsense that they always did. I knew one thing for sure: I looked all around me in Aleppo that day, and I sure as hell didn't see any well-informed journalists.

People could say or believe what they liked, but the reality was pathetic. The journalism profession was dead in Aleppo—again. After Timisoara and its "50,000 dead"; after the Gulf War, Saddam Hussein, and the Iraqi Army, the "third largest army in the world"; and after Kosovo and its "450,000 missing persons," journalists as a whole clearly hadn't learned anything from their decades of misreporting. Their contortions of the truth resulted in them reporting events the way they wanted them to be, not in objectively sharing what was actually happening.

Despite the journalists who actively worked as impediments to reality, the real news on the ground spread fast. Vahan, my Armenian friend, told me that ninety-eight percent of Aleppo was liberated. There were only three square kilometers that were left in the jihadists' hands, and all of the Salah ad-Din district was still surrounded.

Scenes of jubilation were erupting everywhere—perhaps a bit prematurely. Aleppo's complete liberation was at most only a day or two away, and people couldn't get enough of it. Joyful shots lit up the sky, coming from the rooftops, from cars passing by, from groups of people marching and singing in the streets.

One young man from Aleppo, Majd, spoke to me with tears in his eyes. "This nightmare is over—no more sitting helpless while we lose our friends, watch our families die around us. No more bombings, no more shells, no more fear. We can love each other again, without being afraid of losing each other."

Kidnapped in Iraq

The next day, on December 13, the Bustan al-Basha neighborhood opened back up. It had been under the jihadists' control for a long time and had just been freed by the Syrian Army. Syrian flags flew from the tops of the buildings as Vahan and I walked through the district. Each time a new district was freed, we visited it as soon as we could. We walked through a large, pitted lot and saw an old shack supported by sandbags; a burned-out pickup truck was falling apart next to it, and we saw a newer cannon and propane tanks from the Syrian Army. The Syrian soldiers had staked their claim with their big guns, but Vahan had a more primal method for marking his territory: anywhere he saw a trace of the jihadists, he dropped his pants and relieved himself, declaiming that those dogs had ruined his country, his city, and his life. While I understood the sentiment, I chose not to join him in this particular expression of it.

Many Christian families had left their homes, schools, and churches here, and in some places, a few walls were all that remained of the lives they had left behind. But before long, we would come back to that very same area and see businesses opening back up and people selling fruits and vegetables in the streets.

Fimy and I went to visit the destroyed Christian neighborhood of al-Jdayde, which was right behind Farhat Square. We weren't the only ones there, and in the faces of the others who had come to survey the damage, I saw surprise, sadness, and anger. We spent the week walking on the streets and alleys of the Ancient City of Aleppo and even went to where the old bazaar used to be. This covered marketplace had been the site of thriving businesses, run by shopkeepers and passed down through generations, since the 1300s. It had been an architectural pearl in the entire Near East and Middle East, and now all of it had been severely damaged. A solid third of it was gone forever.

But beyond the ruins of the bazaar, the Aleppo Citadel was still standing. That site had been used as a city defense for almost six thousand years, with the construction of the fortress that we knew ending about one thousand years ago. For so many years, I could only see the citadel from far away, but it had survived the war, and now I could really look at it and appreciate it, despite the damage it sustained. We went with a group organized by Syria Trust, a Syrian NGO led by Maronite Scouts. I was there with Fimy, and as the two of us surveyed the scene, hand in hand, emotions of all sorts were running high; all around us, people were smiling and crying, and we were too. Feelings were at their peak—smiles and joy but also shock and tears.

As we walked that day, we saw people offering soldiers laurel crowns. They wanted to give them not just to the soldiers who had been fighting all the way through to the end but also to the wounded, who had sacrificed so much that they couldn't fight at the climax of it all. And we heard the sounds of trumpets in the streets, too, playing in honor of the many fallen who had lost their lives in the Herculean struggle.

On our way home, on Khan al-Harir Street, near one of the entrances to the north of the bazaar, a Syrian Army soldier walking with us shared some of what they had faced in trying to fight back against Jabhat al-Nusra and all of the inhumane abuses they perpetrated. There had been a time, he said, that they set up five hundred propane tanks against the outside walls of civilian buildings and then blew them up to conquer that territory. I could see exactly what he was talking about. There were places where we could walk from one street to the next through big holes in the walls of the houses. They were large enough that heavy war equipment and vehicles could have driven through them. But, even more terrifying, in some places, the tanks had not yet been exploded. I saw them tucked against the walls of homes, grenades taped on and ready to go. Needless to say, we had no wish to end up like a double burst of confetti; we moved right on.

In another spot, not far off, we saw bags of white beans from the World Food Program. I realized what this meant: while the Syrian government had done their best to starve out the jihadists in eastern Aleppo, the jihadists had been getting shipments of food supplied by Turkey. To make matters worse, we could tell from the labels on the food that these supplies had been hijacked from humanitarian organizations. As time went on, we would hear similar reports that confirmed the opinions we formed that day.

The buildings of the eastern neighborhoods were one matter, but, far more importantly, now we had a chance to speak to some of the people who had survived through that occupation. By the time they were rescued, many were bedridden and had to be hospitalized, and sometimes even intubated.

"They shot at us like dogs," one man said, "every time we tried to get out and move down one of the humanitarian corridors. And if someone next to us was shot, we knew we couldn't stop to help them without being shot ourselves."

In Al-Kalima, one of the city's hospitals, an elderly woman with a nervous look told me with great difficulty that she and the elderly man in the next room had been captured and regularly beaten. The look in her eyes made my heart ache. Realizing that she was even afraid of me, I quietly stood up to go and backed out of the room, trying to let her know that I wasn't there to hurt her.

The man next door told us how the jihadists had forced the neighborhood men to work for them, using their knowledge of the city to help them hold their ground and even attack the Syrian Army. "It was the only way we could get rations to feed our families," he said. "But they were predictably terrible if one of us got hurt in battle for them. They withheld the medical supplies that they had in plenty and watched us die in pain."

36

Back to Square One

Sunday, February 16, 2020, somewhere in Iraq, not far from Baghdad.

All four of us captives were lying down on our beds, some with eyes closed, others staring at the ceiling. We remained motionless for hours—sometimes without speaking a single word. It was late that night, but we were all awake.

The sound of terrible screams came through the air ducts, coming from far off, hideous and painful. First, we just heard a man screaming twice, but then we heard a woman four times.

Without moving his head, Julien whispered, "Did you hear that?"

Antoine and I were also motionless. I responded in a low voice, "Yes, they're torturing people up there."

Antoine added, "They must be demonstrators."

We all stayed perfectly still; we didn't want the cameras to see that we were paying close attention to what was happening just above us. Two feelings came over me: I was afraid of being tortured, and I was also relieved that, so far, we hadn't really been beaten or tortured. We were still being held as prisoners, but not being tortured helped me keep things in perspective. Things could have been worse, and for now, we still had hope that we might be rescued.

Two more weeks went by. It had been four weeks since they'd moved us to this place. One night, after we had all just prayed the Rosary, each in our own corner, one of the guards came down into our cell. As I prayed that night—my second Rosary of the day—I had asked for a clear sign of hope that we would be freed. We had all just gone to the small table to split the two cans of tuna among the four of us; that was all our food for the day. It was as we were saying grace that we heard the door, and we jumped to put on our painted ski goggles. We almost couldn't believe our ears as he started talking.

"I have some good news for you all. Tomorrow you'll see a document that we'll ask you to sign, saying that you've been well treated and that all of your property has been returned: passports, cell phones, wedding rings and other belonging, euros and dollars—even in Iraqi currency. You understand of course that it's routine for us to confiscate these things, but you'll get them back tomorrow. After you sign the document, you'll be taken to the Green Zone and received by the UN, and they'll bring you to the French embassy."

We were stunned. Had it really finally ended? We couldn't take our goggles off and look at each other yet, but we knew we all must be feeling the same sense of euphoria, and we thanked him for the news.

He went on. "We see you, you know, through the camera, always praying, especially Antoine. I said to my buddy, 'Look at them! It's impossible that God wouldn't answer them!' And an hour later we got this phone call saying you'll be released. You'll finally get out of here." Then his tone changed a bit. "Abou Dany," he said, "you know how things are between us and Iraq. You know how it goes … no good while it lasted, but it's all over now. Sorry, man."

We told him thank you, that we were grateful, and that when we prayed it wasn't just for ourselves but for him and his friends as well. We told him that we'd keep praying for him, even when we went home. He sounded genuinely friendly as he in turn thanked us for this before going upstairs. When the door closed behind him, we tore off our goggles and threw ourselves into each other's arms, hugging one other and proclaiming victory.

Abou Dany couldn't stop talking about the document we'd sign tomorrow, going over and over it, obsessing about it. To be honest, I couldn't blame him. I thought we must all be feeling the same way. But as it turned out, Julien was skeptical. I didn't understand his reaction and brushed it aside. We picked up praying where we had left off—only this time we prayed in fervent thanksgiving for our earlier prayers being answered. And then we ate and joked, laughing at the joy of going home, of seeing our families, of being able to ask their forgiveness for what we had put them through, of being able to start our lives again. It was all finally going to be over. I stretched out on my bed, and I smoked a celebratory cigarette.

To our surprise, the same man returned only an hour later and told us to get ready to go. We weren't waiting until tomorrow; they were moving us now. We grabbed our goggles, put them on, and then sat calmly on our beds, waiting for our captors to come get us. Fifteen minutes later, we heard the heavy door opening, and they came down. As before, they took us one by one, tied our hands, and brought us one at a time to a vehicle waiting outside. I could tell it was a GMC, just as before.

When they pushed me to the end of the trunk, I could feel Antoine already there. Julien came next and then Abou Dany. Crammed in together again, we experienced the same hell of restless waiting for the car to start as our limbs began aching and cramping. We listened as men moved around outside, loading things, talking, and finally starting up the cars to get on the road. We had only been driving for ten minutes before we began to realize something was wrong. We should have been hearing traffic noise, but instead things were getting quieter. Without saying anything, we all realized that we had been lied to, that we were moving away from the city.

Finally, I burst out in a low voice, "What a bunch of garbage! We're not going to the Green Zone."

Julien had been right, and I felt myself becoming angrier. Abou Dany was heavy next to me, crushing me between him and the side of the car, but nothing could be done. I felt fury rising inside of me, with nowhere to go. My arms hurt, and the cords were cutting into my skin, and it was hard to breathe. I wondered suddenly if they were planning on selling us.

After an hour of driving, each turn taking us farther from civilization, farther from shreds of hope, we slowed down and parked, then sat waiting. We heard restless voices outside. Our drivers got out, and we heard people moving things from another car while we still sat, still waiting. When they finally got us out, it was the same as always, one by one, leading us to an isolated place in the middle of nowhere.

One of them wished us a good night, and we recognized the voice of the man who had told us we were going to be free just a few hours earlier. I asked him, "Sir, can you explain what's going on? You told us we would be released, that we'd be taken to the Green Zone and handed over! What's happening?"

He answered, "Oh yes, tomorrow, tomorrow. Rest in peace now."

But nothing happened the next day. We didn't see a single person. And I realized what their tactic must be here: each time they moved us, they would tell us we were being freed, convince us that the end was in sight, and then when we moved, we would be easy to work with, calm, quiet, and obedient.

The fury rose again inside of me. So many lies, so many un-necessary, detailed, cruel lies. A document that we would sign, being convinced of our faith as he watched us pray through the cameras, trusting God, pretending to feel compassion and friend-ship with us, even acting as though he sympathized and wished us well—everything was fake. And we poor idiots had believed it all. It was pathetic and ugly.

When we were able to open our eyes and take stock of our surroundings, we saw the same black iron beds, mattresses, and dirty blankets from our last basement cell. No doubt that was what we had heard them moving from the other car. This room wasn't any bigger than the last one, but at least it wasn't a basement, and it wasn't as rough and dirty. Everything was made of cement, and I could see that some of it hadn't dried yet. It looked like it had been rapid and shoddy construction work, probably entirely done in just a couple weeks.

The room was rectangular—I'd say two and a half meters by seven meters—without counting a six-square-foot room for the Turkish toilets, which was separated from our living room by an iron door. My bed was at the very end of the room, and I saw a camera on the ceiling above my head. There was another camera at the other end of the room, above the wall to the right of the door, which was not as intense as our last prison door. In the wall above the door, there was a rectangular opening that stretched across the whole width of the room, and we could clearly see the sky from our bunks. We were glad not to have to listen to the buzzing of an old ventilation system anymore, and the light here was softer, not so artificial and glaring. Ultimately, we were at least thankful to be aboveground.

From the permanent look of our surroundings—including the television in the corner and the fact that they had transported all of the furniture, such as it was, from our last cell—it was relent-lessly clear that the promises of going to the Green Zone tomorrow had all been lies.

The next morning, we'd just awakened when the guards opened the door and told us they wanted us to come outside for some fresh air. We were skeptical; they hadn't let us see the sun since the day they'd kidnapped us.

We kept our ski goggles on as they led us, one by one, into a small enclosed space, a sort of inner courtyard surrounded by cinder block walls. But we were outside. Though we still couldn't really see anything because of the goggles, we could catch small glimpses, and we could feel the fresh air, the wind on our faces, and the warmth of the sun on our skin. Against all odds, this bit of sunshine gave us hope for a life that would somehow manage to keep going on. And then the guards said they'd be leaving us here for a bit, that we could take our goggles off as they went back to do a few things in our room.

Amazed, we removed our goggles and looked at each other. We had been aware of it, but in full daylight, we were surprised to see how little our beards and nails had grown away from the sun. We smiled in spite of ourselves, relieved to see each other in the fresh air. We hadn't seen pure daylight in weeks.

Antoine and Julien were looking at a partition of the cinder block wall behind me, and Julien saw something through a chink in the wall. "Look," he said. "It's the outside of that trailer they kept us in."

It was true that the roads we had taken on our last two trips, and the time spent in the car, had been quite similar. But I still wasn't quite convinced. I came to look for myself, and sure enough, he had to be right. Somehow, the realization made me feel faint. I could see the outside of the small space we had come to know so well, that Algeco trailer with the irregular partitions and the odd ventilation system that jutted from its side. All at once we realized it: the construction noise we'd heard the whole time we were in the trailer had been our captors building our new prison cell. I was speechless as this recognition sunk in.

If they had any plans to release us anytime soon, they would never have built a cell just for us. We were going to be here for a long, long time. Someone might as well have just hit me over the head or punched me in the stomach. Here we'd been thinking our time was almost up when, in reality, we were only at the beginning of an imprisonment that would likely last for years on end. Suddenly, the sun felt painful and the air felt cold, and when we went back to our room, I was glad to climb back onto my bunk and pull the blanket over my head, lost and overwhelmed. I wanted to escape in dreams of being free, memories of the past, and unrealistic hopes of what might come to be.

The others also understood what this new realization meant, but somehow Antoine was positive. He told us we needed to focus on the fact that we were no longer in the basement dungeon—a place he'd said he could feel the devil's presence—and that things would not be so wicked here. But despite his talk and encouragement, all I could think was that at this rate, we would all go crazy before being freed.

When I finally looked up from my bed again, I noticed the guards had replaced the camera above the front door with a more modern one that had night vision capabilities. The one above my bed had been reconnected too. And we noticed that the empty space above the door, where we had been able to see the sky, was blocked off by a large iron plate. They had brought us outside merely so that they could add the "finishing touches" to our prison.

One day, I heard a voice I recognized from earlier: it was that strangely funny-sounding man leading the guard when we'd been in the trailer. We'd also heard him once or twice in the basement near Baghdad. We surmised that he must be based by that lousy Algeco trailer; perhaps that was his workplace.

By this point, we were starting our fifth week of captivity, and, to put it mildly, I was depressed. I thought back over the past few hours, weeks, months, and years as I lay on my makeshift mattress, scanning my memories for something beautiful, good, and joy-ful—something to warm my spirit, to move me, to remind myself that everything wasn't pointless. Finally, I found myself focusing on something: Aleppo's Christmas tree.

37

A Christmas Tree for Aleppo

On the evening of December 22, 2016, I was walking on the main road in the Azizieh district of Aleppo when a soldier standing on the other side of the road suddenly started to shoot toward the sky. People all around the city were still bursting out in sudden celebrations at their complete liberation, and within a few moments, I heard other victory shots answering the soldier. Soon, cars around the city started honking their horns, and people opened their windows to sing out patriotic songs. I saw the flags of the Syrian Arab Republic, Russia, Iran, and Hezbollah floating from the windows and watched the evening sky as red streaks of fire shot through, again and again.

"The Kalashnikov rifles are singing with the people!" My friend Vahan was laughing in pure delight as he walked with me.

That same night, my association colleague Benjamin and I had an online meeting so I could update him on our works in progress. We had a lot of different projects going on: pumping groundwater, establishing generators and heating equipment, supplying school and hospital necessities, figuring out university tuition payments for young adults, and, as always, rebuilding the homes and apartments that had been destroyed in the fighting. All of these projects were vitally necessary, and more requests in this vein came in every day, but I wanted to do something more for the people we served, something symbolic to give them a happiness and a hope for continuing joy that went above and beyond the nuts and bolts of everyday survival.

It was Christmastime, and it had been five years since the city had been able to celebrate with a proper Christmas tree. One of the friends of the association, Mr. Choukri, had suggested it. He told us that the Armenian community in the Azizieh district had managed this task until the start of the war, but they didn't have the means to do so right now. It was a wonderful idea, exactly what the scarred and recovering residents of Aleppo needed. But how would we get a real fir tree here? The only wooded areas were in Idlib and Latakia. Idlib was occupied by al-Nusra, and cutting wood was banned in Latakia.

Mr. Choukri told me that the Armenians had usually put up a metal tree with plastic branches. Sometimes, he said, it would be more than five meters high. Given that we couldn't get a real tree in, this sounded like our best option. Mr. Choukri started right in. Only a few days later, I was surprised by how quickly it had come together. I could see it from almost every vantage point in the whole Azizieh neighborhood, and Mr. Choukri was proud to show me how they had decorated it.

We sent out a message to everyone we could in the town and to all of our supporters around the world: "As Christmas is approaching, SOS Chrétiens d'Orient has offered a symbol to the city and its residents—an illuminated Christmas tree, a sign of hope and peace. This is the first time since 2011 that a Christmas tree has been publicly celebrated in Aleppo. After five years of war, it is there, majestically taking center stage, more than thirteen meters high."

One man who lived close to the display found three giant posters to hang on the front of the building next to the tree: posters of

Bashar al-Assad, Hassan Nasrallah, and Vladimir Putin. I chuckled at the display and told them we were just missing Ali Khamenei. When I returned the next day to look at the finished tree, I saw that they had added Khamenei to the poster wall; the whole team was there! I laughed outright, and Mr. Choukri laughed with me, saying they had added the Iranian leader just for me.

This was the big night. With Christmas only a few days away, our "fir" tree was ready. I saw this Christmas as a symbol of the birth of a new peace for the entire population of Aleppo. Hundreds of people on the square had gathered around the tree, some of them singing patriotic songs to the glory of the victorious Syrian Army and their leader, Bashar al-Assad. There were also some women present who were veiled in black mourning, even over their faces, carrying their fallen husbands' weapons as they stood in front of the giant Christmas tree. Whole families came by, civilians and soldiers mixing together, and taxi drivers stopped on their routes. Everyone wanted to stop by the tree to take a picture, to join the crowd that was celebrating. Mr. Choukri had set up a speaker system and was giving a speech.

Without warning, Mr. Choukri turned and called for me to come up through the crowd and to speak for the whole square to hear. This wasn't exactly my idea of a good time, but saying no to this crowd was not an option, so up I went. I couldn't have spoken to a more enthusiastic throng. They cheered as each one of my sentences was translated. I didn't say anything particularly profound; I just told them simply that their city, thousands of years old, would rise from its ashes, would continue on for thousands of more years — this was a city that knew how to survive. As I tried to leave, people wanted to take pictures of me, requested selfies, and asked me a thousand questions. They were all warm and cheerful, friendly and curious, and their joy filled me, flooding my heart with an intense satisfaction.

Kidnapped in Iraq

I knew that I was privileged to be here, that I was experiencing a historic day. I tried to fill my mind with the images that surrounded me, wanting to memorize them, to never forget what was happening that night.

Aleppo's residents had dreamed about this for four years. For four years, they had lived under the steady fire of enemy weapons, watching their friends and families being shot down in the streets, clinging to survival as their homes and businesses were destroyed, as their communities were taken hostage, and life as they'd known it was razed to the ground. They had dreamed of peaceful sleep for four years, and now, finally, it was an interrupted dream no longer.

It's true rebels were still free outside of Aleppo, but inside, the city itself was still liberated. This night belonged to the people of Aleppo, and I was filled with joy to witness their jubilation. It was amazing, too, to see the different ethnic and religious factions mixing together, putting to an end with their joint celebration the favorite stereotypes of our Western media. I saw Sunnites, Shiites, and Christians dancing, holding hands while they shouted and sang together "*Allah Sourya Bashar w bass!*" ("God, Syria, Bashar, and that's all!"), "*Allah maa Jeysh!*" ("God with the Army!"), and so many other chants that I couldn't quite understand. They danced, shouted, and cried for joy—most of them Syrian Sunnites. The Christians were in the minority that night, despite our tree that was symbolic of a Christian feast day.

Syrian television broadcasters were also present, recording the young and old singing in unison in groups along the streets, in the backs of pickup trucks, or hanging out of the windows of cars that inched through the crowded streets. The jubilance was overwhelming, and the celebration around our tree was only one of many in the city that night. There were also live broadcasts of parties in the streets near the university and every other major landmark in Aleppo. Tonight, these people could openly share their joy that their city hadn't fallen. Aleppo had finally been liberated, and on this night, it came back to life.

38

The Hostages of the Free Syrian Army

With Christmas now only one week away, our thoughts turned to what we could do for all the hospitalized refugees who had just been freed from eastern Aleppo. We visited the hospitals frequently; a theoretically simple thing would be to bring gifts for all the children who had been hospitalized. We set about getting it done.

I did my rounds in the Aleppo hospitals each day, inevitably ending up at the enormous St. Louis Hospital, where we felt at home. France built it in the years following World War I, during the French Mandate of Syria. It was run by religious sisters and led by Archangel, a tiny little sister of Italian descent. She and her entire team had been inundated by the tremendous flood of sick and wounded people who were finally free of the jihadists; almost eighty thousand Syrians had been freed when eastern Aleppo was liberated, far more than what the media was reporting. The stories of the men and women we met in the hospitals were overwhelming.

One young girl in the St. Louis Hospital was particularly close to my heart. I always made sure to visit her and her parents, and of course to pray for them too. She survived a bombing on her school but had been badly wounded by shrapnel; all of her friends had been killed in the bombing, which happened near the end of the siege—on November 20, 2016. The shrapnel was lodged in her head, and the doctors couldn't remove it without killing her. For now, she was in an artificial coma.

In another room were three older people whom I thought of as my "survivors." Jean, Georgette, and Colpi were the only remaining residents of a Syrian Catholic retirement home in the Jdeide district where twenty-eight people had lived together at the beginning of the siege. Jean, who wore a cap on his head and had worked for the home, told me their story.

"One beautiful morning, five years ago, we woke up and realized that the Free Syrian Army was in the streets all around our home. Seventeen of our residents managed to escape, but flight was impossible for most of us. I couldn't leave, not when there were people like Georgette." He pointed to his friend. "She's seventy-five, and she'd lived with us for twenty-five years; who would have taken care of her if I had left?"

As winter set in, the bombings continued, and rationing was instituted. The only foods they could get were bulgur, lentils, and pasta. The price of coffee rose to 50,000 Syrian pounds per kilo—approximately one hundred U.S. dollars. Cigarettes were almost 40,000 pounds per pack, so they learned to live without them.

When people started dying, Jean did his best to take care of them. "The first one was Abou Joseph. He was seventy-five years old. The district's imam didn't want him to be buried in the Muslim cemetery. So I pushed him in a wheelbarrow for several kilometers while going through the Kurdish neighborhood. When you push a corpse in a wheelbarrow, nobody stops you. I left it as close as possible to the Syrian Army's lines, knowing that the soldiers would come and find him. But after that, the bombings got so bad that it didn't seem wise to go out, and so when more people died, we buried them in the yard."

Colpi's husband, who had managed the retirement home, died when he went out to get food for the residents in 2015. Colpi herself had been wounded by a shard of shrapnel in her skull. She was fifty, and Jean, who took care of her, was fifty-five. He explained that as she convalesced and grieved her husband, and then as they worked together through the years of the siege, they grew closer to each other. He eventually asked her to marry him, and she said yes.

"And then one day, we looked out and saw the Syrian flag floating in the square near our home. But we didn't quite believe it was all over until the Syrian soldiers came and told us it was time to leave the home. When a Red Cross car came to pick us up, there were only four of us left alive. Maggie, God rest her soul, died just three days after we were freed. She was ninety years old, had grown emaciated and weak, and no longer had the will to eat."

There were people with stories like Jean and Colpi's in every room of the hospital, each with their own stupendous burden of grief and misfortune.

One little boy we got to know, Aboud, was ten years old. He had been riddled with shrapnel and badly burned, and he was being cared for by his uncles and their mother, whom we referred to as "The Courageous Grandmother." Rania Mohamed Hajeali was only forty-eight, and she had a young face under her black veil, but her hands clenched until her knuckles showed white, and her eyes had a look of deep sorrow as she watched her grandson and told us their story.

"On the morning of December 10, our family was getting ready to leave eastern Aleppo through one of the humanitarian corridors when a shell crashed on the balcony of the apartment where my daughter-in-law was trapped by the rebels. The neighbors who found her pulled out her phone, looked though her contacts, and found my number under 'Mama.' And I came running from our home in Tartus, 250 kilometers away."

It had all started for them when Rania's oldest son, Abdel Mouhin, disappeared during the first year of the war. She and her husband had ten children—four boys and six girls. Like all young Syrians, the boys were required to do their military service during the war. Abdel had been kidnapped by the terrorists in Douma, where he was a military student, in 2012. Rania's husband couldn't bear the grief of not knowing what had happened to his dearest child, and he died only forty days later.

"This was in the early days of Aleppo's siege, and friends of our second son, Morhaf, thought it was possible that the rebels hadn't taken him too far away, that maybe they were holding him just on the other side of the city, in the eastern neighborhoods they'd just taken. He wanted to go find and rescue his brother. I was proud of him for his courage, but like him, I worried what it would mean for his own family if he, too, went missing—he and his wife had five children of their own.

"My daughter-in-law told him that they would all go together. Whatever happened, she said, they would not be separated. And so, in January 2013, Morhaf and his whole family moved into eastern Aleppo. It didn't take the rebels long to locate them and confine them to quarters, but they didn't take their phones, and they didn't kill them—yet. Every few months, when the cell network would come back on, however briefly, he would call and tell me that they were okay, that they were surviving, that they were still alive and hadn't died yet."

But when the Russian Air Force initiated heavy bombings of rebel-held locations, all through eastern Aleppo, the rebels tightened their grip on Morhaf. They said they wouldn't let him leave unless he called one of his brothers in the Syrian Army, convinced him to go AWOL, got him to trade places with Morhaf himself, and then convinced him to join the rebel forces.

Rania's eyes got misty as she continued to speak. "Twenty days ago, when the bombings intensified and the humanitarian corridors opened up so civilians could get out, the rebels monitoring Morhaf and his family knew they would try to escape. And so, the first chance they got, they shot him in the open street, in front of my daughter-in-law and their oldest son. As they took his body away, and their children all came out and began to cry, she forced herself to quiet her own screaming and tried to tell them that he would be okay, that they were just taking him to a hospital, that he would be back—but she knew he was dead."

By that point, she knew they had to move quickly, and that very night they packed what they needed to leave. But as the bombs continued to fall, they couldn't get out. It was while they watched and waited for a lull that a shell exploded on their balcony, where she stood with her oldest son. It severely burned her, and it badly injured little Aboud, whom we saw before us in the hospital that day. It was a blessing the other children were far enough away from the impact that they were not hurt; it was at this point that the neighbors had come in and called Rania.

After eight anguished hours on the bus, Rania and her brother-in-law finally arrived in Aleppo, a city they didn't know that was in a state of utter chaos, choked with violence, and in the death throes of the siege.

"I walked right up to a military officer and asked him to show me where the front was. They were astonished at first, but when I explained that I was there to grieve my son, who was a martyr, and to rescue his family, they gave me a pass and ordered the soldiers to let us through. As we moved forward through one of the deserted corridors, we heard the echoing of the bombings all around us, and halfway down we heard people shouting, warning us not to come any farther.

"As we stopped and waited, we saw them coming in the distance. An elderly couple was pushing a vegetable cart toward us; it held my little grandchildren and the bloody bodies of my daughter-in-law and grandson, and I assumed they were dead. The old couple turned to go as quickly as they had come, and I barely had a moment to thank them before they were gone. Then we in turn moved quickly to pick up the handles of the cart and bring our family back to the Syrian Army's side of the front."

When they made it back to safety, Rania was able to stop, at which point she realized Aboud and his mother were in fact still alive. She brought them to the hospital, where they all were now. The only one they were missing was Morhaf; they never found out what the jihadists did after they dragged him away.

Before I left Aleppo for my next trip, I went to see Antoine Audo, the Chaldean Catholic bishop. As we talked about the state of affairs in the city, and about the people who remained to pick up the pieces after all the violence of the past years of siege warfare, he confirmed much of what I surmised must be the reality of the situation.

"The rich people of Aleppo left long ago for Lebanon, and that's been a loss to Syrian society we won't recover from anytime soon. And of course, like Rania's family, another group of people found safety living in the provinces toward Latakia and Tartus. The blow upon the bruise came when a third of our young people ran away from military service to take refuge in Germany. And now you see where we are today: before the war, there were 150,000 Christians in Aleppo. Today, at most, there are fifty thousand left. The people who fled were those who could afford a trip and a smuggler. The people who stayed behind were the impoverished and the patriots—sometimes both. Think back to France during World War II. Can you imagine if your population had fled in 1940? There would never have been any resistance."

He paused and sat for a while before sharing his final thoughts —thoughts I didn't fully understand. "Did we not have the right to defend ourselves? Or were we simply unwilling to die for such a cause, because the president of our country is a dictator? It is still our country—such reasoning seems very strange to me. And I, for one, am proud that I have stayed to defend my country, when so many others have fled in despair."

I felt disillusioned as I went back to the office. I'd heard similar arguments before: "Bashar al-Assad will disappear one day—not Syria." Syria was here for the long haul, no matter who the current ruler was. Not to minimize the devastation of the war, but what kind of people leave their country because things get hard? This sort of desertion was a consistent pattern that I saw everywhere. If you love your country, the logical thing to do is to stay and fight for it. But Europe forgot this lesson a long time ago, though our cemeteries are filled with men and women who died to keep our country independent. They didn't run away. As the British say, they kept calm and carried on. They didn't give in.

39

Some French Deputies to the Rescue — a Delegation on the Front Line

In the weeks that followed, Aleppo's fall—or liberation, depending on who was talking—continued to take center stage in the world's news. International supporters of the Free Syrian Army were enraged to see the balance of war shifting to Bashar al-Assad's favor. France was a part of this response as well; news that "the worst man on the planet" had taken back Syria's second-largest city with the help of the Russians and Iranians didn't go over well at the Quai d'Orsay, the Parisian home of the Ministry for Europe and Foreign Affairs, where politicians were choking with rage.

Meanwhile, journalists who'd never set foot in Syria organized demonstrations in Paris. Some clones of Bernard-Henri Lévy—a pro-Kurdish and pro-Islamic French contemporary philosopher with a knack for controversial politics—who were completely ignorant of the situation, outrageously advocated for war, as they had done for the Libyan Civil War in 2011 and the Iraq War in 2003. They didn't understand what they were asking for, not for one second. Ultimately, they got carried away feeling like they were doing something important, dressed warmly in the safe streets, supporting an incoherent message, and buying a good conscience for a cheap price. Some of my friends in Paris sent me pictures and videos of these clowns on the street, making me laugh a little. Crowds like this had always seemed ridiculous to me—and, as far back as I could remember, they had never prevented history with a capital "H" from happening.

It was in this context, on January 5, 2017, while I was in Damascus for two days, that I learned that several French deputies had arrived from Paris at the Dama Rose Hotel: Thierry Mariani, Jean Lassalle, and Nicolas Dhuicq. Jean Lassalle surprised us with his delightful singing and a few jokes, and we were curious about the journalists who had accompanied them—Pierre-Alexandre Bouclay from *Valeurs Actuelles*, Charlotte d'Ornellas from *Boulevard Voltaire*, Marie-Baptiste Duhart from RTL, and Astrid de Villaines from LCP. A representative from Franceinfo was also present.

Because of snow on the roads, Bashar al-Assad had provided a plane for the French politicians to reach Aleppo from Damascus. We flew together and arrived in Aleppo in time to celebrate the Twelfth Day of Christmas with the Apostolic Armenians in the battered district of Villat. Holy Mass was celebrated by Catholicos Aram I, who had made the trip from Antelias in Lebanon. From there, we'd go to visit some of the neighborhoods that had just been freed; I was still astounded at their ruins.

Alexander Ivlef, a Syrian friend, was traveling with me. He had been a French teacher in Aleppo's French Cultural Center before the war. During that time, French President François Mitterand had come to Syria to close the French consulate in Aleppo. He thought there were too many open French consulates in the world. When Ivlef and his colleagues heard about his plans, they got the entire civilian delegation together to go from Aleppo to Damascus to meet with him and try to change his mind. They politely reminded him that the consulate in Aleppo was the first

French consulate to open anywhere in the whole world. He had in fact been unaware of that and, in the end, decided to keep it open. But as it happened, President François Hollande went on to desert Syria, recalling Éric Chevalier and closing the French embassy in Damascus, politically and culturally severing the ties of diplomacy between our two countries.

Thierry Mariani stood in front of the shuttered embassy doors, speaking to the press. "Syria may be a rival, but it is not an enemy like Saudi Arabia and ISIS. France may not agree with Syria on everything, but this is exactly why we need an embassy. We don't dialogue with those we agree with but, rather, with those with whom we differ. We're part of what used to be the French consulate in Aleppo. Quite simply, there is no more French diplomatic or consular representation in this country. We even had two high schools, one in Damascus and one in Aleppo, that had sister schools in France. Those Syrian schools are still open, but with no ongoing help or recognition of any kind from France. And just last night, we were speaking with the president of the Syrian Chamber of Commerce; he reminded us that, once upon a time, thanks to the French Mandate of the 1920s, Syria had been a French-speaking country, but, however much Syria might remember it, France has forgotten it."

After we left the empty building, we made our way to the Jibreen Camp, where some of the recently displaced people were being held temporarily. As eastern Aleppo communities were cleared after the occupation, anyone left was sent here; the Syrian Army needed a staging ground to make sure terrorists weren't slipping through, hiding as innocent civilians. We didn't have long to visit here, but our three French representatives made the most of their time, asking plenty of questions and trying to get a realistic picture of the conflict and its effects.

As we approached the camp, the children there rushed toward us, as children do, asking for smiles and attention. When they saw the cameras, they got very silly and started posing, convinced that they'd soon be famous back in Europe. The women, on the other hand, were reserved and dressed in black, and they smiled only with hesitation. The men didn't even leave their shacks.

Interpreters with us translated for the children, relaying their requests to us. Some asked for toys, while others wanted notebooks and pencils so they could go back to school. They thought we could bring them anything, make anything happen for them. It was touching—and sad. Many of these little ones had been born during the conflict, and they didn't even know what school was. Their little smiles enlivened their young and prematurely wounded faces.

The wheels in my head spun as we turned away from the children; I was imagining how much paperwork we'd have to get through in order to bring any supplies to such a place, and yet these were little children, asking for help. If it weren't for the red tape, it would be a relatively simple thing to bring them little toys and notepads. And it didn't matter if they were the jihadists' babies, as I was sure many of them were. Children were children, and they didn't even know what *jihadist* meant. Many of them in fact had no legal existence, born as they were without papers or status to women who were coerced or abandoned or had given themselves over in desperation to survive after their husbands had died. We had to find a way to help them.

Back at the airport, the plane was waiting for us, ready to bring the delegation back to Damascus.

"How long is the flight back?" asked Nicolas Dhuicq.

"Well," I said, laughing, "if we don't get shot at, it should only be about forty-five minutes." As it turned out, this was a poor choice for a joke.

While we waited, Pierre-Alexandre Bouclay and I talked with one of the soldiers, exchanging e-mail addresses so he could get some of the pictures the journalists had taken of him; he wanted to send them to his fiancée. And then a sudden explosion, not far off, made us turn around.

"That was a close one!" said Bouclay.

Just as suddenly, a second whistle pierced the skies, followed by the crash of targets being obliterated, and smoke and debris shot up into the air. Now Bouclay really yelled, certain that we were about to be hit. I felt like I'd lost consciousness but stayed awake, and I realized a rocket had exploded to my left, just a hundred meters away. A rocket? Something wasn't clicking—I couldn't understand what was happening, but it did occur to me to be grateful that I hadn't been hit by shrapnel.

I realized the others were running toward the terminal entrance. I took off after them as the earth trembled under my feet, convincing me that with the next rocket blast I'd lose my balance, fall to the ground, and very shortly meet my maker. But we all made it inside, and we barricaded the entrance as the rockets outside continued to fly around the building. There was an old, ornate chandelier that hung from the ceiling, and as we pressed ourselves up against the walls for support, pale and trembling, we watched the chandelier shake mightily.

Time dragged on, and our immediate panic marginally subsided. Mariani took it upon himself to try to make us laugh in an effort to relieve the tension, even if only a little. He took out his tablet and looked up some '80s music videos. Surprisingly, it worked, and we found ourselves smiling, even if a bit tensely, as he continued on with stories about his trips and political adventures.

Jean Lassalle, not to be outdone in trying to make people laugh, stretched out his tall frame, covered his face with his beret, and said, "Just wake me up when the terrorists arrive, okay? Or if the plane is ready to go."

By this time, night had fallen outside. We saw flashes of automatic weapon shots behind the tarmac, and we knew this meant that the jihadists were only a few hundred meters away. Deputy Dhuicq, who was an expert from the National Defense Committee, carefully noted the sounds coming out of the night and, with great enthusiasm, explained to anyone who would listen the minutiae of the ballistics being used against us—he could identify the caliber of each weapon as it fired. Not surprisingly, not everyone there shared his thirst for such knowledge.

As the explosions picked up again, crackling faster and louder, a young woman who was a radio journalist was livid, and she was certain we would die or be kidnapped here. Bouclay tried to reassure her that we were hearing friendly shots, that there was really nothing to worry about. "No, no, don't worry. These are friendly shots!"

She managed an almost withering look as she glowered at him and hissed, "Friendly? Friends? Don't you think you're going a little too far?"

But Bouclay responded without hesitation. "All those who don't want me to die are my friends! By all means, choose your camp."

As it turned out, this young woman, who arrived in Syria full of prejudices and ill-informed opinions, would go on after this visit to be one of the most honest reporters of the whole group. We would have much to thank her for in the end.

All things told, we waited for three and a half hours in the airport while al-Nusra fired rockets at us. When things had been quiet again for a while, the soldiers with us tossed decoys into the dark off and on for an hour, making sure the jihadists weren't still lurking in the shadows, waiting for us to come out. Finally, they gave us the green light to leave, telling us to grab our things and run quickly and quietly, under cover of darkness, to the plane that still waited for us. And so, wheeling suitcases behind us, we bolted across the tarmac to the dark plane. We made it inside, shuttered all the windows, and covered with our coats the lights we couldn't turn off; any bit of light seen from the outside would turn us into obvious targets.

As the pilot took us up in the air, guided by candlelight, he came on over the intercom with some encouraging words. "If we're not killed by a rocket during the first five minutes, then we'll definitely be out of the woods."

We learned later that the rockets were being fired at us from Rashidin, a fiefdom of Jabhat al-Nusra, about fifteen kilometers from the airport. They would in fact claim credit for the attack just hours after we left.

Benjamin turned to Thierry Mariani and said, laughing, "This'll make a great story to tell when you're back at the assembly!"

As I looked at the journalists and tried to gauge their reactions to Benjamin's comments and everything that they had just been through, I felt some doubt that they'd be in any hurry to relive the experience, in any way.

When I finally made it to my hotel room in Damascus that night, I thought about the stories the journalists should have shared at the start of this war. When they should have denounced the complete Islamization of the first Syrian revolutionaries, almost nothing was said. Where there should have been questions and concerns about such goings-on in the geopolitical conversations of international newsrooms, there was a big void. The Free Syrian Army was consistently painted as the underdog "rebels," standing up to their terrible dictator. Even when the violence of the siege of Aleppo reached its peak, and again during the city's liberation, the French TV stations continued to paint a picture of poor rebels being crushed by overbearing Russians and Syrians. In France, many chose to collaborate with Hitler rather than forging ties with Stalin. And we thought that Mao looked like a great visionary, and that Phnom Penh's capture by the Khmer Rouge in April of 1975 had been fantastic news for Cambodia. Later, in 1986, when the SS20 and the Pershing missiles confronted each other in Berlin, we even had a fashionable slogan: "Better Red than Dead." Now, in the 2010s, nothing had changed. Our nationwide, decades-old lack of foresight and clarity was terrifying.

The next day in Damascus, we had a remarkable appointment: we were expected at the presidential residence, where we would meet Bashar al-Assad. A friend had even found me a suit to wear so I could look at least somewhat presentable.

I had just stepped from the car and was following everyone else, climbing the stairs to the house, when I looked up and saw the president standing just a few feet above me, welcoming his guests without ostentation or ceremony. I was surprised by how approachable he seemed, and I said a quick "Hello, Mr. President" as he shook all our hands in turn. The flashes of cameras on my right momentarily blinded me, but I moved ahead when I saw that he was inviting us to come into the room off to the left at the top of the stairs.

I mostly watched and listened as the French deputies had lengthy discussions with him, but I was gratified when, at one point, Thierry Mariani mentioned the work of SOS Chrétiens d'Orient in Syria and pointed to me.

Bashar al-Assad looked at me for a few moments, while nodding his head in approval. I was a little uncomfortable with the scrutinous gaze of such a man on me, and I didn't quite know how to react when his eyes met mine, but he smiled. And then he expressed his views on how important it was to preserve the presence of Christians in Syria and the Middle East. "Christians ensure peace and understanding among people. They contribute to unity and peace. It is when the Christians are compromised that we have more and worse civil war; without their vanguard in Syria, the Muslims would take us back to the dark ages of the seventh century."

40

Deir ez-Zor – the Siege Continues

Back at my hotel, the staff watched the news on the TV in the lobby; the reporters were sharing images of the siege in Deir ez-Zor, which would reach its climactic point and eventual resolution later that same year—in November 2017. A Russian television team had been able to enter the city in a helicopter to capture the images being shared now.

Deir ez-Zor is isolated in the eastern Syrian desert, meaning that anyone stuck in the city had no way out. Their only option was to fight until they died. A friend of mine who was a Syrian journalist made it in one night on a military flight, flying as we had with all the lights off. They'd gotten in, and he'd gathered information for reporting as he'd wanted, but it would be another ten days before they had a safe window to take off for Damascus again.

After he made it back, sick with hepatitis C, he sat down with me and shared the details of how rough the situation there actually was. "There were grandmothers and seven-year-old children standing beside the Syrian Army, with cigarettes in their mouths and Kalashnikov rifles in their hands. They were on the warpath, ready to retaliate against ISIS in case they tried to inch forward. Deir ez-Zor is like Stalingrad! Every square centimeter counts, and both sides defend and fight over it bitterly."

In short, it sounded like things in Deir ez-Zor looked like a medieval siege. Unlike Aleppo, there wasn't any way to allow the city to breathe. And because it was so hard for members of the media to get in and out, there wasn't any international media hype to shed a light on the siege, for good or ill.

The setup was like this: the city was split in two, with the Syrian Army controlling the southern section of the Euphrates River, including the airport, and ISIS controlling the northern part of the river, supplied with water from Iran. In the Syrian Army's section, the Deir ez-Zor Airport's line of defense had been weakened in a bombing. The official line was that it had been the fault of the American Air Force, when, in an "error," they had killed between sixty and eighty Syrian soldiers and let ISIS take over the hill that overlooked the airport. The current heart of the conflict was on this hill, which meant that the road connecting the city to the airport was cut off and no supplies or reinforcements could get in. If the Syrian Army didn't survive this skirmish, if Deir ez-Zor fell, we all expected that there would be a massacre, just as there had been in 2014 when the Islamic State group massacred around a hundred civilians after invading and taking the city's northeastern neighborhoods.

41

Fortress of the Kurds

July 31, 2017

"*Deus in loco sancto suo, Deus qui inhabitare facit unanimes in domo, ipse dabit virtutem, et fortitudinem plebi suae.*"

The words echoed through the cool room. Outside, the heat was oppressive.

"*Exsurgat Deus, et dissipentur inimici ejus et fugiant qui oderunt eum, a facie ejus. Gloria Patri.*"

"God is present in His sanctuary. God makes those who are of one mind to live together in His house. He Himself will give strength and power to His people.... May God arise, and may His enemies be dispersed. May those who hate Him flee before His face. Glory be to the Father."

We were attending Mass in the heart of what had once been Syria's greatest crusader fortress. As the calm silence and darkness surrounded us, here in the chapel in the Fortress of the Kurds, the centuries-old connection to the Catholics of Syria's past was palpably beautiful.

Krak des Chevaliers, a massive and impregnable medieval lime-stone fortress near Homs, was first home to Kurdish forces in the 1000s. It was given over to the keeping of the Knights Hospitaller

Kidnapped in Iraq

Crusaders in the 1100s, and I could imagine those knights and feel their presence around me as I prayed, as if the words of the ancient Mass were awakening their souls. I pictured them here, eight hundred years earlier, with their coats of mail, each covered with a white tunic marked with a red cross. They wore their sheathed swords as they prayed, always ready to fight for Christ. A shiver ran down my spine as I remembered them, and I hoped that, in some way, they could appreciate what we intended to be a beautiful tribute to them after all these centuries of silence.

I felt like an apprentice who had come to seek wisdom from those who had fought for the honor of European Christianity. I closed my eyes and thought back on the history of the place, momentarily distracted from the Sacrifice of the Mass being celebrated before me. But given the beauty of the Mass, I couldn't be distracted for long. Father Aubry, a priest of the Fraternity of St. Vincent Ferrer and the assistant religious adviser to SOS Chrétiens d'Orient, was celebrating Mass according to the Dominican rite, which was similar to the traditional Latin rite that would have been celebrated here in the Middle East, here in this very room, during the thirteenth century. I had never had such a sense of being part of a sacred continuum, and the humility and awe it provoked were astonishing.

After Mass and the Rosary, a local man came to speak with us. He was amazed to see all the foreigners here, most of us volunteers with our association. While we already knew the story to a certain extent, we listened as he told us how this architectural jewel, the pride of the region, had been taken over by the al-Nusra jihadists, with the aid of the Lebanese Islamists, on March 8, 2012. It was two years and two months before the Syrian Army managed to wrest it back. Not surprisingly, it had sustained some damage, but, as had happened so many times in the past, through earthquakes and wars, they would find a way to repair it, to preserve it for the next millennium of Catholics who would follow in their footsteps.

Also present were two little religious sisters from a neighboring village in the Valley of Christians. Sister Lydia, who was obviously very moved, told us with tears in her eyes, "It has been many years since I've seen this ancient Mass celebrated, and never in this place. The beauty of it surely brings us closer to Heaven. What better way for us to find the strength to continue hoping for peace for Syria, and in your own country of France, both of which have suffered so enormously. When people come together, as people from our two countries have come together today, God will surely bless our actions and intentions."

Her faith, sincerity, and simplicity were edifying. Especially after such a celebration of Mass, it was surely a day overflowing with an embarrassment of riches and blessings for us all.

42

Christians in Chains

It was 2018. In the past few months, we had witnessed the almost complete disappearance of ISIS in Syria. The territories to the northwest of the Euphrates River had fallen into the hands of the Turks, except for the city of Afrin, which, together with all the territories to the northeast of the Euphrates River, was still being held by the Syrian Democratic Forces. Despite the difficulties, the SDF—that is, the alliance between the Kurds and the Free Syrian Army's former jihadists—was still holding on. And in fact, in October of 2017, Raqqa, the ISIS "capital," had fallen to the SDF. Thousands of jihadists ran away in a large convoy, taking the road to the north, and not a single one of their trucks was intercepted. They had vanished as they moved toward Turkey.

But they hadn't disappeared for everyone. Some Syrian officials claimed that the Turkish government would end up using the jihadists to accomplish their own goals, and in fact just three months later, on January 20, 2018, the Turks launched Operation Olive Branch, moving toward Afrin to fight against the SDF. And the world looked away. The Kurdish forces had done all the groundwork to get rid of ISIS, and now, as the Turkish troops joined with and supported the jihadists in moving back against them, the Kurds found themselves alone and abandoned by Europe and the United States.

Syrian politics and military maneuvers, however, were not all that came up on our radar that year. One day, my phone rang, and I saw that it was François-Xavier Gicquel, the operations manager of SOS Chrétiens d'Orient. He had called to ask me what I knew about the state of Christians in Pakistan, and he went on to talk about how most of them were held as modern-day slaves, bound by debts and unable to choose their own way of life or achieve financial independence.

Slavery in the twenty-first century? This seemed absurd to me, and I wondered why I hadn't heard anything about it before now. François-Xavier asked me to go with him on a trip to northern Pakistan to see what we could do about organizing the release of Christian slaves. I was eager to make the trip. This was absolutely the sort of work that our organization had been formed to undertake.

The background of the situation was this: In 1947, India was divided into two vast territories: modern-day India for the Hindus and Pakistan for the Muslims. But Christians, who were in the minority, were excluded from the division, and they became almost entirely landless. Christianity in Pakistan, specifically, was recent, dating only from the English occupation at the beginning of the nineteenth century. In India, however, it had been present from the very beginning, thanks to the evangelization of St. Thomas the Apostle. And with the British occupation of India, the number of Catholics in India rose even higher—many of the soldiers in the British Army were in fact Irish Catholics, and their presence was a source of some evangelization. But both in India and in Pakistan, regardless of the legitimacy and tradition of Christianity in the two regions, owning land was difficult for Catholics.

SOS Chrétiens d'Orient had created a program to free those treated as slaves, entering into negotiations with their "owners." In order to inform and improve this program, and at the request of St. Paul Church in the village of Pansara, François-Xavier and I flew to Punjab, where members of the Christian community in Pansara waited for us.

The customs officers at Faisalabad International Airport took a long time to check our passports and look over the letter from the parish that had invited us. We could tell they weren't pleased with our coming there. Pakistan is almost entirely Muslim, and the 2 percent of the population that is Christian is not viewed favorably. But in the end, the officers had no legitimate reason for detaining us, and they had to let us pass. As we went through, we saw a large crowd of people waiting to welcome us.

I met one of the men who was there, Ladou. François-Xavier had told me about him ahead of time. He was the one who handled all the administrative burdens for Father Parvez, the pastor of St. Paul's Church, who had invited us. Ladou, smiling and friendly, was clearly glad to see François-Xavier again. It was my first trip, but François-Xavier had been here twice before.

As we made our way to the village of Pansara, we had to go through a police checkpoint and announce our purpose there yet again, telling the guards that we would be in Pansara for a week. It was cold there, and they were all wrapped in coats and hats as they inspected our papers and then let us pass.

Once in Pansara, we made our way through some of the streets, eventually finding ourselves in front of an iron gate that enclosed a compound. It was a secured residential neighborhood, and we had to wait for a guard to slide open a big door to let our car go through. We saw a small building on our right, which we learned was a school, and there was also a little white church, built in the style of Indian architecture.

It was the custom there to dress as the locals, so after our arrival, we quickly changed our clothes. We looked like real Pashtuns, or rather, Pathans, according to the local name, as we went to meet Father Parvez, who welcomed us around a table. There were some young people coming and going as we sat and talked, and they watched us with smiles on their faces, talking to each other and sometimes laughing. Father Parvez told us some of them had been slaves.

I turned to him and asked what I hoped didn't sound like a foolish question, but I wanted to understand. How did people become slaves? What happened to put them in such a situation?

"Well, it's like this," he said. "Because the Christians have no land, their economic situation is very difficult. At one point or another, they almost all hit a moment where they need to borrow money to survive, either for food or medical expenses, or perhaps to pay a wedding dowry or for the education of their children — there will always be something. The people who loan the money often own big farms or brick factories, and they arrange the debts in such a way that, through inflation and interest, they can never be paid back. The debt spiral continues to drag the Christians down, and while each wage they earn in the factories or farms is immediately paid back to the lender, it is never enough to pay off the debt and never enough to get them out of the dilapidated housing that the debt lords provide. In the end, they effectively belong to these carrion crows, working off the money until they die, at which point the debt is passed to their children."

He rose from the table. "That's enough sitting and talking for now. Let me show you around our campus here. The school is mostly made up of students from very poor Christian families, but there are also a lot of Muslim students. Many of the children come from families whose debt we've worked to reduce."

As he opened a classroom door, the students immediately rose and greeted him. The teacher stopped his activity and bowed in respect, as was the custom there. There was a brief pause, and then, in chorus, the students all said "hello" and "welcome" to us—in English. When they sat down again, I saw they had a dirt floor that doubled as a table, as they had no desks. Their schoolbags were in fact plastic bags, which they sat on since they had no chairs. But their small booklets and notebooks were carefully and tidily stacked beside them, and the students themselves were clean, with impeccable uniforms and bright, smiling black eyes. I had never seen such order and happiness in the best of French schools; they clearly lived a virtuous poverty here.

At this point, Father Parvez excused himself as he sent for his car. He had an appointment with someone that day but wanted to bring us to see Christ the King Colony when he returned.

When we went out that afternoon, François-Xavier explained what the colony was—namely, a village construction project that would provide homes for several hundred families. Currently there was room for just over one hundred families, but Father Parvez hoped to acquire another parcel of land to add to the first, thereby increasing the capacity to three hundred families. He was able to raise funds through the church and buy the land directly from the government. So far, fifty families had lived there for the past seven years, after being freed from rich Muslims who'd enslaved them in their brick factories.

Father picked up the thread from there and told us about how the Islamic Republic's Pakistani government had been working on enforcing human rights in their society, knowing that without these assurances, they would never be respected or welcomed on the world stage and so would have limited or no access to such benefits as the global economy. But with so many varied tribal affiliations in their populace, not to mention the interference of fighters from the Taliban, al-Qaeda, and ISIS, progress was slow.

"Have you seen any improvements in day-to-day conditions?" I asked him.

"Well, yes," he said, "but with many complications. Thirty years ago, the government started giving lands to the Christians, but the Muslims disputed this, causing enough problems that they stopped it. Now, for the past few years, and despite continued pushback from the Muslims, the government has allowed lands to be sold to the Church. And we, as an organization, can then turn to the individual Christian families and help them get established on this land. But none of that is any good unless we can first bail them out of their indentured slavery to the rich Muslims."

The road to the colony was mostly unpaved and very bumpy, but when we arrived, we were greeted by a row of tidy houses, and we could see more behind them. As soon as we got out of the car, a little crowd of families came from the houses and gathered around us. Children ran forward in excitement, then retreated shyly to hide in the saris of their mothers and older sisters. But the men greeted us warmly, hanging garlands of flowers around our necks, and the women waited for us to walk past so they could throw grains of rice and rose petals in our faces, showing their acknowledgment and gratitude for what we were trying to do. Father Parvez said it was thanks duly given, and he reminded us that it was because of funding from our association that all these families lived here freely while their children went to school.

As they invited us, we went into some of their homes, which helped us get a good sense of how they were really able to live. The homes were bright and clean, and the land around them housed livestock and gardens that enabled the families to share meat, milk, and fresh produce.

"Freeing them from slavery is one thing," Father told us. "But then we have to help them find a way to build a future. With the homes and farms here, and with businesses built in this colony that provide them with a revenue, they can actually build savings and provide an education for their little ones."

From Christ the King Colony, we went to visit a brick factory with Father Parvez. He had set up an appointment for us with the owner there. In that area of the country, there are a lot of brick factories, and the smog left the air foggy, while the smell of burning constantly hung in the air. As the car slowed down and turned into a big, vacant lot, I was struck by the ugly landscape and the gray sky. I looked up to see chimneys, built on manmade hills, spitting out a steady stream of smoke. And then I saw some men in rags on both sides of the chimneys. They looked permanently bent over and exhausted by the heavy loads they carried on their shoulders.

Our driver parked the car by a small shack, and we saw a man waiting for us on the stoop. He sat at a table, with tea in one hand and a rosary in the other. He had several dozen men and women who worked in his factory, and he was relaxed and casual as he smiled at us and sent one of his stewards to get us some tea. He and Father Parvez began talking in Urdu, so we couldn't understand the details of their conversation, but Father told us they were working out the details of a deal. An entire family would be released in just a few more weeks

With Father Parvez translating for him, François-Xavier asked the owner a question.

"Doesn't it bother you to lose a whole family of workers?"

But the owner shrugged, unconcerned. "Not at all! There will always be more indebted families who show up tomorrow to replace them."

We realized that he wasn't trying to be cynical or ugly. He was just stating an ordinary fact of life as he had always known it.

When we looked more closely at what was happening by the chimneys, we realized that what we thought were hills were in fact enormous furnaces. One group of slaves would put the bricks in on one side. After they had baked, the bricks would be pulled out on the other side with long hooks that were attached to the ends of sticks. The heat was blindingly intense, and I couldn't imagine the reality of working in such conditions, day in and day out.

Father Parvez spoke quietly to us, in a way that told us not to react to what he was saying. "Sometimes, they say they have accidents here, but we know that sometimes they are also punishments. Workers are sometimes pushed right into the furnaces and burned alive."

As I worked to control my horror at such a thing, I looked around behind the furnaces and saw workers who were shaping the soil that would be baked into the hard bricks. They were squatting as they worked, men and women together, some as old as seventy, and even little children, some younger than six years old. As I looked at the men and women, I realized I couldn't really tell how old they were—their faces and bodies were prematurely aged by the harshness of their work. One old man was even dragging himself along the ground to get his work done, and like everyone else around him, he breathed in the dirty smoke from the coal furnaces as he worked on the assembly line. While rain might momentarily cool them down, it also meant that any bricks in progress had to be remade.

"The hard truth," Father said, "is that, despite all we might do, these types of factories aren't going anywhere anytime soon. The cities continue to grow, and so the need for bricks for new buildings remains constant. What you see today is happening in thousands of brick factories all over this country—there are two million slaves in Pakistan. We do what we can, but there is always more that needs doing."

When we returned to the parish compound, we sat and continued talking with Father, listening as much as we could. He was a scholar, and he liked to talk about everything—history, religion, spirituality, and societal phenomena. The conversation took us all over the world and into the complexities of the Pakistani mindset. It was during this afternoon that I learned Father Parvez had also been a writer. As if fighting back against slavery, providing homes to hundreds of families, and being a spiritual leader to all his parishioners weren't enough, he'd also published at least a dozen books.

43

Deir ez-Zor

As things had stabilized somewhat in Deir ez-Zor in late 2017, we decided in March of 2018 that I should make a trip to the city. Sebastiano, one of the other members of our association, and Alexis, my assistant, would travel with me. It had been ten years since my last visit to this city, and it seemed an eternity away—not just in time but also in distance. I was anxious to see what the city looked like after so many years of violence, but the road was still uncertain, even though it was finally and officially in a demilitarized zone. Rather than driving from Damascus, we decided it would be safer to fly to Qamishli, in the far northeastern part of the country, on the Turkish border. Once we got there, we'd find a car to drive to the city. As was almost routine at this point, our plane took off with all lights turned off for safety.

When we arrived, Father Gabriel, al-Hasakah's Syrian Orthodox priest, was there to welcome us and drive us to the city. Like us, he also wanted to see the extent of the city's devastation. Not surprisingly, the road to the city was full of roadblocks and checkpoints, and along the way, we had for ghoulish company the frames of cars and trucks that had been burned out, dismantled, and left to rot along the road. To be honest, it was quite similar to the roads that led in and out of Aleppo, and in each burned-out car I could picture all too clearly the civilians whose purposed flight to safety had ended so horribly. Of course, there were larger vehicles that had been destroyed too: supply trucks, military vehicles, and others.

We were making progress toward the city, but we couldn't come at it directly. As we wound our way through villages on the circuitous journey, we saw evidence of the violence that had been perpetrated even in these more remote places. When we stopped to buy some bottles of water, one shopkeeper told us there had been massacres throughout the countryside, including in his own village, "before Hezbollah came to release us." And though the flags of Hezbollah were hung everywhere, and the battle-hardened faces of their fighters were present on every street corner, we could still see the graffiti the invaders had left on the fronts of buildings and road signs; the efforts to paint over it or scrub it away hadn't yet been fully successful. Nevertheless, men worked on repairing the roads and rebuilding their homes, and children were back in school. Life was in the process of returning to normal.

Our car finally stopped on the banks of the Euphrates River. We couldn't drive across it, as there were no more bridges; they had all been destroyed in the battles between the Syrian Army and ISIS. I looked across to the opposite shore and saw Russian soldiers. They had constructed some sort of floating bridge that was attached to two amphibious machines that ferried the bridge back and forth, from one bank to the other. Father Gabriel asked one of the soldiers if we could borrow one of the inflatable boats to get across, and they took us over.

Our first stop was a visit to the airport, which had been held under a fierce siege. I found myself thinking back to heroes like General Issam Zahreddine, a Druze warrior beloved by the Syrians and feared by ISIS. I imagined the years of intense fighting that he and his men—and the residents of Deir ez-Zor, whom he was fighting to protect—must have experienced. And then I recalled the times when the American Army had bombarded the Syrian Republican Guard, weakening them in front of the enemy. This targeting "error" had caused significant damage to one of the Syrian Army's strategically held locations, dividing it into two isolated sections, which made the soldiers holding those sites incredibly vulnerable to the attacks of ISIS militants. Eventually, despite all their setbacks, the Syrian Army kept at it until they broke through the south and west of the city, and the siege was shattered.

We moved on, walking through the sections of the city that had seen the most destruction. When I had visited so many years ago, all the churches had been in a row along Cinema Fouad Street. But that had been on the front line, and now all the churches were almost entirely gone. All that was left was piles of stone rubble, except for the Syrian Orthodox church. It too had been severely damaged, and large portions of the roof had caved in. We picked our way through the rubble, found the cross, and stood it back up, grounding and supporting it in a pile of fallen stones. We had been warned to be careful where we put our feet as we walked and worked in the city, and we took the warning seriously; there were mines all through the area, and locals told us that people were killed or maimed every day.

Our time that day went quickly. After 2:00 in the afternoon, crossings of the river were suspended until the next day, and we realized when we checked our watches that we only had an hour left to make it back. As we carefully picked our way over the broken streets, we stopped by the remains of an old bridge. It was lying in pieces in the river, and I recognized it from my last trip. It had been built by French engineers a hundred years ago, and I remembered that, last time I had seen it, I had taken a long dive off it to swim in the Euphrates. I decided, in the spirit of returning the city to what it once had been, I should do the exact same thing now, and I leapt into the water for a very brief swim, rushed as we were. From then on, it was a ritual for me: every time I visited Deir ez-Zor, I would swim at the site of this old bridge and remember what it once looked like.

We made sure to take some pictures of the city as we hurried back to the crossing, realizing that we would in fact be there past 2:00. But, luckily for us, we traveled with our priest. Although no one was technically allowed to cross this late in the afternoon, everyone in Syria—Syrian Army soldiers, Hezbollah, Russians, Afghans, and Kurdish militiamen from the PYD—hold an immense respect for clergymen, no matter the religion they represented. This was not the first time being with a priest had opened doors for us and made things easier. Sure enough, when we finally made it back to the crossing, they readily bowed and made an exception for us, ferrying us back to our car on the other side. We went directly to the plane and back to Damascus.

As it happened, the situation in Damascus was not great when we returned. Violence had picked back up, and it would continue for some weeks. It wasn't until early the next month—April 4, 2018—that I was able to write in my journal that negotiations were underway to arrange the withdrawal of the jihadists from Eastern Ghouta, a district in southeastern Damascus.

As we had seen in other scenarios, directed by Russian influence, the agreement was made to transport the jihadists from their Ghouta location (the Yarmouk Camp) to Idlib (on the Turkish border). The buses had arrived to evacuate and transport the terrorists, and in return, they would turn over the cities of Kafraya, Foua, and Eshtabraq, including their besieged and kidnapped civilians.

By April 12, 2018, Ghouta was completely freed. A few days later, we took advantage of the opening of the humanitarian corridors in Douma to meet the civilians there and to bring powdered milk and other necessities to the children.

Meanwhile, in the north of the country, Aleppo was still holding militants at bay through its western periphery, even though the city technically had been freed since December 22, 2016, almost a year and a half earlier. But the fact of the matter was that as Aleppo continued to be partially besieged, it continued to be partially shelled.

44

Ashura in Damascus

In August of that year, 2018, back in Damascus, I was invited to celebrate Ashura by a Syrian-Iranian friend, Amir, and his mother. Each year, at the time of this memorial, millions of Shiites come together to commemorate the assassination of Husayn, the prophet Muhammad's grandson, which took place in the year 680.

I found Amir and his mother at the end of the Hamidiye bazaar, right in front of the Umayyad Mosque. A security cordon had been set up here, and the area was closed from the esplanade that faced the great mosque all the way to the alleys that bordered it. Iranians were only allowed in if they had their papers with them. We could see Hezbollah watching from behind the barriers.

We walked through the alleys together until we reached the Roqiye Mosque, which was all white and had a large red flag flying from its dome. As we approached the entrance, we separated; Amir's mother went into the women's entrance, while he and I went in through the men's.

The crowd just inside the entrance was huge—hundreds of people jostled each other, most of them Iranians and Afghans. Civilians, clergymen, fighters, and expatriates were all there, trying to find a place in the crowd, and everyone was dressed in black.

In the center of the crowd, two large circles formed, each with about twenty men in it. As the rest of us watched, the men started chanting back and forth at each other, crying out lamentations of war in lyrical crescendos, beating their chests, swinging their arms, and punctuating each refrain with a loud cry of the prophet-martyr's name. It was as though the louder each man chanted, and the harder he beat his chest, the more devoted he was to Husayn and the more he won the respect of the crowd around him.

Even the people who weren't in these two circles chanted Husayn's name as they moved toward a tomb that I imagined must contain the relics of Roqiye, the man for whom the mosque was named. They, too, beat their chests and repeated his name endlessly, while above it all, another man looked on. He had a microphone, into which he spoke the word "Husayn" over and over, as though to keep the momentum of the crowd going.

And then the chanting stopped, and all at once the room was dead quiet. Everyone sat cross-legged on the floor and looked up. One man faced the crowd in the darkened room, and then he started talking. He gently and seriously told us about the Battle of Karbala, the battle in which Husayn died. Soon, moans and sobs punctuated his story, which was then interspersed with spontaneous prayers to Heaven. He even periodically collapsed as though overcome with grief, as was the custom.

As I sat, surrounded by the crowd, they repeated a collective sighing and weeping in a chorus, and I was surprised to see that while I wasn't alone in seeing some comedy in such a display, many of the men there had real tears in their eyes. The grief over a man dead some thirteen hundred years was very much alive and present to them in this moment. The storyteller finished his tale and fell silent, a silence that lengthened and thickened through the whole room. The atmosphere felt heavy with sadness, confusion, and despair.

Quietly, he began to speak again. He brought us out of history, back to the present moment, telling us that we were in fact here today, but we were also still in Karbala, with Husayn, at the battle in which he died. "Karbala was not yesterday. Karbala is today. The usurpers have returned, and the fight isn't over with. Look around you. They're very close. Yazid and his men have come back. They have returned to make our blood flow, but we, we are Husayn's sons. We could not be there to prevent the first Karbala tragedy, but we can make sure that we never allow it to be repeated today!"

Every one of his sentences invigorated, reinforced, and revived us and made us feel invincible. In unison with the crowd around him, he punctuated each sentence with "*Allah ma salle allah o Muhammad va hàle Muhammad!*" – "May God's salvation be on Muhammad and his family!"

I'm not Shiite, but eventually even I found myself carried away, even if only briefly, by the power and sweeping feeling of such an experience. Only moments earlier, the room had been immobilized by the heavy weight of despair, and now we were emboldened by courage and thirsty for a fight. The emotional rollercoaster was wild, and it was with a bestial fierceness that the crowd left the mosque, ready to sacrifice all for the cause.

45

Wedding

Ashura wasn't the only event I was celebrating that August. There was something much more exciting and much more personal on the schedule: Fimy and I were finally getting married.

I had sent invitations all over Syria, and almost everyone was coming. As for our families, even though it was only my mother, my aunt Anne, and two of my cousins who were able to be there, all of Fimy's family made it. And though my family was small in numbers, about fifty of my friends from France, mostly former volunteers, traveled to join us that day, including my two old friends Sébastien and Nicolas, whom I'd known since I was a kid. Everyone was gathering in Beirut, and I chartered a bus to take them from there to Maaloula, where we would have our ceremony. I had come to Maaloula ahead of time with my three groomsmen, Ladislas, Damien, and Sebastiano, ready to welcome our guests.

On the day of the wedding, Fimy arrived in a limousine with her mother and bridesmaids. Our old favorite driver, Ramez, brought us men up to the top of the village, by the Monastery of St. Sergius, where there were motorcycles waiting for us. We climbed on, revved up, and then drove down through the streets of Maaloula, carrying flags of the Sacred Heart and a French flag from the Old Regime, holding them up so they could fly in the wind behind us.

Our guests were waiting below to cheer our arrival at the steps in front of St. George Parish.

Fimy's brother walked her down the aisle as the choir sang the "Canticle of Moses" loud and clear. As if the emotion of the moment weren't overwhelming enough already, this favorite song of mine pushed me over the top. I suddenly felt incredibly overheated and then burst into tears. I stood up straight and tried to get control of myself, but it was no good, and I sobbed like a little kid while my groomsmen laughed with me, then whispered to me that I was being moved by the Holy Spirit descending upon me, overwhelming my heart.

Our army of priests faced us, and the ceremony began. I was proud of our priests; we had the representatives of so many Eastern Christian traditions there with us that day, as well as priests from various Latin Catholic churches. Father Toufic was Melkite; Monsignor Abdo Arbach was Homs' Melkite Archbishop; Father Elias was from Maaloula's Greek Orthodox church; Father Qassis was a Syrian Orthodox priest who had come from Aleppo; and the Franciscans, Abounas Michel and Fadi, were also there. And, from France, Father Augustin had come from the Fraternity of St. Vincent Ferrer, Father Hervé from the Diocese of Toulouse, and my spiritual father, the Franciscan Father Emidio, was also there to support me.

We exchanged our wedding rings and our vows, and the choir sang the song of coronation: "Lord, our God, crown them with glory and dignity ..." Crowns were put on our heads, according to the Byzantine rite, and hand in hand, Fimy and I, followed by our bridal party, walked three times around the altar. Father Toufic blessed us and prayerfully exhorted us to dedicate our lives to the hands of the Virgin Mary, the Mother of Jesus, from now until the hour of our deaths.

After the formal ceremony, we celebrated all night long in the school courtyard next to St. George Church. When the dinner and dancing finally wrapped up, some of our guests weren't finished partying yet, so they climbed the Catholic mountain, where we had celebrated the Feast of the Holy Cross. They lit their way with their cell phones, and they fueled their journey with a five-liter bottle of vodka. Beyond tipsy, they stayed up to watch the sunrise and then slept on the mountaintop in the cold early-morning air.

So many of our guests had traveled so far that we had planned a weeklong celebration for them, wanting to give them more than "just" the day of the ceremony and also wanting them to remember our wedding forever. Thus, on the very next day, we all climbed aboard the bus and headed to Aleppo. Monsignor Jeanbart had opened his bishop's house to us, giving everyone somewhere to sleep. With the help of Alexandre Ivleff, a friend who has an inexhaustible store of knowledge of the city, we showed them Farhat Square, Old Aleppo, and the well-nigh eternal citadel.

The next day, we went on to Mhardeh, where Mr. Simon al-Wakeel and his wife, always warm and hospitable to us, welcomed our whole crew. We all ate together in an outside restaurant, kept good company by my special wheeled suitcase; full of all kinds of alcohol, it was an endlessly popular catalyst during our week of revels.

Later that week, we visited Nabel al-Abdallah in Sqelbiye. He had invited us all to come and have lunch and spend the afternoon. He opened his pool for us, and it looked like there were a dozen pigs roasting on spits nearby. We laughed at this; we knew the jihadists were at most seven meters from this location, and we were sure they could smell the forbidden pork. We laughed even harder when Nabel showed us some tattoos on the skins of the roasting pigs: they had been named and marked with the word

Erdogan in "honor" of the Turkish president. Between the alcohol, which flowed like the water in the pool, and the mountain of pork, which we consumed with great delight, we finished our week of revels in a manner that was far from halal.

All too quickly, the week was over, and it was time to get back to business. But just as we had hoped, we would keep the memories with us forever.

46

The Offensive in Idlib Starts

The center of the war had moved. We saw it focused in Aleppo from 2012 to 2016, and then in Deir ez-Zor, and now, through all of 2018, Damascus was the city that hung in the balance. But the Syrian Army was making real progress in emptying the pockets that harbored al-Nusra and ISIS, gradually clearing out the checkerboard of battling neighborhoods.

Just as quickly as Damascus was cleared out, Idlib filled up. Day after day, convoys of defeated jihadists were transported there. We hoped against hope that they would die there. Letting the killers live seemed surreal to us; we couldn't believe they could just go, with no trial or retaliation after the way they'd terrorized the country all these years.

During most of the years of the war, the Syrian Army had to concentrate its efforts on the western part of the country, abandoning eastern and northern Syria. Consequently, the Kurd fighters from the PYD in northeastern Syria were left to their own devices. Turkey did not appreciate the Kurdish stronghold growing along the border, especially since it had its own strong Kurdish population on the other side of that same border. Turkey's leaders knew it was likely that the Kurds on either side of the border would try to join together, seceding from both Syria and Turkey to form their own independent state of Kurdistan. This would mean a significant loss of Turkish territory—and eighteen million Turkish Kurds. And so the Turks backed ISIS in its efforts to destroy the hope of a Kurdistan. When eventually Syria was able to refocus its attention on the area, it was also loath to part with the Kurdish territories and, as Turkey did on its side of the border, sought to maintain the region as part of the Syrian state.

While assistance from the United States for the Kurds and their interests has in turns increased and vacillated, U.S. aerial support allowed a firm unification to grow among three Kurdish cities on the Turkish border: Qamishli, Kobani, and Afrin. The Kurds had the idea that, together, these three cities could be the seed and center of their Kurdish state. But this was too much for the Turks, and they didn't take long to respond. They sent military support to back the jihadists in Idlib, which they knew would complicate matters for the Kurds, and launched a number of military operations over several years to confront the issue: "Operation Euphrates Shield," "Operation Olive Branch," and "Operation Peace Spring." The pocket of the country surrounding Idlib quickly became a primary focus of Turkish attention, especially as the Turks knew they could use it to negotiate and bargain with Syria. In a nutshell, Erdogan let Syria know that as long as it allowed its Kurds along the northern border to threaten the sovereignty and integrity of the Turkish state with possible Kurdish secession, Turkey would keep its troops in Idlib, continue backing the terrorists centered there, and not surrender the city back to the Syrian government.

Nevertheless, the Syrian Army had launched a somewhat successful offensive on Idlib in February 2018, taking back some of their Syrian territory. By that point, there were about three million people crowded into Idlib, a population primarily made up of fighters from what had been Jabhat al-Nusra, the Syrian offshoot of al-Qaeda. In an effort to distance themselves from al-Qaeda, al-Nusra, in 2016, had changed its name to Jabhat Fatah al-Sham. From there, it evolved to join with other Islamist groups and changed its name yet again, becoming Hay'at Tahrir al-Sham. But we all knew that it didn't matter what they called themselves — in the end, they all operated under the same principle of Sharia law, rife with beheadings and terror. In our circles, when people talked about the Free Syrian Army, these were the people they meant. These were the men whom Turkey protected and supported, in many ways, for years on end, even going so far as to set up observation and control towers along the perimeter of their area.

And so two Syrian detachments positioned themselves strategically to contain any potential expansion of territory from the Idlib center. General Maher al-Assad and his men, supported by Iran, were on Idlib's western side. General Suheil al-Hassan, also known as the Tiger, was positioned with his troops on the eastern side and was supported by the Russians.

Despite an agreement that Russia and Turkey had made to demilitarize Idlib on September 17, 2018, the Syrian Army launched an offensive against the rebels and jihadist groups in that area on May 6, 2019. In response, the Islamists took revenge on the handful of Christians in the province.

One of these Christians, Suzanne der Karkour, was found murdered, and my Facebook feed filled up with prayer requests for the repose of her soul. Fimy had known her — she was one of her mother's cousins. She'd been massacred by the jihadists while she was walking to a neighboring village; she went there on foot every day to teach Arabic to the children in the village church. Although she had previously retired from teaching, she offered these classes for free, concerned as she was that the war was interfering so much in the children's education and in their future.

Kidnapped in Iraq

One day, when she didn't show up for her usual class, the priest at the church where she taught became worried for her and sent out a search party. They found her the next day, in a field by her own house: her murderers had attacked her only moments after she had started down the path, and before killing her, they had burned her face with cigarettes and sliced her hands. Even worse, when a doctor performed her autopsy, he found clear evidence that she had been raped by multiple different men over a period of twelve or more hours, the last time just that morning, hours before the priest and his friends found her body. Suzanne had been a virgin, and she was in her sixties.

After events such as these, some of the journalists who had earlier referred to these people as freedom-loving rebels began to change their tune. We hated that their eyes had been opened at such a cost, but now at least they were calling the terrorists by their proper names.

47

Raqqa, a Kurdish City

The city of Raqqa was in north central Syria, roughly midway between Aleppo and Deir ez-Zor. Since 2014, it had effectively been the capital of ISIS, but in 2017, two years ago, it fell back into Syrian hands. It had been the Kurds, in fact, supported by Western armies, who had been key in orchestrating its recapture. As their capital yielded to heavy bombings, the jihadists had fled farther north with their families.

It was difficult for us to get to Raqqa from Damascus. It would be easier if we came by way of Jazira, but regardless of the route we chose, we knew we'd only have a small window of time to make the trip. The American President Trump had announced the withdrawal of American troops in northeast Syria on October 9, 2019; once they were gone, we knew Turkish forces would move in. And in fact, with the help of their mercenaries, they did quickly seize the Syrian territories along the border between Tell Abyad and Ras al-Ayn, in a swath thirty kilometers wide. They got all the way to the M4 Motorway at Tall Tamar before the Russian and Syrian armies moved to surround them, halting further progression. The Kurds in the region were isolated, and the uptick in military advancements meant new waves of displaced people would be moving south for shelter, especially in al-Hasakah and Raqqa. There were more than 150,000 displaced people in this region, all of whom had run away from the Turks and the Turkish mercenaries who mutilated, raped, and plundered whenever they could.

I decided some of us should go there as soon as possible to see what we could do to help, so I traveled with two volunteers, Wael and Arthur. We left Damascus in the early morning on Monday, November 4, 2019, to fly to Qamishli. We arrived late that same morning and traveled on immediately to al-Hasakah, where the city and its surroundings had suddenly become an open-air camp of displaced people.

A young man named Saad was there to welcome us. He was originally from al-Shaddadah, a city farther south, but he had lived in al-Hasakah for a long time. He managed the humanitarian affairs for the Syrian Catholic church in that city. He shared with us that he knew of about thirty thousand people who had managed to settle into houses, hotels, or squats, and a few very lucky ones who had been able to find lodging with relatives in the city. In addition to assisting with housing needs, where and as we could, we focused on providing food for the refugees: Saad helped us organize a massive baking scheme. Together, we were able to supply forty-eight thousand loaves of unleavened bread, in addition to nine thousand liters of water.

He also offered to make a donation of blankets and food for sixty Christian families from the city, and working with the network of public schools in the city, he gave us the means to open up seven of the fifty-eight public schools as temporary housing for 1,950 families—that is to say, around 9,000 people. His help was invaluable. Each family settled into their own classroom in the schools. It wasn't a lot of space, but it did at least give them shelter and some modicum of privacy. As we helped them get arranged, we saw pieces of chalk on the floor, a few scrawls left on the chalkboards on the walls, and small chairs and tables piled up on each other in various corners of the building and on the school playground. This had been a fully functioning school not that long ago.

Then Saad led us outside the city, to a place called Tall Tamar. The scene that awaited us there was striking. We watched as a refugee camp was established before our very eyes, with tents going up and machinery hard at work, as thousands of helpless people waited. We saw humanitarian workers handing out food supplies in tents, and endless lines of women and children waiting for food.

"Where are the men?" Arthur asked.

Saad explained that all husbands and brothers old enough to work would go into the city every day, trying to find a way to support their families' needs. While they looked for work, their wives, sisters, and children would get the food supplies, enough for two days at a time, from the humanitarian workers who were there on the ground.

"Winter is just around the corner," I said. "How can they get by? How can they stay warm and fed under such temporary and minimal conditions?" It was unrealistic for any family to have a sense of security when they didn't know if they'd have food in another two days.

The next day, we moved on from al-Hasakah to Raqqa, bringing with us five hundred blankets and six thousand loaves of unleavened bread. There were about 6,500 families in need of shelter there as well. Since 2012, the city had been passed back and forth from the Free Syrian Army to the Jabhat al-Nusra Front, from the Islamic State to the Syrian Democratic Forces (alliances of PYD Kurds and Sunni Arab groups who are close to the Free Syrian Army). It had been stuck, without a break, in the middle of a years-long military tug-of-war, and it showed.

Kidnapped in Iraq

We drove on some of the M4 Motorway's back roads, which had until recently been a front line. One young woman, Havrin Khalaf, had been horribly treated when she'd been captured on this route by the jihadist mercenaries whom the Turks used in that region. At the age of thirty-four, she worked all her life to promote what she saw as the common good, connecting different ethnic groups that share a common interest against both the Syrian government and ISIS. The terrorists had made her pay dearly for her work, raping her and mutilating her chest.

Our drive to Raqqa took about four hours, and yet again, we were astounded by the scene that lay before us. The scale of the damage here was far beyond what we had been used to seeing in Aleppo, with a level of devastation and destruction we had not witnessed elsewhere. All over the city were huge empty places where we could see only the barest remaining outlines of the buildings that used to stand there, structures that had been entirely reduced to fields of rubble. The air force had had a field day here, and I was more than a little dumbfounded about all the press the situation in Aleppo had elicited when clearly this was so much worse.

When we reached the town center, we stopped to get a quick lunch in al-Naim Square. Before the war, it had popularly been called Paradise Square, but now it was known as Hell Square because of what ISIS fighters had done when they occupied the place. They'd drive their tanks and wave their black flags in triumphant processions, filling the square sometimes with their military equipment, broadcasting images and videos to showcase their strength around the world, inspiring fear and hatred.

But, far worse, this place had been the scene of many public executions, especially beheadings. Their victims were always dressed in orange, and the executioners always in black. Their weapon of choice was a sword; they'd swing it through the air and then hold up the severed heads by their hair for everyone to see, waving them like trophies in front of a crowd that was forced to be there for hours to witness one execution after another, a crowd that was threatened until the watchers shouted their coerced infatuation with each murder. Then they'd toss the heads to their children to use as soccer balls, or they'd be mounted on pikes around the square, displayed as a warning and to induce terror and obedience. The rest of the bodies would be dismembered, and various other pieces of the victims would also be placed out on display. Like the terrorists' other exploits in this square, the beheadings were filmed and broadcasted.

Not everyone was beheaded, however. If they discovered any homosexuals, the jihadists would throw them off the roof of the highest building on the square, or from the city's highest bridge. If they survived that, they would then be stoned to death; the ISIS criminals said that this was the way to wash their sins away.

Aside from the "crimes" that warranted beheadings, stonings, or being thrown from rooftops, ISIS had a myriad of reasons for punishing the most insignificant acts of daily life as though they were desecrations of Sharia law. They would always refer back to the Islamic texts—the Koran and the Sunnah—for some sort of justification, as though proving that they were in the right, and then proceed with their daily punishments of the people, some of which ended in amputations or even crucifixions. Such punishments were meant to be warnings to anyone who thought about disrespecting Sharia law.

But now the tide had changed, and those 6,500 families had come to Raqqa for refuge. It wasn't entirely safe, as there were still various pockets of ISIS fighters hidden throughout the city and its suburbs, but they no longer had the rule of the place, and it was safer for the refugees than the alternative of staying in their various home villages.

Before we left the city, one of Saad's colleagues pointed to a stadium in the distance and told us we should go see it. Like the square, he said, this "black stadium" had been the site of imprisonment and execution for many of ISIS's victims. As we approached, we saw a massive crowd gathered around, and when we looked into the stadium, we could see traces of old black ISIS flags that had been torn down. There were new flags up now, showing the victors' colors—yellow, red, and green. The flags of the SDF were also there, and those of Asayish.

The flags weren't the only objects inside. We saw dozens of pickup trucks, full of armed civilians, shouting and singing along with the crowd. Voices over the loudspeakers, resonating through the stadium, urged on the chanting of slogans and the recitation of cheers and patriotic, religious catchphrases. I had seen such gatherings before, where slogans were recited over and over to the glory of Assad, the Syrian Army, and Syria. Here, the praises went to Abdullah Ocalan and his fighters from the PKK and the YPG/YPJ. I saw kids who were barely thirteen, with cigarettes in their mouths, waving Kalashnikov rifles toward the sky. Farther away, some young Kurdish girls, wearing the uniforms of the YPJ fighters, posed with their Kalashnikov rifles over their shoulders and their signature colorful scarves around their necks. I knew, much to my dismay, that such a sight was an unbeatable image of propaganda, guaranteed to make every Western feminist support the Kurdish cause.

Arthur, standing beside me, had a question in the same vein. "One day, we'll have to stop and ask ourselves a serious question: Is a female fighter who is celebrated for killing like a man really a step forward for the feminine cause?"

48

News of a Plague

March 20, 2020, somewhere in Iraq, not far from Baghdad.

A guard had just entered. He was new; we hadn't seen him before, and we didn't recognize his voice when he asked Abou Dany how our morale was and how we were doing. Abou Dany answered him honestly: we were annoyed, hopeless, and fed up with being here.

But rather than reprimanding him for such frankness, the guard cut him off, saying, "But you're leaving soon! Just three to five more days and you'll be released."

Abou Dany sounded nervous as he laughed and responded, "We heard such promises before, so many promises of freedom. We're beyond believing it anymore. You've promised us so many things. You've often said that we'd be free. So, forgive us, but we don't believe you."

"Well," the guard replied, "you've never heard such promises from me before, because I'm new here, but I mean what I say."

Abou Dany relayed the conversation to us again, though we had been able to understand most of it ourselves. Hope in freedom wanted to resurface, but what Abou Dany had said was true—we had been told such things before, only to find ourselves in miserable despair when we inevitably discovered that we had been deceived.

I wouldn't let myself believe it, and I turned to talk to Julien. "We can forget about it! I'd be surprised if they let us go before the year is up, and honestly that's the idea that I'm trying to accustom myself to. No more hoping for release every few days or weeks." All at once, I was completely depressed.

"Maybe now is the time to start that hunger strike," he replied.

We had talked about doing such a thing before but had never made a firm decision on it. He really liked the idea, but I looked at Antoine and could tell he was less on board. We were already down to one meal a day, and I knew we'd all lost quite a bit of weight. If we did decide to do it, it would be because it was our only weapon, the only way we could exert some sense of power and control. If we stopped eating and grew weaker, we would lose our value as hostages. Presumably, by this point, they wanted us to stay alive for something.

Another guard came back into our cell and stopped next to me, pointing at me. "Why isn't this guy smiling?" he asked Abou Dany. "Why isn't he happy?"

This wasn't the first time one of the guards had asked this question, had wondered why I looked more depressed than the others, why I was sleeping during the day and awake at night. I fought to control my temper, fed up as I was with the questions. Did they really expect us to be happy?

And so I turned to Abou Dany, allowing him to translate. "Why do they want me to be so happy all the time? Thank him kindly for his concern and tell him I said that we're angry because we're being imprisoned for no reason. We're being treated like outlaws with no justification and no explanation."

The guard raised his voice in response. "But you're a thug! You entered the country like an outlaw!"

"Really?" I said, sarcastically. "Like an outlaw with a *visa?*"

He didn't have any answer to that, and so he changed the subject. "And why did you marry a Syrian woman?"

"Is there some rule against me marrying a Syrian woman? I had every right to marry her."

He suddenly sounded much more serious, and he began to shout at me. "No, you don't have the right! No right at all!"

I turned my head away, knowing that I was moments away from being hit if I didn't shut up. He was waiting for me to give him a reason. Just two days earlier, they had struck Antoine hard on his neck because he'd taken off his darkened ski goggles while we were outside getting air.

He left without hitting me, but I sensed that some sort of step had been taken, that things would be more ugly and harder among us and our guards from now on.

Abou Dany was muttering at me. "Now you've done it. Now they're going to start torturing us."

Abou Dany is nothing if not comforting.

The guard whom we'd first thought of as the comedian had also come that day with the new guy, but his visits were commonplace. He'd always speak in his funny voice, say my name—"Aleksandeeeer!"—and then pretend to treat us nicely. But he was the one who had lied to us the most about our supposed freedom, making a game out of comforting us and then dashing our hopes. Ultimately, he was not funny at all—only deceitful. He would joke to himself by calling me Abou Joseph, and then would ask me how my son was doing—as if I knew. I was sure he was trying to hurt me by teasing me about my family.

When the two guards finally left that day, I punched the metal frame of my bed in frustration; the only result of such an exhibition was that I tore the skin on my hand so badly that I needed a huge wad of toilet paper to try to soak up the blood. The next time the guards returned, they wanted to know what had happened to my hand. It was clear, then, that at least they weren't watching the cameras all the time. One of them surprised me by cleaning my wound, and I heard voices and saw shadows around me, but they were disembodied from behind my goggles.

More guards came in again the following day and wanted to know how our morale was. Abou Dany answered for us, saying we had never felt so low and that we wanted to speak to someone in charge, that we wanted to make sure our families knew we were alive.

"You really will be leaving soon," the guard replied. "But we want to warn you: there's a virus raging through the world right now. Tons of people are dying everywhere, and no one knows how to stop it."

We listened incredulously, wondering what new story they'd invent to torment us next.

"France is on the verge of chaos," he was saying. "And all of Europe has closed its borders."

He kept going, but I stopped listening. He was sharing lots of details, talking a long time about all of this, but they had given us full details of other scenarios before, making us think that we would be getting out, only to lock us up again. I wouldn't fall for it another time, especially not with such a wild tale.

We sat that night watching our one TV station, a continuous broadcast of American films with Arab commercials every ten minutes. The reruns were endless, so much so that sometimes we'd see the same movie three times in a single day. Last night, *Outbreak* had played again, and I was sure the guards were just making up a story based on that.

"They really are assholes," Julien suddenly said. I was surprised to hear such an outburst from him, but I knew he was as exasperated as I felt. "An epidemic! I can't wait to see what they're going to come up with next."

The following day, we heard them open the door again, and we reached for our ski goggles. Someone said that the *liwa*, the colonel, was here to see us. Suddenly, my heart started racing, and we all sat up straight and still and listened intently. If he were really here, something big must be going on. It had been a long time since he'd come to talk with us.

His voice filled the room. "I have very good news for you—you'll be with your families in less than a week."

I'd waited for this moment for months, but still, I realized that I couldn't quite believe it, couldn't quite trust what I was hearing.

"I didn't come to see you earlier because I had no news to give you," he was saying. "But things have changed now. A scourge has fallen on the whole world. There's this virus that's killing a lot of people, has spread all over the planet. It's called corona."

Here we go again. He was laughing at us. Corona? Like the beer? I almost started laughing out loud at the absurdity of it all. I wondered what he'd been smoking before coming here to lie to us and mock us.

"Before next Sunday, you'll be brought back to French authorities at your embassy. And when you have been returned, you'll pass this message on to your French leaders: You'll tell them that if we ever find French citizens on Iraqi soil, they will not be treated so well as you lot have been. We will execute them immediately. You will tell your leaders that France must immediately stop lending any kind of support to ISIS."

He turned to one of the guards and told him that, after he left the room, he should change the channel on our television to the BBC.

"Watch it," he said. "And you'll know that what I'm saying is true." The door slammed behind him.

Now we began to wonder if maybe he wasn't making it all up. We took off our goggles and turned to the TV. As the BBC switched on, controlled by our guards outside, we saw images of empty streets in capitals around Europe. I was dumbstruck. An empty Paris, in the middle of the afternoon? What was going on? It was the same in images from Rome, Berlin, and Madrid. Anywhere we did see individuals, they hurried along, heads down, with most of their faces covered by masks or scarves. And the BBC was reporting thousands of deaths, numbers coming in from all over the world.

We didn't say anything. It all seemed too absurd to be real.

And then I started to wonder, and I realized that I was connecting some dots, that a few questions I'd had suddenly made sense. There was a road within earshot of our prison, and usually we heard trucks and traffic on it all the time. But a few weeks ago, the sounds had suddenly ceased. The guards had also started insisting that we clean our room regularly, which they never used to do, giving us various detergents to scrub everything down, under threat of punishment if we didn't comply. And they had been so unusually "concerned" when I'd cut the skin on my hand, wanting to know what had happened and ready to clean and bandage it before it might get infected. I didn't want to believe them, didn't want to trust that they were actually being straight with us, but as the pieces all started clicking together, I began to realize that it must be true. The virus was real. It wasn't an invention.

We turned to each other, all of us reaching the same conclusion, realizing that we really were getting out. Our kidnappers didn't want to be responsible for us if we died of this thing while being held by them, and so they were releasing us. There was a global panic, but our small group was being freed because of it.

49

Last Trip

Two days later, on Wednesday, the guards started coming in and out of our room, emptying it of furniture. Surely then, I said to my friends, they must be moving us today. Abou Dany reminded me that they had said "before Sunday"; he took that to mean that we wouldn't be moved out until Saturday. But, sure enough, just a few hours later, they came back in, told us to stand up and get our things, and said that we'd be leaving in an hour.

We were still vacillating, still not sure if this were really true. So many times before we'd been told to get ready to go, only to be piled into the back of another car and brought to a new prison. Sure enough, there was another big GMC vehicle waiting for us outside. But this time, they had tied our hands in front, meaning our circulation wasn't cut off and our arms didn't hurt so much, even though they still piled us in, blindfolded. We listened to the roads they drove on, for about ninety minutes, and realized they were in fact taking us back to Baghdad. We wondered why there weren't any roadblocks.

When the car stopped, they took us out one by one, leading us into a house. The one who took my hand seemed warm and friendly, and I was sure we had "met" him before. They lined us up against a wall, and we stood there, waiting and listening, as people came and went through the doors on either side of the room.

After some time, both doors shut, and we heard a command to remove our ski goggles. That's when we realized we were alone with the *liwa*. I slowly and carefully removed my goggles, fearing the worst, but all we saw was this man standing in front of us. We had never seen him properly before, and to a certain extent, we still couldn't see him properly. A cap came down just over his eyebrows, and a khaki face mask covered most of his face, coming up just below his eyes, which were all we could see.

He held up a cell phone. "I'm going to take a video of each of you and ask you some questions. You'll tell me who you are—your first and last names, birthplace, and family situation, if you're married, single, if you have children, your children's names, and what you do for a living."

We all nodded, ready to comply. When my turn came, as was usual here, he wouldn't believe that I was French. He said I looked too Iranian to be French and concluded that I still must be a liar. And, just as in the past, there was nothing I could say that seemed to convince him otherwise. At this point, it definitely was not worth arguing, so I shrugged, and then he took the video of me and moved on.

When he had finished with all the recordings, he reiterated some of what he had said earlier and gave us further instructions on the nature of our release. "You make sure your people know this was never about money. There was no ransom here, and if anyone says there was, they're lying. This is about the clear and consistent pattern we see of your French government supporting ISIS and terrorism in Iraq. We have the proof of this, in multiple documents that we've uncovered, that we can release at any time if France refuses to withdraw from the country. You tell your government that the French are not welcome in Iraq. Next time any of you or your countrymen show up, you'll be met with instant execution."

He paused a beat, then looked at his watch.

"It's two in the morning now. An embassy vehicle will come pick you up before eight tomorrow evening."

He turned sharply on his heel and left the room.

We tried to sleep, but none of us could. I watched the night through the window; I could see some palm trees and factories in the distance and a canal full of stagnant water much closer.

At one point, I heard Abou Dany speaking to himself, his voice and words revealing the panic that we were all trying to keep at bay. "They're still just playing with us! They're going to kill us; we're all going to die."

But, sure enough, at 8:00 p.m., some men came back into the room. They brought back our passports, which we hadn't seen all these months, and they asked us to verify that all our papers were in order. We took a moment to flip through everything and were relieved to see that it all checked out. Someone opened a door to the outside, and we saw cars waiting for us—lights on, engines running. They tied our hands in front again and, to our surprise, led us to sit in the seats rather than cramming us into the trunk space.

We drove for about twenty minutes, and then we were taken out and led into a house. I felt somehow, with each stage of this trip, that my life was coming back.

There were a lot of people here, surrounding us as they moved and talked, and I saw bright lights and heard a TV in the background. I could also smell food. The person who led me into the room used my first name when he spoke to me and was polite. He brought me to a seat and told me I could take off my ski goggles. Just as last time, I took them off slowly, and when I looked around, I saw my friends all sitting next to me. We realized that we were no longer in some outlaws' outpost, no longer in a dark hole; this was an official Iraqi government office.

I turned to see the person who had brought me here, but he asked me not to look at his face and even held his hands up so I couldn't see him. Still, I could tell he was smiling and that he was young, maybe only nineteen or twenty. He was tall and thin and surprisingly well-dressed, though he had thick, long hair that came down his back and hung around his face as well.

The other man with us was small and stocky but strong, and he wore a tasteless suit. As he talked in general terms about how Iraq was in crisis, how our imprisonment was unavoidable in such chaos, and how Iraqi forces had used every tool available to try to find us, I scanned the room, curious about all the people who were coming and going, the men all heavily armed. I saw one I thought might be a brother of the kid who had brought me in. His hair was the same, but he also had a huge beard that was colored with henna in spots, and he wore a cap on his head.

There was another guy behind him who was completely dressed in black. His T-shirt was a bit too tight, and his belly was almost visible. He had a big mustache with a little beard, and his hair was flattened in the back. He noticed me looking at him, and his eyes met mine with some discomfort. I didn't speak to him, but something in his look made me think he felt sympathetic toward us, that he felt bad for everything we'd been through.

We weren't there long before it was time for us to head back out to the car, which, according to what everyone said, would bring us right to the French embassy. As we climbed back into the car, something caught my attention. One of the men standing nearby was looking away, trying to make sure we couldn't see his face, though I recognized something about him. I suddenly caught a glimpse of his cold, dark eyes and realized that this was the *liwa*. His silhouette and clothing matched those of the masked man who'd recorded our messages earlier, the man who'd seemed in charge of our kidnapping from the start. What was he doing here with the Iraqi government officials?

But this was not the time for me to ask such questions. The car started off quickly, and we were in Baghdad soon. I recognized the streets and knew we'd be at the embassy in just a few moments. But they pulled the car off to the side of the road just before we got there, told us to get out, and pointed down the road as they closed the doors behind us, ready to pull back out and leave.

"The embassy is just up there," the driver told us. "Just walk up to the gate."

The car idled for a moment, the driver making sure we got going in the right direction, and then it quickly turned back the way it had come.

We didn't hesitate—no goggles, nothing tying our hands, no guards by our side. Still hardly believing it, we walked down the city street, listening as our flip-flops smacked against the sidewalk, echoing oddly and comically.

The buildings on this street were protected behind tall, thick walls, which had barbed wire running along their tops. Security forces stood along the road; one of the soldiers stopped us, asking us where we were going, and then pointed us on to our destination.

We stood in front of the French embassy for a moment, and then Antoine reached up and pushed the intercom button by the front gate.

"We're the hostages," he said. "We're the hostages, and we've just been released. I think you are expecting us?"

Another gate opened off to the side, and a large vehicle came out into the road behind us. A security guard got out of the car and came to us immediately. "You're the Frenchmen? You're the hostages?"

When we nodded, he handed us face masks with a quick ex-planation about the virus, then instructed us to climb into the car. As the vehicle drove us back onto the embassy grounds, the guard said he was very surprised that the militiamen had just released us onto the street, with no talking and no negotiations with their French counterparts. He explained that usually the most dangerous moments during a hostage crisis were when the hostages were kidnapped and when they were returned. The way they dropped us off avoided all the tensions of a normal trade-off; we were fortunate, he said.

50

A Liberating Virus

Once they had brought us inside, they showed us around the public areas a bit, including a gym in the basement, before leading us to the apartment where we'd temporarily stay, complete with a kitchen, bath, and bedrooms. They had laid out clean clothes for us on the beds and had left a few packs of cigarettes for us as well. When I went into the bathroom, I saw a scale on the floor, and I stepped on it. I had lost fourteen kilos, or just about thirty pounds. Later that same night, a military doctor examined us, spending about an hour with each of us, seeing if anything in addition to our rapid weight loss looked problematic.

Given the lateness of the hour, once all of this was done, we weren't able to call our families until the next day. For some reason, the number I had for Fimy didn't work, so I called my mother first instead. She burst into tears when she recognized my voice, relieved as she was after all this time to know that I was alive, that I had been returned to the French authorities, that I would be coming home soon. She gave me my wife's new phone number, and I called her right away. This time, I was the one crying over the phone; I couldn't stop myself, and I honestly didn't feel the need to do so. I couldn't wait to hug and kiss Fimy, to pick up my son and hold him close. As it turned out, we would have to wait a few months longer—because of the virus, travel was severely limited, and France was not currently allowing any flights in from Syria. The three of us who had been kidnapped would be brought back to France on a military transport from our current location in Baghdad, but Fimy and our son, along with so many other domestic and civilian travelers, were not allowed into the country.

After we finished talking with our families, we sat down with government officials and authorities at the embassy to go through one debriefing after another. They wanted to learn any and all information they could to help them discover and hopefully neutralize the men who had held us for seventy days. Every detail we could remember was important; together with the authorities, we wanted to be sure that this would not happen again with other French citizens. To that end, we also delivered the message that the man with the dark eyes had emphasized so strongly, that Frenchmen would continue being threatened on Iraqi land as long as France continued supporting ISIS, and that, if it came to it, they had compromising files that they could release at any moment that would put France's stability in serious jeopardy.

It was Saturday night. Abou Dany had gone with the Iraqi authorities the day before to be reunited with his family in Erbil, and we would be leaving for Baghdad International Airport in an hour. We bid a fond farewell to the people who had taken care of us at the embassy; then we went out to the car. It was dark, and moving through the city streets, we saw few lights on. We didn't even have to stop at the roadblocks; the diplomatic flags on the cars guaranteed us easy passage all the way to the airport.

There was a small group of men standing on the tarmac, waiting for us, and they showed the driver where to park. As we got out, we were able to get a full view of the military transport plane—a sturdy old Transall—that would take us home. The back hold was open toward us, with light spilling out. Four men stood in the opening, arms crossed, wearing aviators' uniforms. As we walked toward the plane, our pilots broke out in smiles, threw their arms up, and gave us each a hearty greeting, welcoming us home.

It was a stupendous and at the same time numbing moment, surreal in its relief. The three of us looked at each other, and we all had tears in our eyes.

"God the Father didn't abandon us," Julien said.

"And the Motherland came to find us," said Antoine.

I was too overcome to say anything at all.

We climbed on board, and before the door shut, I looked behind us, back into the darkness, to say goodbye to the men who had returned us to this warmth and light. A crew member came to take our luggage, such as it was, while another took our temperatures and asked us some health screening questions. When we went to sit down, we buckled ourselves into harnesses on the canvas seats, facing each other on opposite sides of the plane. The Transall laboriously started down the runway, and all at once, we were off the ground. There were no portholes or windows, but knowing that we were leaving the country was enough for us. We looked at each other and smiled triumphantly, and then we threw back our heads and laughed for the sheer joy of it all.

I glanced around and saw a suspended stretcher hanging from the ceiling—a makeshift bed. At the end of the hold, just in front of the cockpit, much to my surprise, I saw a kitchen table spread with a red-and-white checked tablecloth. I assumed this meant we'd be eating at some point, but all at once I was so tired that I didn't have the mental energy to figure out anything else. One of the pilots had suggested that we try to get some sleep once we reached cruising altitude, so I got up and tried to climb onto the stretcher. But with all the weight I had lost, all the muscle mass that had disappeared, I couldn't get up there on my own; I had to ask some of the crew members for help. It didn't matter to me, though, and I fell asleep with a smile on my face, thinking about seeing my family again so soon.

It was only an hour later when I woke up, and I saw Julien and Antoine sitting at the table with Camembert cheese, red wine, and homemade cakes. The crew members had thought of everything for us, and the familiar feast they had conjured up was beautifully spread out on that cheerful tablecloth. We consumed the food and drink we loved and had missed, our wineglasses clinked, were emptied, and were then refilled, and it was as though we were already home. Again, we found ourselves deeply touched by the warmth and thoughtfulness of these soldiers, our countrymen.

After the long flight, with two stopovers, we landed at noon the next day at the military airport in Vélizy-Villacoublay. A senior manager from the Quai d'Orsay, accompanied by his assistant, welcomed us on the tarmac and explained the social distancing measures, the meter that we were to keep between ourselves, and all the new rules.

"I know it will be hard for you to respect all of this, but please don't kiss or hug. We're well aware of how difficult that will be, especially in a situation like this, but it's important for you to keep to these rules and stay safe. We're all doing everything we can to combat this virus, and a lot of things have changed since your disappearance. You'll have to get used to these new ways of doing things, the sooner the better."

And then he showed us how to greet people by bumping elbows or touching the tips of our shoes together. To be honest, part of me wondered if he could possibly be serious.

Finally, we were done talking with him, and we were allowed to move past security and through to the other side of the windows, where we knew our friends and families were waiting to see us. First, I saw Benjamin and François-Xavier from the association, and then I saw my mother and my sister. We fell into each other's arms, virus be damned, and out of the corner of my eye I saw Antoine embracing his wife and daughters, and Julien running to his parents.

My sister shouted with joy, no longer able to keep her exuberance in check. "You're here, Alexandre! You're home! You're finally home, finally back with us!"

After what was far too brief of a reunion for any of us, we had to temporarily leave our families again; we were due for a complete health exam in the Bégin Military Teaching Hospital in Vincennes. As we drove there, we watched out the car windows and saw streets that were almost entirely empty. It was Sunday, and the few people out were wearing masks. Everything was strange.

Our health exams didn't take too long, and that same night, Antoine, Julien, and I were driven by some of the officials from the Quai d'Orsay to the Saint-Lazare neighborhood in Paris, where our families waited. Together with some of the team from SOS Chrétiens d'Orient, our families were waiting for us in a big apartment. We embraced again, then ate and drank to our heart's content, and we tried to catch up on everything we had missed for the past few months. Suddenly, as though to remind us that the world had changed in the time we'd been gone, the whole roomful of people got up as if on cue at exactly 8:00 p.m., went to the windows, opened the shutters, and applauded into the street, waving and cheering in company with the neighbors across the way.

"Wait, what's going on?" I asked, voicing the question for all three of us.

Our families told us this was something that happened every night now, around the country. It was a custom that had been started in response to COVID-19, a way that everyone could show their appreciation for the doctors, nurses, and other caregivers who were on the front lines of the fight. And it was a way for everyone to feel united when so many people were living in isolation. It reminded them that ultimately they weren't alone, that they fought this fight together. We slowly nodded as they explained, but I was sure I wasn't the only one of the three of us who was still more than a little confused about a response like this to an illness. Perhaps we had stayed in Syria too long, where life and death hang in the balance every day. As we tried to understand where the others were coming from, they talked about hundreds of people dying every day because of this illness, and, once again, I felt like I was slipping into a science fiction movie.

The next morning, it was time for the three of us to part ways. It was oddly nerve-wracking to say goodbye to Antoine and Julien. After all, we had been together for twenty-four hours a day for almost ten weeks. But of course, at the same time, we were all eager to get through the last bit of our journeys, to finally, really make it home.

My mother and my sister and I were taking the TGV toward Cholet on the Montparnasse train station platform. The lines wound endlessly as people did their best to respect the social distancing rule, standing a solid meter away from each other. When I finally got to the front of the line and the travel official went to stamp my tickets, one of the agents asked my identity and purpose for traveling.

I explained that I was returning home from Baghdad after being held in captivity for two months somewhere in Iraq. I could see from his eyes that he was suspicious of my answer, but of course I couldn't read his whole face—most of it was covered by the mask he wore. He took out his phone and googled my first and last name, watching me closely while the search results loaded. Sure enough, there were already some news stories telling of our captivity and release and showing our pictures.

His eyebrows went up, and he shook his head and let out a sharp sigh, almost a whistle, as he handed my ticket and documents back to me. "My apologies, sir. People tell us so much nonsense, you know. Hard to know what to believe."

Finally, by the end of that day, I was back home in Cholet. But I felt strange. I suddenly felt lonely and empty. It was like I didn't know what to hold on to. All at once, I felt dizzy.

Sleeping was hard that night. I lay awake for hours, and when I did finally sleep, I had a nightmare in which I was being forced to say goodbye to my son, knowing that I would never see him again. I woke suddenly and found myself sitting straight up in my bed. I took a breath and reminded myself that I was safe, that I was here in my mother's home, that everything was fine. I would see my son again; I would see Fimy again. My sister was just a short walk away, and I was no longer imprisoned in an Algeco container.

Gradually, the days began to go by more smoothly. I started writing so that I wouldn't forget things, and also to help me process them and sort everything out. And when I could, I went for walks. The streets in Cholet were empty, and on the news, I heard people talking about conference calls, telework, part-time unemployment—and fines and arrests for breaking COVID-19 restriction rules. It was a whole pile of things I didn't really want to understand. I sensed that I'd been frozen, like the character in *Hibernatus* with Louis de Funès, and that I had returned to a world of the future that was even more crazy, absurd, and irrational than the one I had left.

It was during these weeks, too, that news from family members, friends, and acquaintances reached me almost daily. Their calls, e-mails, and texts overwhelmed me, and I found myself almost sinking under their kindness and goodness as I did my best to try to answer everyone. At the same time, I was aware of the somewhat ironic fact that I had moved from one confinement to another. But, in truth, I appreciated the gentler return to living in the real world that the lockdown afforded me. It was good to have so much quiet time with just my family. Overall, I knew it was making for a much more gentle transition than I might otherwise have had.

My good friend Nicolas, who had come to Syria two years earlier to help us celebrate our wedding, came by one afternoon to pick me up and take me to spend the evening with a small group of our other old friends. He always struck quite a picture: he had a glass eye, for one thing, and as he drove his Mercedes up to the corner, he had a cigarette in his mouth, his shirt was open down to his navel, and I could see a large scar on his chest, just below the gold chain he wore around his neck. As I hopped in to join him, he took off down the road with a squeal of burning rubber, shouting into the wind, "Time to outrun the lockdown, buddy!"

I laughed with him, happy for anything to distract and help me let off a little steam. He drove me to our friend Jeremy's house, and I was happy to see that another old friend, Chamo, was there too. They were getting things ready for a barbecue.

The four of us ate, drank, and laughed until nightfall, and the way they handled everything that had happened to me made me love them all the more. They didn't insist on talking about it, knowing very well that I might not want to, but let me know in subtle ways that they were happy to listen to anything I wanted to say. These dear old friends of mine were Cholet townies, but their care was straightforward and exactly right, refined and precisely what I needed. Somehow, they got me, and I tried to tell them so.

The atmosphere suddenly became a little too sentimental. Without warning, Nicolas cried out, "In any case, you got us praying for you, you son of a gun. You've been trying to get us to church all these years, and now look—you dragged us there from the other side of the world. You're a real bastard, you know that, right?" We all burst out laughing, and I was reminded that God has a great sense of humor.

The lockdowns were letting up, and restaurants and businesses were reopening. As I started being able to walk more, I realized I was nervous being out in big public crowds, that I didn't like not knowing who was around me, not knowing how to track strangers. I realized I didn't want to spend time in the downtown area; I much preferred being on the quiet side alleys to sitting or walking in the big main square.

The biggest thing I discovered, in these first months after our release, was how many people had prayed for us, how they had spread the word and organized huge numbers of people through their Christian networks and social media outlets to ask God for our freedom. Swann, my little cousin, had started some prayer chains via Facebook for us to be released. Rosaries and Masses (including Gregorian ones) had been organized in the four corners of the world—Myanmar, Peru, Ethiopia, and even Sweden.

I was so touched to discover this, and I wished that I could have thanked each and every one of them individually. I knew it was thanks to their prayers and sacrifices that God had granted the grace of our freedom, had allowed us to come home to our loved ones. And to think that He had used a tool like the coronavirus to bring us home! The thought of it was incomprehensible. He had also used our absence to bring many people back to prayer, back to church. There had been Masses and weekly prayer meetings in the Franciscan monastery, and unbelievers, lapsed Catholics, and

Muslims had all come together, some there and some in other places, to pray for us to be rescued. Some of them got in touch with me, reminding me that, years ago, I'd asked them to go with me to Mass. Now, just like Nicolas, they laughed, relieved at my freedom and chuckling that I had finally gotten them to church.

Later I would learn that Angélique, a friend of mine who had once been a volunteer in Aleppo, had led Rosaries in Nantes for our release. She had fallen out with God, so to speak, had been angry with Him for one reason or another, but since then, she had experienced a remarkable reversion in her faith.

I also remember the phone call Julien made to his father from the French embassy in Baghdad on the morning after our release. His father told him, in a trembling voice, that he had started believing in God because of him. For Julien, this was a perfect answer to one of his biggest questions: Why did God allow such a thing to happen to us?

It was stories like this that showed us a glimmer of the indefinable blessings that had resulted from our ordeal. Thanks to the prayers of the whole world, we had been able in some way to find the strength to offer our sufferings to God. In turn, He had touched the hearts of those who had prayed for us, had brought them back to Himself. Already, we saw the fruits of this trial. Who knew how they would multiply over time in the years to come?

Though I meditated with gratitude on the prayers and conversions of my friends, my contentment was far from complete: I sorely missed Fimy and baby Joseph. We did of course get to spend a lot of time over video chats, like the rest of the world during those days, but I couldn't wait to hug them. International airports remained closed, and the whole world stayed on lockdown as healthcare workers and government officials did their best to turn the tide against the virus. It would be another two full months before border restrictions loosened, allowing Fimy and little Joseph to come to our family's home in France.

Reunited at last, we had a wonderful summer together, visiting our friends wherever restrictions allowed and simply spending time together, overjoyed to finally be able to see each other face-to-face. When September came, Fimy and Joseph went back to Damascus for a few weeks. While they were gone, we had an ugly reminder of the reality that we seemed to have left in the past.

On October 16, 2020, a young religious fanatic—an eighteen-year-old Chechen—slit the throat of a French teacher named Samuel Paty and then beheaded him. This happened in Conflans-Sainte-Honorine, just forty kilometers from Paris.

France, as it had done before, went into a state of shock. And, like a bad habit, almost as though such rituals could ward off evil spirits, it started its medieval processions of verbal contrition, explanations, and expiations, fueled by demonstrations, wakes, and empty speeches. It sickened me that, yet again, everyone was sidestepping the real issue, not naming the enemy, declaring that Islam is love. The truth still was that in fact the people of France had become hostage to the immigrants they had allowed to enter, immigrants who did all the manual labor, garbage-collecting, building, cleaning, and sweeping that kept our country running, everything that Frenchmen themselves had no stomach or brawn or pride to do on their own. We had let the devil into the house, disguised in workmen's clothes, and then we were astonished and grieved when his pitchfork struck.

Thirteen days after the murder of Samuel Paty, a Tunisian man—an Islamic extremist—slit the throats of three congregants in the Basilica of Notre-Dame de Nice before being wounded by Nice's municipal police.

It is hard not to see the pattern of the gangrene of Islamist thought spreading from the violence I witnessed in Syria to towns and cities in my own country. Ultimately, though, while we can mark individual instances of its spread, the way it sinks into people's hearts and colors their minds is more difficult to identify, let alone prevent or contain. And because of that, defining the root of the problem, naming it, is also difficult. People attribute it to radical Islam, the Muslim Brotherhood, Islamist politics, or to Wahhabism and its creators and supporters, which include Qatar, Saudi Arabia, and Turkey. The thing is, it's also politically inconvenient to name these groups as enemies while simultaneously profiting from arms deals with them on the one hand and talking about being open-minded to different ways of life on the other hand. And so we allow our enemies to mow us down while we stand up, look them in the face, and refuse to recognize them for what they are. Intellectually, the mental gymnastics that allow such a thing are fascinating to behold—and the spiritual and patriotic weakness that gives free rein to such exercises is nothing short of pathetic.

Signs of the Syrian devastation followed me home like a bitter cold. I know this story; I've seen it before, and I've seen what its consequences are. France isn't Syria, of course. But thinking that our secular republic is strong enough to face aggressive Islamism is a serious mistake. Nature abhors a vacuum, which is exactly what a secular republic creates. With such a "foundation," our society is so meaningless that Islam is able to move right in and fill the holes in each heart that yearns for something more, something bigger, something deeper. Deep in the heart of every man and woman, no matter the emptiness that their society might advocate, is a native need to have a sense of meaning and purpose, and they will find it in Islamic radicalism if nowhere else. After all, man cannot live on bread alone.

Epilogue

Today, Syria is a relatively bloodless country. The Syrian state re-captured 90 percent of its territory, thanks in particular to its two allies—Russia and Iran. But the human cost of this operation has been exorbitant. Nearly seven million Syrians have fled the country, seemingly permanently. A civil servant from the Quai d'Orsay told me that, in his opinion, Bashar is living a dictator's dream: "He has purged his country of all opposition. All those who didn't want to live under his rule are abroad. The only ones left are active or passive supporters. If he's intelligent, now would be the time to carry out political reforms, but will he do it?"

The problem for Bashar al-Assad, of course, is that though he has managed to stay in power, he is now in a great deal of political debt to the two allies who saved his bacon and who don't share his agenda. Iran is at severe odds with Israel, an adversarial relationship that could at any time ignite into a conflagration. As an ally, Syria would have to get involved, though it is only just barely getting back on its feet after its own terrible civil war. Russia, at least, would benefit from a calm Syria. With such a relationship as has been built up between the two countries, Russia could easily put down economic roots in Syria, by the sea, that it could use to reap significant financial rewards.

Kidnapped in Iraq

On that note, not everyone in Syria lost the war. The oligarchy there made a fortune for ten years. Those who did the actual fighting know that they shed too much blood, sweat, and tears to now, in any justice, be suffering from the economic restrictions that Western countries have imposed on Syria. Their state of poverty has been aggravated while the war's copious spoils have lined the coffers of the new affluent class in their country—the Syrian oligarchy. The rank and file among the soldiers, and all of the laborers and shop-keepers who, with their families, bore the brunt of the evils of the civil war, feel betrayed by the economic outcome and are waiting for real social reforms for the country. Those Syrians who stayed instead of running when things got so difficult now begin to think that their presence only lends credence to the rule of a mafia that runs their country. They fought to defend their lives and the life of their country, and now they see that their efforts have fueled a power that does not respond to their needs, let alone honor their sacrifice.

The economic crisis there has sparked protests and demonstrations as the price of staple goods has skyrocketed. Syria's bread-basket has been destroyed, olive groves have disappeared, and the coastal regions along the Valley of Christians have burned. There are still frequent fuel shortages and power outages, meaning people can't transport goods or heat their homes in winter. But certainly none of the Syrians have the stomach for another war, so they protest the poverty without actually questioning Damascus's central hold on power. Bashar al-Assad's Russian ally, however, is becoming impatient with him as he struggles to propose a way out of the crisis. And, ever watchful, Turkey maintains its positions throughout northern Syria, the cross-border area, and the troublesome province of Idlib.

How could the world's journalists seem to think that the Free Syrian Army was a group of good guys? How could they not see that most of the militias gathered under its banners were in fact masquerading jihadist groups? Could it have been willful igno-rance? If those journalists really wanted the truth, all they had to do was look at the people fueling, supplying, and supporting the Free Syrian Army: Saudi Arabia, Qatar, and Turkey—what great "democracies." They are of course religious dictatorships that, through their proxies in the Free Syrian Army, were attacking a secular authoritarian regime.

In its role in the Syrian Civil War, the Muslim Brotherhood has lost a battle, but its adherents are by no means finished. Noth-ing is over for them. It is written into their creed that they cannot support any political model unless it is the Islamist model, which means they will never stop trying to take over and dismantle any governments that do not align with them. One step at a time, one pawn at a time, in one manner or another, they move forward, get knocked back, and then keep on coming.

Hafez al-Assad, after having crushed the Muslim Brotherhood in Hama in 1982 after six years of latent war, accepted numerous concessions—and these concessions led to a new conflict thirty years later. It weakened the rule of secularism by allowing the Muslim Brotherhood to open its prayer rooms in the Ba'ath Party's establishments, and then by allowing the building of more mosques throughout all of Syria than there had ever been in the complete history of fourteen hundred years of successive caliphates. Assad, the son, who was confronted with the consequences of his father's policy, would pay the bill.

For ten years, Syria has been entangled in a fight in which the Syrian nation has been attempting to survive in the face of Islamism and its different sponsors. Wahhabism has been defeated, but the Muslim Brotherhood, which the Turkish President Erdogan sup-ports, still holds territories in the northern part of the country. The

Idlib region will probably be nibbled away over time, but what's to be done with the three million refugees, three quarters of whom are these Islamists whom the authorities have transported by bus from the four corners of the world?

When I look at Syria, I see a message and a warning for the Western world. Diversity can lend a richness to a society, for sure and certain, but without the proper supervision of diverse ways of life, conflict will inevitably ensue.

Our imprisonment opened my eyes, allowed me to see through the curtain that was already unraveling one step ahead of us. And, at the same time, it only reinforced my deepest convictions. In retrospect, I was able to see those ten weeks as an intense Ignatian retreat. They began with sheer terror and outrage, but, while my state of mind at the end of it all was by no means perfect, I had at least progressed in acceptance, in trust of God, in the ability to hand our future over to Him. It was like a purgatory on earth, an imprisonment in which the soul would be tortured but purified. During those weeks, I had more than enough time to think back on all my sins and flaws, the many mistakes I had made, my failures, bad actions, and bad thoughts. There was nowhere to hide from my own weaknesses, almost nothing to distract me, and the routine torment of clarifying reflection on my own insufficiencies became a fire that purified me from the inside.

There was nothing except being face-to-face with myself and, in the end, with God. The ugly places of my soul, which I had become accustomed to and skilled at hiding, rose to the surface, uncovered and then excruciatingly purged by divine light. As though this were not enough, God's silence was added to this painful trial. He allowed us to wait, without answer, without knowing what might happen, and so demanded not just a purification of the blemishes in our souls but also the addition of an increase of faith.

Epilogue

After we were freed, I began to understand one thing more about such darkness—the Lord gives you what you ardently desire once you're finally ready to do without it. This had certainly been the case with our freedom. I wasn't always very good at it, but I tried, in the end, to look for the positive. My fellow prisoners and I tried to schedule our lives around regular prayer and a common meal, trying to live as willing monks rather than coerced prisoners. And, finally, I became convinced that we would be staying there for quite a long time. It was only days after that interior acceptance that we were released. What a divine irony, and by such a means! This was a second chance—and I took it as a sign and a hope that the Lord gave me.

Sophia Institute

Sophia Institute is a nonprofit institution that seeks to nurture the spiritual, moral, and cultural life of souls and to spread the gospel of Christ in conformity with the authentic teachings of the Roman Catholic Church.

Sophia Institute Press fulfills this mission by offering translations, reprints, and new publications that afford readers a rich source of the enduring wisdom of mankind.

Sophia Institute also operates the popular online resource CatholicExchange.com. *Catholic Exchange* provides world news from a Catholic perspective as well as daily devotionals and articles that will help readers to grow in holiness and live a life consistent with the teachings of the Church.

In 2013, Sophia Institute launched Sophia Institute for Teachers to renew and rebuild Catholic culture through service to Catholic education. With the goal of nurturing the spiritual, moral, and cultural life of souls, and an abiding respect for the role and work of teachers, we strive to provide materials and programs that are at once enlightening to the mind and ennobling to the heart; faithful and complete, as well as useful and practical.

Sophia Institute gratefully recognizes the Solidarity Association for preserving and encouraging the growth of our apostolate over the course of many years. Without their generous and timely support, this book would not be in your hands.

www.SophiaInstitute.com
www.CatholicExchange.com
www.SophiaInstituteforTeachers.org

Sophia Institute Press is a registered trademark of Sophia Institute.
Sophia Institute is a tax-exempt institution as defined by the
Internal Revenue Code, Section 501(c)(3). Tax ID 22-2548708.